KNIT

WEAR

LOVE

FOOLPROOF INSTRUCTIONS FOR KNITTING YOUR BEST-FITTING
SWEATERS EVER IN THE STYLES YOU LOVE TO WEAR

AMY HERZOG

PHOTOGRAPHY BY KAREN PEARSON / PHOTOGRAPHY CREATIVE DIRECTION
AND STYLING BY KAREN SCHAUPETER

STC CRAFT / A MELANIE FALICK BOOK / NEW YORK

Sweater knitting doesn't have to be daunting! With a comfortable understanding of your own style and a few basic tricks, you'll be making wardrobe staples in no time.

CONTENTS

INTRODUCTION

Whether it's an occasional hobby or a deep passion, knitting can offer us many things: a chance to relax and be creative, a challenge to overcome, the pleasure of looping our experiences and memories into something tangible.

Fundamentally, though, our knitting experience and process *is* a productive one. We're *makers*. Our sticks and our string and our brains all get together and create something that has utility, for us or for our loved ones. Handknitting an item is not the fastest way to get it (and often not the least expensive, either!), but it *is* the most satisfying.

Hand knitting allows us to imbue our garments and our gifts with love and good thoughts and to make them exactly as we wish them to be. In this book, I urge you to use your talents and your passion to give yourself one of the greatest gifts of all: garments that are uniquely, beautifully you.

I hope my first book, *Knit to Flatter*, started you on this journey by helping you understand the kinds of silhouettes you like to wear and how to modify a sweater pattern so that the result will fit you perfectly. But there's more to a sweater than just the silhouette and the numbers.

Many of us tend to think of our sweaters as projects, but fundamentally, our hand-knit sweaters are clothing. In fact, our handknits are essentially *couture*—wait, don't put the book down! *Couture*, these days, is shorthand for

haute couture: the by-hand creation of a clothing masterpiece that is priceless, elegant, and intended for something other than daily wear.

But there was a time, not so very long ago, when *all* clothing was created to match the individual's measurements and specifications (whether by a fashion house, seamstress, relative, or oneself). And the original meaning of the word *couture* is simply the making of clothes for an individual. I think it's time for us to reclaim this word, because when clothing is made for you, and only you, wearing it feels like nothing you've ever experienced before.

All of us spend our days in clothing that was made for someone else (I affectionately called her "Ms. Average" in *Knit to Flatter*). Wherever we aren't the same as Ms. Average, our clothing tells us "You're wrong." Hundreds of times a day, our clothes tell us things like "Your arms are too long. Your legs are too short. Your shoulders are too broad." But custom-made clothing moves with you; it makes you feel *right*. Clothing that's made for you sends the message "You're awesome, just the way you are." This may sound like a luxury, but as sweater knitters it's one that we can create with our own two hands.

For most of us, fashion isn't really about feathers and beading or impossibly high heels and dramatic makeup on a runway. Fashion, in our real lives, is about clothing that drops seamlessly into our daily experiences, that's creative, fits us perfectly, and is intimately personal.

Our clothes express who we are, in the here and now—and *that's* the kind of couture I hope you'll achieve in your sweater knitting.

I wrote *Knit to Flatter* to help you learn to love your natural assets and build a wardrobe full of sweaters you love to wear because they fit properly and look great. I focused on shape and proportions and the simple concept of creating visual balance.

Knit Wear Love is the next step in the "love thy self, in thy sweater" journey. Here I help you create garments that not only suit your shape but also your sense of *style*. Sweaters are inherently flexible, changeable things. In the pages that follow I teach you how to look beyond a pattern's main photo and explore how you can turn any sweater into a garment you can't wait to wear.

In *Chapter One*, I explain how to identify your personal style (as it applies to sweaters, anyway) through a series of fun mood boards and exercises.

In *Chapter Two*, I deconstruct sweaters into their fundamental parts and give you lots of practical information about changing this or that to create the sweater of your dreams. Once you've identified your style and have your "sweater personality" in mind, this chapter gives you the technical tools you need to knit sweaters successfully.

Next I present what I call *meta-patterns*:

instructions for making the eight most popular sweater silhouettes—pullover, cardigan, vest, tunic, cowl, wrap, tank, and bolero—each one in three gauges and twelve sizes, with multiple options for style customization.

To show off the flexibility of the meta-patterns, I am happy to present a cast of six amazing models (some of whom you'll recognize from *Knit to Flatter*), each one a different shape and size. For an example of how different the "same sweater" can be, check out Courtney and Morgan in their pullovers on pages 42 and 49!

The meta-patterns are set up so that you can easily adapt them to suit your choices of size, gauge, and style. I'll be honest though—there are a lot of numbers included in these patterns. So, to make your knitting easy, for each one I've provided a worksheet that you can fill out with the numbers that pertain to the size and gauge of your specific garment. You can photocopy the worksheets in this book or download fresh copies from my website: www.amyherzogdesigns.com/knitwearlove. You'll be amazed at how quickly your sweater knitting goes when there is just one set of numbers to follow!

I wrap things up with a crisp checklist for moving forward in the creation of your own sweater wardrobe. Sweater knitting can sometimes be intimidating, so I leave you with a short reminder of the most important steps to getting a sweater you adore.

I'm honored to be part of your sweater-making journey. My goal is to help you create sweaters that immediately become favorites in your wardrobe: the ones that make you look and feel your best.

UNIQUELY YOU:
YOUR SWEATER STYLE, DEFINED

Making sweaters that suit you is easy if you have a comfortable understanding of your own style. Discovering your own style—and translating it into the materials and shapes you'll use when knitting your sweater—is what this chapter is all about.

While pattern photos invite us to step into a very specific daydream about the life of the model wearing the sweater, all sweaters are much more alike (and flexible!) than those photos might suggest. Though sometimes it can be difficult to imagine, the look of a sweater can be changed completely simply by using a different yarn or color. In this chapter, I step through the specifics of finding your own fashion style and translating that style into yarn, color, and fabric choices that will make any sweater you knit one that you love to wear.

I've selected eight major fashion styles to showcase here and throughout the book. If more than one of these appeals to you, of course that's fine! We all have different facets of our own style, and it's great to be able to express those through clothing. It's likely, though, that you have a main style and a couple of backup singers (so to speak) that you'll turn to time and time again. If after reviewing these style overviews, you're still not sure how they apply to you, check out the fun exercises that begin on page 18.

VINTAGE / Vintage clothing borrows the best ideas from decades past and carries them into a current setting—without too much messing around. For an outfit that doesn't feel strictly retro, they work especially well when paired with a current trend or silhouette. Visible darts, substantial waist shaping, and tailored details are all common for vintage (and vintage-inspired) pieces.

FIBERS Natural fibers, often in single-fiber yarns rather than blends, play most faithfully to vintage styles. Conventionally plied yarn construction is also the most well-suited to this style.

FABRICS A sturdier, elastic fabric tends to be best for the structure and tailoring involved in vintage styles, often in a lighter-weight gauge. (Hint: Since these styles often come from time periods when women had fewer clothes and wore what they had a lot, to channel the vintage vibe, ask yourself: Could I wear this fabric day in and day out?)

COLORS While there are definitely exceptions, overall, most vintage clothing tends toward a subdued but not neutral color palette. Allover color, Fair-Isle patterns, and intarsia are all common, but typically without the hyper-saturated, extremely bright colors we might see in more contemporary pieces.

ICONIC SWEATER EXAMPLES Fair Isle ski sweater; "sweater girl" pullover with ribbed waist; high-collared polo-shirt pullover.

CASUAL / Casual clothes are ones you can really live in—their more relaxed shapes and fabrics let you go from errands to lunch to curling up with a good book, and while they might occasionally include a bit of detailing, they're not afraid to get a little grubby either.

FIBERS Casual sweaters demand both comfort and a hard-wearing, not-too-fussy set of fibers. Cotton, wool, hemp, and linen—particularly in super-functional blends or constructions that lend elasticity and memory to the yarn—are great choices for this style.

FABRICS The relaxed silhouettes of casual clothing offer some flexibility in the structure of your knitted fabric. Your fabric can't be so loose, however, that you lose the hard-working nature of these pieces! (Hint: We expect a lot from our casual clothing, so it's a great idea to knit a large swatch and thoroughly wash and live with it for a bit before making a final decision on these everyday, rough-and-tumble staples.)

COLORS Silhouette and simplicity, more than color, tend to lend a casual feel to a piece.

ICONIC SWEATER EXAMPLES V-neck cardigan worn open; scoop-neck tunic; oversized "sweatshirt" sweater.

Don't be afraid of color, but keep it slightly muted.

Vintage typewriter, £100, Urban Outfitters (urbanoutfitters.co.uk)

Small-scale stitch patterns in lighter weight yarns give a vintage feel.

Think clean, crisp shapes out of traditional materials.

You'll expect to get a lot of use out of these sweaters, so make sure your fabric is up to the challenge. Play with your swatch to see how it behaves over time.

Casual sil-houettes are relaxed, com-fortable, and undemanding.

Shapes are
slightly
relaxed and
allow lots
of movement.

SPORTY
style

ALL GOOD DAYS

RASCAL

73

Rub, stretch,
and get a bit
rough with your
swatch to ensure
it's durable and
flexible enough.

Pockets are a
fun, functional
detail.

SPORTY / Sporty styles serve your body's needs in every respect. They're comfortable, move well and freely, and have a touch of the practical in them. They tend to appear simple rather than ornate, though they often include engineered details that serve a functional purpose.

FIBERS A sporty garment requires materials that are on the soft side, wick moisture well, and don't demand a lot of fuss. Natural fibers like wool or cotton with the occasional high-tech blend are par for the sporty course, and think springy. (Hint: Check out the sporty wrap on page 134 for a yarn with climate-controlling fiber blended in!)

FABRICS Great elasticity and movement are required in any sporty style, along with a hard-wearing durability that doesn't remember what a fabric shaver even looks like. To last well, your sporty stitches should spring back with energy when you stretch and then release them.

COLORS Sporty clothing is often either in a decidedly neutral shade or an extra-fun color that adds spirit to your workout. (And sometimes both!) But that's far from a strict rule—wear whatever color makes you want to get up and move.

ICONIC SWEATER EXAMPLES Kangaroo-pocket hoodie, post-workout wrap, raglan-sleeved pullover.

BOHEMIAN / Unconventional and intricate, bohemian clothing derives its unique look from eclectic detailing and unusual combinations. Mix and match different colors and textures to your heart's content—the more, the merrier.

FIBERS Bohemian looks typically rely heavily on natural fibers, particularly inelastic ones with nubbier textures like linen, hemp, and tweedy silk blends. The intricate colorwork so often associated with these styles works best in a lightweight, smooth yarn with an extensive color palette.

FABRICS Fabrics tend to be either quite dense (colorwork pieces especially) or quite open (think an allover lace piece). Trims of all textures and varieties are common for this style. (Hint: To achieve a truly bohemian look, try combinations of knitted-on lace, several different stitch patterns, and/or rustic yarn textures.)

COLORS Colors within bohemian pieces can be busy and are often detailed, but tend to remain within blues and earth tones more than any other color group.

ICONIC SWEATER EXAMPLES Colorwork poncho, Fair Isle tunic, belled-sleeve openwork pullover. **(See mood board on page 12.)**

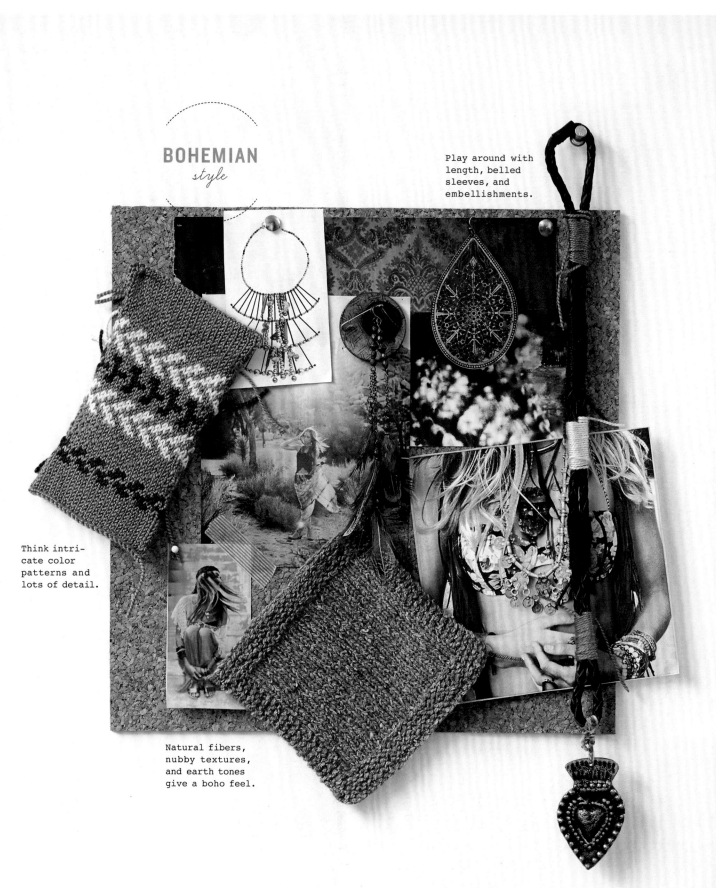

BOHEMIAN
style

Play around with length, belled sleeves, and embellishments.

Think intricate color patterns and lots of detail.

Natural fibers, nubby textures, and earth tones give a boho feel.

Think bold
color and unus-
ual shapes.

Modern styles
tend to be
eye-catching,
clean, and not
at all fussy.

Geometric
influences in
stitch pattern
or color lend a
modern flair.

MODERN
style

Silhouettes
tend to be sim-
ple and sleek.

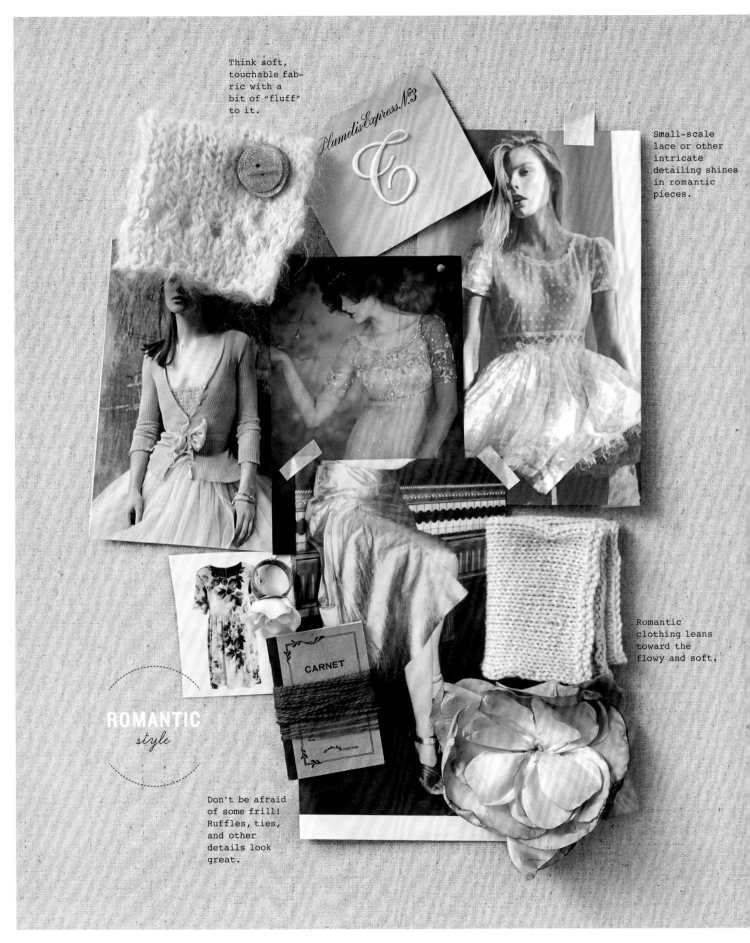

Think soft, touchable fabric with a bit of "fluff" to it.

Small-scale lace or other intricate detailing shines in romantic pieces.

Romantic clothing leans toward the flowy and soft.

ROMANTIC *style*

Don't be afraid of some frill! Ruffles, ties, and other details look great.

MODERN / From bold uses of color and stark lines to ultra-minimalist designs that place all focus on shape, modernist fashion tends to be eye-catching, clean, and generally highlights one main design feature.

FIBERS Anything goes in terms of fiber for modern pieces, though crisp stitch definition is often a good bet, and yarns with a substantial halo will probably marry least well with a modern design.

FABRICS Denser gauges tend to be better choices for most modern pieces, with stitch patterns that present clean lines and crisp edges. (Hint: If the design isn't about the fabric itself, continue swatching until you get a fabric that serves the main focus of the piece.)

COLORS Modern designs tend to work best in subdued neutrals (when the color of the piece isn't a focus) or eye-catching, bright color combinations (when it is).

ICONIC SWEATER EXAMPLES Such a list must inevitably become dated at some point, but as of this writing: color-blocked boatneck, ultra-soft charcoal gray tunic, sleek curved wrap, and asymmetrical hems or necklines. **(See mood board on page 13.)**

ROMANTIC / Soft, gentle, and decidedly feminine, romantic pieces are typically detailed, curvaceous, and delicate. Waist shaping often features prominently, as does a soft, floaty fabric and plenty of curved detailing.

FIBERS Softness tends to reign for romantic clothing, whether natural fiber (think bamboo, silk, fine alpaca) or synthetic. This style tends to make great use of alternate yarn constructions or especially fluffy materials.

FABRICS Movement, curve, and drape are the name of the romantic game, and these lightweight garments can often call for a more open fabric than you'll see in other styles. Look for yarns that don't lose their shape at larger gauges, fingering- or sport-weight yarns, or even try laceweight held doubled! (Hint: Romantic looks pair especially well with fabrics that have a bit of a halo. Try your yarn at an ever-so-slightly loose gauge compared to the ball band's specified number, and see if the spaces in between your stitches fill in with a soft "glow.")

COLORS If any style can be said to have a color profile, romantic is it. Pastels, lighter neutrals, and metal tones all speak to a romantic sensibility.

ICONIC SWEATER EXAMPLES Ultra-soft, long-sleeved cowl (on or off the shoulder); ruffled V-necked pullover, sheer-fabric boatneck.

CLASSIC / Classic fashion focuses on silhouettes, fabrics, and pieces that have stood the test of time. Clean lines, elegant tailoring, and subtle touches give a timeless style no matter what the occasion.

FIBERS Classic clothing tends to focus on natural, long-wearing fibers like wool, linen, silk, and cotton—all in traditional blends and constructions.

FABRICS Typically, these pieces lean toward the structured and tailored; this is best achieved through knit fabrics that have a reasonably "snug" gauge like that listed on the yarn's ball band. (Hint: If you place your swatch on a table so that the wrong side is showing and pull your stitches apart a bit, there should be tension. When you let it go, the fabric should spring back into shape, even with an inelastic fiber.)

COLORS No one set of colors truly captures the classic style. On the other hand, any color iconic enough to call a specific time to mind (e.g., neon and the 1980s) will clash with the timeless goal of classic fashion.

ICONIC SWEATER EXAMPLES Crew-neck textured or cabled pullover; fine-gauge crew-neck cardigan; structured blazer.

AVANT-GARDE / Avant-garde fashion catches your eye and pushes the envelope. Unexpected pairings, concepts taken just the tiniest bit over the edge, and inventive new shapes are all hallmarks of fashion's risk-takers.

FIBERS These pieces love shiny silk or bamboo blends, highly elastic and sturdy wool, and yarns with unexpected or eye-catching drape. New yarn constructions, alternative fibers (steel? bring it on!), anything crispy, crunchy, slinky, or otherwise noteworthy—all will find a great home in the avant-garde closet.

FABRICS Stitch patterns and gauges that look unusual marry well with this style. Try an especially snug or loose gauge, oversized stitch patterns, dropped stitches, exposed seams, and the like. (Hint: It's a really great idea to work a large swatch, to be sure you can envision the garment at scale—not surprisingly, that is hard to achieve with a 4" [10 cm] square!)

COLORS If it's eye-catching and bold, it can be avant-garde. This style does wonderful things with subtly (or not-so-subtly) variegated yarn, deep, saturated colors, and super-bright brights.

ICONIC SWEATER EXAMPLES Dropped-stitch pullover with unfinished edges; military-style cropped jacket; knee-length jacket.

CLASSIC *style*

Shapes lean toward the structured and tailored; think crisp seams and clean details.

Choose natural, long-wearing fibers like wool or cotton blends.

These timeless colors and shapes would work equally well on both you and your gram.

AVANT-GARDE *style*

Whatever else, think: eye-catching!

Make your sweater a statement piece with new yarns or fibers and unusual gauges.

Be inventive and unusual in shape, color, and fabric.

You might already be resonating with a style (or three), but if you're not, don't worry! These exercises will help you hone in on your own platonic sweater ideals and prepare you to pick up your needles with confidence.

Finding your own style!

EXERCISE #1

PROJECT VS. CLOTHING

Instead of thinking about sweaters as projects you want to knit, think about them as clothing you want to wear. Not sure what you'd like? Don't think too hard, just jot down some quick answers to the following questions.

What kinds of fabrics and textures do I like to wear?

What do I pull out of the closet time and time again? How do I feel when I wear these pieces?

When do I wear sweaters, and why? Do I have a "gap" in my wardrobe?

EXERCISE #2

YOUR FAVORITE SWEATER

Lay out your favorite sweater (storebought or handmade) and spend some time looking at it. Note its silhouette and shape characteristics:

Now write down up to five reasons why this is your favorite sweater:

Finally, write down up to three features you'd like to change about it:

Compare these lists to the eight styles on pages 8—17. Any definite "Yes!" or "No way" comparisons?

DESCRIPTIVES

Close your eyes and start to craft a wardrobe entirely from your imagination. Come up with between 5 and 20 words describing that wardrobe, and write them down.

Think about the 8 major styles. Which are best described by your adjectives?

STYLE NOTES QUIZ

Write down some off-the-cuff answers to these questions. The next time you're enchanted with a pattern photo that looks nothing like your life, pull these words out! You'll be able to have your sweater—and wear it, too—if you customize it to suit your style.

My favorite sweater is _____.

I love wearing these colors: _____

I've never looked good in the color _____.

My biggest sweater pet peeve is when_____.

I feel best when I'm wearing a _____neckline.

No matter what, a sweater needs to be_____.

These fibers make me happy: _____

SANITY CHECK

When you are looking at a photo of a sweater that you're seriously considering knitting, it's easy to get distracted by the pose, setting, and details, so be sure to take time to really assess what you're looking at. If the sleeves are a length you don't usually wear, ask yourself why not—and whether you might be able to change them to a length you wear regularly. If you suspect you're reacting more to the setting and model than the sweater itself, imagine it in your own closet.

   Finally, do a sanity check to make sure you're not crushing on a fantasy rather than making a decision based on your real life. Ask yourself the following:

What would this sweater look like laying on the table? (Answering this question will help you to distinguish between the fantasy of the photo and the reality of the garment.)

How will this sweater look on me (honestly)?

What would I wear with the sweater?

Where can I imagine myself wearing it?

What changes could I make to this sweater to make it perfect for me?

SWEATERS, DECONSTRUCTED

If you've read Chapter One, you likely have a good handle
on the types of styles, fabrics, and colors you'll be happiest
wearing. That's great! This awareness will help you make
your next sweater perfect for you.

While sweater-knitting is nowhere near as complicated as that heirloom lace
shawl you may have been considering, there is some important technical know-
how involved in creating a great garment. This chapter lays it all out for you in
plain English, from size and structure to seams and stitches.

Making a sweater that's perfect for you is rarely a straightforward matter
of finding a pattern you like and following it exactly as written. Usually a few
modifications are needed. But don't despair! My approach to sweaters is simple:
You start by picking a pattern and size that are mostly right for you, and then
you make small changes from there. For example, if you love the open style of
the cardigan shown on page 67 but lofty alpaca isn't going to fit well into your
lifestyle, you might replace it with a smooth linen. Or if you adore the modern
pullover on page 45, but scoop necks are more your style than asymmetrical
ones, it's easy to change the front neckline shape. Guidelines to these kinds of
changes and more are all here for your reference.

CHOOSING A FLATTERING SIZE AND SILHOUETTE

Even a sweater in a style you love will lay unworn in your closet if it doesn't fit well and look great on your body. My first book, *Knit to Flatter*, is a comprehensive resource on fitting and flattering, and if you want to delve deeply into these subjects, I hope you'll check it out.

But, for now, let's begin with a quick recap. There are two main fit/flatter components to consider when making or buying a sweater: the way the sweater visually balances your underlying body shape, and how well it fits you.

SILHOUETTE / BALANCE

Although we may not always realize it, most of our innate preferences boil down to our body's inherent shape, and clothing that highlights or adjusts (part of) that shape. Think about it—we spend tons of time (way too much, in my opinion) with a side-view of ourselves in the mirror. But when was the last time you walked up to someone sideways?! Others see us straight-on and focus on the outline, or silhouette, of our bodies instead.

Body shape is crucially important—because as much as we ourselves like to obsess about numbers, *the rest of the world can't see them*. The human eye is pretty abysmal at absolute size, actually. (How many times have you been convinced that the project you're knitting measures 14" (35.5 cm), only to measure it at 8" (20.5 cm) instead?) We're much better at seeing *outline* and *silhouette*, and we're down-right exceptional at seeing *balance* and *imbalance*—and therein lies the key to body shape and clothing.

Fundamentally, our body shape either appears balanced from top to bottom (what I call proportional), our bottom half draws the eye (what I call bottom heavy), or the top half draws the eye (what I call top heavy). Which body shape you are might surprise you! It's all about the apparent and relative width of these parts of our silhouettes—not about how big or small we *think* they are.

Your clothing can change the way your body shape looks, if you want. There are four main principles:

1. **To widen** part of your body, place a horizontal stripe or visual element there.
2. **To narrow** part of your body, place a vertical stripe or visual element there.
3. **To lengthen** part of your body, stretch one solid piece of fabric/texture/color over the whole section.
4. **To shorten** part of your body, break it up into lots of different vertical "chunks" of color/fabric/texture.

Most of us are happiest when we appear balanced. So if one part of your body appears imbalanced on its own, you can change that if you like. Here's a brief recap of the guidelines I presented in *Knit to Flatter* for achieving balance in your shape.

Proportional figures should ensure that visual elements on the top of the sweater are balanced by those on the bottom (e.g., a wide horizontal collar paired with long, belled sleeves or a longer sweater length).

Top-heavy figures are often happiest when narrowing visual elements at the top (e.g., a deep, narrow V neckline) are paired with broadening visual elements at the bottom (e.g., deep hem treatments or longer sweater lengths).

Bottom-heavy figures are often happiest when elements that broaden their shoulders (via a wide collar, for example) are paired with narrowing or plain elements at the bottom (such as shorter sleeves and a plain, folded hem).

Of course, other things might be going on with your figure too—you might have a straight or curvy waist, you might have an especially long or short torso—we could go on analyzing ourselves forever! But if you stick with a basic notion of your own body shape, and an understanding of how the lines embedded in your clothes change that shape, you're well on your way to sweaters you love to wear.

FIT / SIZE

The single most important sweater advice I can give you is to *start by choosing a size that will fit your shoulders well.* A good shoulder fit is the most important—and most challenging—part of sweater-knitting. Shoulder fit can be challenging because there is no single shoulder measurement that works across all sweater constructions. Fit is typically determined by bust circumference instead. But there is a way!

To get a great fit in the shoulders, first, take your upper torso circumference by wrapping a measuring tape snugly around your torso, as high in your armpits as it will possibly go. Remember to keep your arms and shoulders in a neutral position, and breathe normally!

Compare this measurement against the finished bust circumferences in the patterns, choosing the size equal to or greater than your upper torso that represents your desired amount of ease:

A close fit of 0-1" (0-2.5 cm) above your upper torso will give you space to wear a single thin layer in the shoulders;

An average fit of 1-2" (2.5-5 cm) above your upper torso will give you space to wear an average layer comfortably in the shoulders;

A relaxed fit of 2-3" (5-7.5 cm) above your upper torso will produce a comfortably oversized fit in the shoulders.

BODY SHAPES

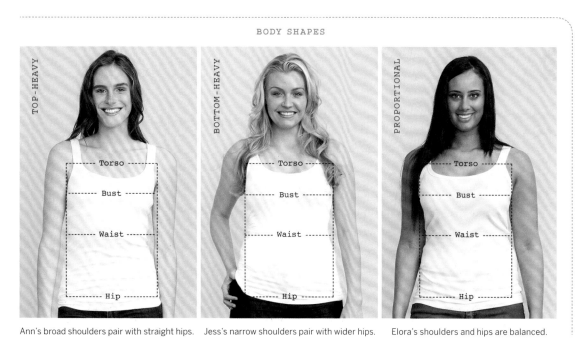

TOP-HEAVY

BOTTOM-HEAVY

PROPORTIONAL

Torso — Bust — Waist — Hip

Ann's broad shoulders pair with straight hips.   Jess's narrow shoulders pair with wider hips.   Elora's shoulders and hips are balanced.

Choosing a "base size" in this way will ensure that the most complicated modifications (recalculating that sleeve cap) are unnecessary. You may need to change a few simple things, though. So once you've chosen your "base size," compare all of the other measurements for that size against your own body measurements. When a base size measurement is very different from your own body measurement, you're likely to need a modification to ensure a great fit. (And that's okay! It's totally normal to need modifications.)

To make your mods, draw out a dummy sweater schematic with the base size's measurements written on it, as in the illustration below.

As you compare these numbers against your own body, you'll notice the places that need to change. Cross off the numbers that are wrong for you, and write the correct ones in. (For example, in my own case, the body and sleeve lengths of most sweaters are too short for me. I also need a little extra room on the front of the sweater, only in the bust, to accommodate my larger bustline.)

Length modifications are usually a snap: Figure out which part of the garment requires more (or less) length, and then knit for longer (or less) than the pattern specifies.

Width modifications require you to adjust the stitch counts from what's printed in the pattern, to match your own body's needs. (To carry my own example further: I've selected a 38" (96.5 cm) base size, but require a finished full bust circumference of 41" (104 cm). My back bust stays at 19" (48.5 cm), but I'll widen the front bust on my sweater to measure 22" (55.5 cm).)

If you're changing stitch counts or making big changes to length, you'll need to determine a new *rate of shaping* for the relevant portion of your garment. That sounds complicated, but it just means that you might need to know how often to work your shaping!

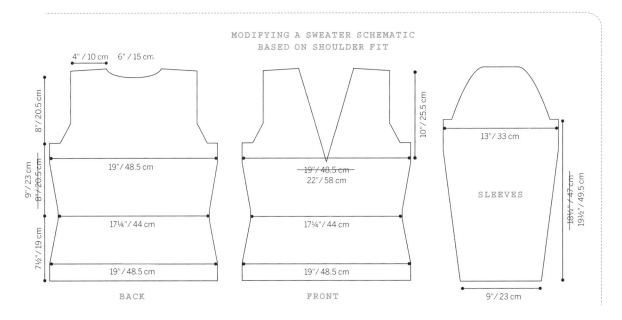

MODIFYING A SWEATER SCHEMATIC
BASED ON SHOULDER FIT

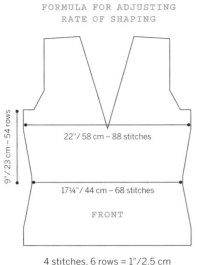

FORMULA FOR ADJUSTING
RATE OF SHAPING

9" / 23 cm – 54 rows

22" / 58 cm – 88 stitches

17¼" / 44 cm – 68 stitches

FRONT

4 stitches, 6 rows = 1" / 2.5 cm

TOTAL ROWS: 54

SHAPING ROWS: 10
(Adding 20 stitches, 2 stitches per increase row)

RATE OF SHAPING: 4
(54 / 10, rounded down to nearest even number)

INCREASE INSTRUCTIONS:
Work increase row every 4 rows 10 times

Determine any rate of shaping—from CO to waist, waist to bust, in a V neckline, or on a sleeve—with this simple formula:

**Rate of shaping =
total number of rows / number of shaping rows
(rounded down to the nearest even number)**

The total number of rows is equal to the vertical distance in that portion of your body, multiplied by your row gauge; the number of shaping rows is equal to the number of stitches added or removed divided by two (since you typically shape two stitches per row).

Speaking of waist shaping...

I'm doing something slightly sneaky with the waist shaping in these examples, and in fact with all of the sweaters in this book. I've located the shaping along vertical dart lines

rather than keeping it at the side seam. This kind of shaping better matches the way most bodies are shaped (always a good thing, in sweater knitting). But there's one more important benefit: Doing so allows the shaping on the front and back of your sweater to be entirely different. You can change the stitch counts on the front and back of your sweater's body completely independently from one another—the only rule is that the stitch counts need to match your own fabulous self!

SWEATER PROCESS:
FROM SWATCHING TO SEAMING

Some people are intimidated by the idea of knitting a sweater, but when it comes down to it, most sweaters only require basic skills. If you can cast on, keep a consistent gauge, increase, decrease, and bind off, you can knit a sweater. The difference between a sweater looking not-so-great and fabulous lays in the details of the process: from choosing the right style (see Chapter One) and size (see above) to choosing the right yarn, swatching well, and knowing how to finish the seams (see below).

SWATCHING

I know, I know. I can hear the groans already. For so many knitters, swatching feels like a frustrating prerequisite to getting to the fun part of starting a project. But swatching is truly crucial. It will tell you if the yarn you are considering really is right for a sweater you'll want to wear. It will also tell you what gauge it wants to be knit at in order to look and feel great.

Most instructions tell you that you absolutely must match the gauge (the number of stitches and rows per inch) in the pattern in your swatch or you're setting yourself up for all sorts of problems. And so we knit the same yarn with the needles called for in the pattern and then we try bigger ones and smaller ones until, if we're lucky, we match the pattern's gauge. We slog along until the ruler tells us we're right and we can start.

I'm here to buck the trend and tell you that the most important reason to swatch is to figure out whether you want to *wear a fabric*. Who cares that the gauge is perfect, if the fabric is uncomfortable?

The second most important reason is so that you can use it to *discover* your true gauge. If you approach swatching as a way to *discover* your gauge, rather than *match* gauge, you'll be much happier with your finished sweater, and you'll probably enjoy how much more control you have over the process. Once you have a swatch that looks and feels good, you can rework the numbers in the pattern if you have to.

So please, let's let go of the pattern's numbers for a bit and, instead, look at swatching as a means of taking control of our knitting and achieving sweater happiness. A good swatch:

Has to be large enough to truly tell your gauge and give you a good feel for the fabric. I think a roughly 6" (15 cm) square is sufficient. (Hint: if you're tempted to skimp, cast on fewer stitches and knit for longer, rather than wimping out on your swatch after just 3" (7.5 cm). To get a good predictor of your gauge, you need your hands to be in their "knitting groove"— and that usually just doesn't happen for the first inch or three.)

Has to be cleaned the way you'll clean your garment. If you're going to care for your handknits by using a wool wash and getting them wet (my favorite method), you'll need to do the same with your swatch. There's no other way of knowing how that fabric will look after it's been cleaned! Washing the swatch will also show you the yarn's bloom. (That is, how much the strands of yarn "plump up" and "fill in" the spaces between stitches when they get wet.)

Has to be measured precisely for gauge. It can be incredibly difficult to estimate fractions of a stitch or row when we're measuring gauge. The difference between 4.3 stitches to the inch and 4.4 stitches to the inch is hard to discern when we're staring at a knitted square, but it makes a gigantic difference in the size of your sweater! So instead of measuring a 4" (10 cm) square and trying to decide exactly how many stitches and rows are in that 4" (10 cm), I recommend outlining the maximum number of stitches and rows you think will give you a good gauge estimate (see illustration below).

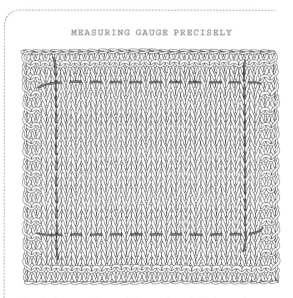

MEASURING GAUGE PRECISELY

Precisely measuring a whole number of stitches and rows rather than fractions gives a much better gauge estimate.

Then, count the whole number of stitches and rows you've outlined. (Something like 37 stitches and 51 rows, say.) Now, measure the exact number of inches those stitches and rows take up—your ruler will helpfully give you the exact fraction of an inch you're looking for. (Something like 5⅛ [5.125] inches and 4⅞ [4.875] inches, maybe.)

Divide the stitches by the inches, and the rows by the inches, to get your precise stitch and row gauge. (In this example, 7.2 stitches and 10.5 rows to the inch.)

STRUCTURE

Let's face it—handknit sweaters aren't the lightest garments on the planet. And yet, we'd (ideally) like them to stay anchored on our bodies, retain their shape, and allow us to move comfortably when we wear them. This makes structure an incredibly important feature of any sweater. There are three main ingredients to the overall structure of your garment: fabric, construction, and your body.

FABRIC

When you're knitting a scarf or a shawl, size and structure are (almost) irrelevant. If you like the fabric and want to wrap it around your neck, you're done. This isn't true for a sweater, though! Good sweater fabric contains enough structure to help the garment stay in place on your body even through movement.

What does that mean? Essentially, that your knitted fabric has enough elasticity and memory that *moving one stitch also moves all of its neighbors*. This elasticity comes from the knit stitches themselves and the way they're formed—quite aside from any elasticity (or lack thereof) in the yarn you're using.

For a sweater fabric to hang properly on your body when there are a couple of pounds of it, stitches shouldn't be able to move and act independently of one another. If they can, the second that sweater goes on your body the fabric will start to droop, sag, and bag.

To examine your fabric's structure, place your swatch on a smooth surface (like a table) with the wrong side facing up. Gently stretch and release the fabric; it should be relatively easy to stretch, but it should bounce back quickly when you let go. If it's hard to stretch the fabric, you won't get great movement. In this case, try needles one size larger. If the stitches don't spring back together quickly, your fabric doesn't have enough structure. In this case, try needles one size smaller.

CONSTRUCTION

All sweaters are essentially three cylinders (body and two sleeves), joined somehow at the shoulders. This is true no matter what sweater silhouette you choose, whether you knit it in this direction or that direction, all-in-one, or in pieces, with your eyes closed or open (kidding!).

The different ways of joining those shoulders *are* the different sweater constructions (raglan, drop-shoulder, yoke, set-in, etc.). Different construction styles give you different precision in the fit of your shoulders, with different weight-bearing points when the sweater is worn.

I chose the set-in sleeve construction for the sweaters both in *Knit to Flatter* and in this book. The set-in sleeve construction rests the weight of your sweater on strong seams and provides the most precise shoulder fit of all construction styles.

Finally, whenever you're thinking about the overall structure of a sweater, you also need to consider how *your own body* will come into play. Square shoulders will add their own structure to a sweater and anchor it in place. The fabric and construction style of the sweater can be a little less structural, since the body picks up some of the slack.

Sloped shoulders will encourage that sweater to slide down (and sometimes off) the shoulders. This is particularly true for a sweater without a lot of structure in the shoulder area; V-neck raglan cardigans worn open spring to mind. If you have sloped shoulders, the fabric and construction of the sweater need to be a little more structural to compensate.

FINISHING

Finally, when you're done knitting a sweater, you're not truly done with your project. To get a great garment you want to wear for decades,

your unfinished piece(s) need a little tender-loving care—typically called "finishing" by knitters everywhere.

There are lots of good books on finishing (see Recommended Reading on page 190) but, honestly, the best advice I can give you is to take a finishing class at your local yarn store. For finishing more than anything else, I think it's helpful to have someone standing over your shoulder while you're working, giving you the guidance you need to get things right.

That said, I do want to share the three most important parts of finishing a sweater with you: blocking, seaming, and edging.

BLOCKING

In all cases, I wholeheartedly recommend wet-blocking. Not only does it help your knit fabric achieve all of its lustrous glory, evening out your stitches and fluffing up beautifully, but it also makes your sweater a snap to seam. To properly wet-block your sweater, first soak it in

SHOULDERS

SQUARE SHOULDERS

SLOPED SHOULDERS

Francesca has square shoulders, which add structure to a sweater.

Courtney has sloped shoulders, which may cause some sweaters to slide off; to compensate, she may want to choose styles with more structure.

cold water (I like to use some wool wash, too). Let it sit in the water for at least 15 minutes (more is okay). *Carefully* get the excess water out of the pieces without lifting or stretching them. I like the spin cycle (SPIN ONLY, and on a low speed setting) of my front-loading washing machine, but another method is to place your knitted pieces in a colander, squish most of the water out, then lay them gently on a towel. Roll up the towel and walk on it to eliminate the excess water.

Next, lightly pin your pieces to the correct dimensions—either to a blocking board or something else. (I use interlocking exercise mat tiles.) You're producing 3-D fabric here, so don't get crazy with the pins! Only pin the bits required to make seaming easier—around the armhole, the bicep, at the bust, and hip. (Let the waists roll free.) Let the sweater pieces dry thoroughly before proceeding.

(And yes, if you can't wait to wear that sweater, it's perfectly legal to prop a fan nearby and help the "air drying" along a little bit!)

SEAMING

Seams are beautiful things—they not only provide structure to a sweater but subliminal instructions to the fabric about where it should anchor to your body. Mattress stitch is my favorite seaming method. I used it exclusively on the samples for this book, and I highly recommend it. It's worked with the right sides of your knitting facing up and lying next to one another. (For stockinette stitch, this means you want the smooth side facing out.)

One (admittedly slightly dorky) visual aid when working mattress stitch: When I was a girl, I was taught to look at my knitting and see

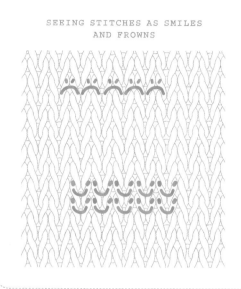

the knit stitches as little smiley faces staring up at me. One whole stitch is a whole smiley face; half of one stitch and half of the next form a frowny face, instead.

Thread your tapestry needle with yarn (often the yarn you used to knit your sweater, unless it's a tweed or some other yarn that's not smooth) and scoop your tapestry needle underneath your knitting and back up again on one piece, then the other. You'll get a "zipper" effect that you can then pull snug every inch or so.

Exactly what part of your knitting you "scoop up" depends on which kind of mattress stitch you're performing:

Vertical mattress stitch is used on side seams, or whenever you're joining two pieces of knitting together along their side edges. Use your tapestry needle to "scoop up" the bar *between* the edge stitch and its next-door neighbor. (That's between two smiley faces.) You're sewing yarn through the space between one stitch and the next.

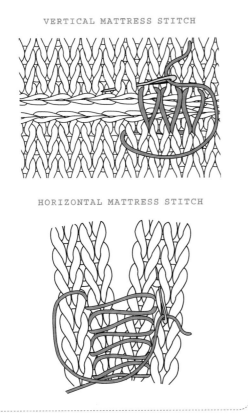

VERTICAL MATTRESS STITCH

HORIZONTAL MATTRESS STITCH

Horizontal mattress stitch is used when joining shoulders, or whenever you're joining two pieces of knitting together top-to-top or bottom-to-bottom. Use your tapestry needle to "scoop up" both legs of an entire stitch on one piece knitting, and then the other. When seaming two tops together, you'll see the smiley faces on your bottom piece of knitting, but since the top piece of knitting is upside down you'll see "frowns."

You can combine the two very easily by using your tapestry needle to "scoop up" a bar on one piece of knitting, and both legs of a stitch on the other.

Once you've mastered your shoulder seams and your side seams, you're ready to tackle the sleeve cap: that mix of horizontal and vertical mattress stitch that can seem so daunting. Never fear! Here's an easy way to go about ensuring a great set-in sleeve (hint: Your sleeve cap seaming will be easier if you work your decreases one stitch in from the sides):

1. First, use an openable stitch marker to pin together the bind-offs at the underarm to the bind-offs on the sleeve cap.
2. Then, use another marker to pin the exact center of the top of the sleeve cap to the shoulder seam.
3. Finally, place more markers about an inch apart around the sleeve.
4. Now pick up your sweater and give it a light shake. Adjust pins as necessary. You're ready to seam!

Perfectly done mattress stitch gives you an almost giddy feeling as you zip lines of neat little stitches together. If you're nervous about tackling a whole garment, start with a few swatches for practice! Once you're confident in your mattress stitch, you'll be amazed at how wonderfully finished your sweaters appear.

EDGING

Now that you've put your sweater pieces together, you've (likely) still got one more thing to do, and that's knit a finished edging onto any raw, unfinished parts of your sweater. In a pullover that's typically the neckline; in a cardigan, it can be the button band, too.

Often, the exact number of stitches you pick up doesn't matter so much. (Knit fabric is deliciously forgiving in that way.) But you need to get close to the right number—too few stitches and your edge will pull in and pucker. Too many and you've got an unintentional ruffle happening.

But what number is that right number? You can figure it out precisely by calculating the length of the edge you're trimming and multiplying by your stitch gauge . . . but you can also use the following rule of thumb: When picking up stitches along a vertical edge, pick up approximately 3 stitches out of every 4 rows. When picking up along an edge of bound-off stitches, pick up one stitch in every bound-off stitch. And when picking up along a diagonal edge, pick up approximately 4 stitches out of every 5 rows (along a straight edge) or even 5 out of every 6 (along a curve).

After you've knit a few rows, pay close attention to whether any puckering or ruffling is happening—if it is, rip out your edging, adjust your rate of pick-up, and do it again.

NEXT STEPS:
MAKING THE DESIGN YOUR OWN

Fit and finishing are incredibly important, but for me, the fun part of personalizing a sweater lies in the *design*. Playing around with different stitch patterns and neckline and sleeve shapes will help you take any pattern and turn it into the best sweater ever—for you.

STITCH PATTERNS

When making a design your own, changing out some or all of the pattern's specified stitch patterns is a very powerful tool. Some stitch pattern adjustments are easier to work around your fit modifications and some are harder. In this section I tell you everything you need to know to play around with this important adjustment.

Of course, stockinette stitch and ribbing make for a pretty fantastic sweater (and if you don't believe me, go to your nearest store and see what's being sold there). So please don't

feel that it's in any way necessary to make a sweater that's fancier than you want to knit. (Personally, I find stockinette both soothing to knit and utterly wearable!)

But some knitters definitely want their sweater projects to include a knitting challenge or some extra visual interest. Adding panels of a different stitch pattern, or changing the pattern's main pattern stitch or edge pattern stitch, are great ways to do so. With that in mind, here are some handy tips and guides for using stitch patterns in your sweaters.

SELECTING A STITCH PATTERN

Your first choice in adding a stitch pattern to a sweater is selecting the stitch pattern itself! It's likely that there are tons of great stitch dictionaries in your local bookstore, and all of them are full of options for your sweater (see Recommended Reading on page 190). The first step in any stitch pattern selection is to *swatch it in your chosen yarn*. This is crucial: Not only will it tell you whether the stitch pattern you're considering is even a remotely good substitution idea, but your yarn's fiber content, gauge, and construction will have a dramatic effect on the stitch pattern's appearance.

So swatch, and be sure you like the way the pattern is knitting up in your yarn instead of just admiring the picture in the dictionary!

The second step is to consider whether your stitch pattern will affect your shaping.

USING AN ALLOVER STITCH PATTERN

Some stitch patterns are easy to shape. In those cases, feel free to work them all over. (That's what I did for the Classic Pullover front on page 42: I worked shaping as written, keeping my existing stitches in the established pattern, and it worked out great.) If you're using an allover pattern, check out the "centering stitch patterns" section below.

If you're swapping out the main stitch pattern entirely, note whether your stitch pattern has a drastically different gauge than stockinette stitch (or whatever the main pattern stitch is for your sweater), and adjust stitch counts if necessary.

You can also include a different stitch pattern in panels. In this case, gauge is a little more flexible. A good rule of thumb is that the size of your sweater won't change dramatically when your panels are knit/purl-based (the textures used in the Vintage Vest on page 84 and the Classic Cardigan on page 63 are good examples) or incorporate small eyelets. For cables, which "suck in" the fabric, cast on (or increase) one additional stitch for each crossed stitch in your cable panel. So if you'd like to run a 2x2 cable up the front of your cardigan, cast on 2 extra stitches.

PLACING STITCH PATTERNS

While, of course, you can place a stitch pattern wherever you like on the body of your sweater, there are easy (and not-so-easy) places to incorporate them. Here's a quick run-down:

Using a stitch pattern on the edges of your sweater's body and sleeves is a great, easy way to change things up a bit. All of the complicated shaping in the sweater takes place after you've changed to Stockinette, making this use of stitch patterns incredibly easy. It's no coincidence that I used this trick to achieve several different styles in this book: For example, I changed up the edge stitch

of the The Cowl (page 94) to achieve Bohemian, Casual, and Romantic looks.

Placing a vertical panel around the side seams of your sweater's body is another great way to achieve an interesting look without working any shaping in the pattern. Since waist shaping is located along vertical darts in these sweaters, there's usually a couple of inches at each side seam that are free and clear for easy stitch patterning.

Placing vertical panels in the center of your sweater's body is a third easy, attractive way to place stitch patterns within your sweater. Keep the panels between 30 and 50 percent of the width of your sweater front (or back) for the cleanest look. You can start the stitch patterning at the hem and work it all the way up to the neckline or change it up a bit and start (or end) at the waist. I did this on the back of the Casual Tunic (page 121), and it provides fun, unexpected visual interest.

CENTERING STITCH PATTERNS

When you're working a stitch pattern over the full width of the piece, as is the case if you're altering the edge stitch or working a pattern immediately after the edge stitch, you want your cast-on stitches to be an even multiple of your pattern repeat.

(Not sure what "a pattern repeat" is? It's the portion of your stitch pattern that you work over and over again. The number of stitches in a stitch pattern is often specified as a "multiple of x plus y stitches." The "x" is your pattern repeat, and "y" is the number of stitches you work at the beginning and/or end of the row around the repeated sections. Here's an example: If your stitch pattern is multiple of

STITCH PATTERNS: (Left) Small textured patterns in lightweight yarns give a vintage feel; (right) Unfussy lace in a relaxed tunic lends a casual air.

8 stitches plus 1, like the Arrow Lace pattern for the neckline of the Bohemian Wrap [page 141], that means the stitch pattern will repeat evenly over 9, 17, 25, 33, ... stitches.)

Sometimes, the sweater's cast-on stitch count just won't work out evenly for the stitch pattern you've chosen. No sweat! You just need to center that pattern repeat on your stitches. (This is most likely to happen when you're working over a larger pattern repeat. For example, the Cherry Stitch pattern for the Avant-Garde vest on page 81 is a multiple of 10 stitches.)

Here's how to center a stitch pattern: The basic idea is to incorporate as many stitch pattern repeats as you can, and choose an unobtrusive stitch for any "remainder" stitches. *(Note: I'm using the Cherry Stitch pattern from the Avant-Garde vest shown on page 81 in this example.)*

1. **First, take your total stitch count and find the nearest repeat multiple below that number.** This tells you how many repeats you'll be able to work. For the Cherry Stitch, I'm looking for a multiple of 10 stitches, plus five, to center my repeats: I want to start and end with a cherry.

   For the sample shown, the pattern called for a CO of 76. 75 is the largest multiple of 10 plus 5 stitch counts underneath my CO, giving me 8 cherries across the back of my sweater.

2. **Subtract that multiple from your total number of stitches.** This will tell you how many "remainder" stitches will be left after working the maximum number of pattern repeats possible.

   For the sample shown, I've got 76 – 75 = 1 remainder stitches.

3. **Divide this remainder in two.** This is the number of stitches you'll have, on each side, outside of the stitch repeat. If this is a small number, just work them in stockinette, garter, or whatever other plain stitch pattern looks best. If this is a larger number, investigate (and maybe swatch!)

to see whether it's possible to work a partial repeat on the sides. If it's an odd number, you'll have one stitch more at the beginning or end of your row. Don't worry, it will look just fine.

For the Avant Garde vest shown, I worked 1 stitch in Reverse Stockinette before starting my pattern repeat, and ended after working the final cherry.

NECKLINE CHANGES

No matter how perfect the fit, if the style of a sweater doesn't suit you, it's not going to see a whole lot of wear. If you hate wearing boat necks and the sweater has a boat neck, even if it fits you well, you probably won't wear it. Fortunately, necklines are pretty easy to adjust. Here's how.

CHANGING OUT A NECKLINE SHAPE

When changing a neckline shape, you'll be removing the same number of stitches as in the original pattern but in a different way. There are just a few different neckline shapes in sweater knitting:

A V neckline removes all stitches evenly over the entire neck depth (minus about an inch at the very top). To determine the rate of shaping, take the entire depth of the neckline (in rows) and divide by the number of stitches to remove on each side of the neckline. Round down to the nearest whole number.

Example: I want to change the scoop neck of the Casual Tunic (page 121) to a V neckline.

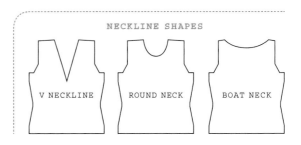

NECKLINE SHAPES

V NECKLINE   ROUND NECK   BOAT NECK

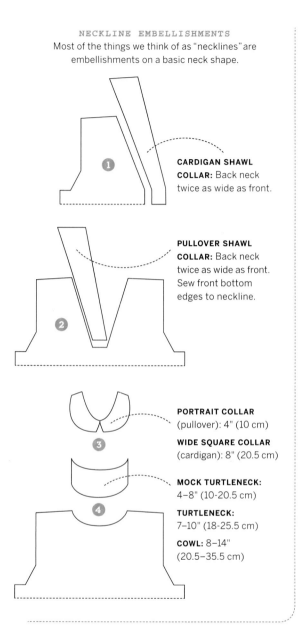

Most of the things we think of as "necklines" are embellishments on a basic neck shape.

CARDIGAN SHAWL COLLAR: Back neck twice as wide as front.

PULLOVER SHAWL COLLAR: Back neck twice as wide as front. Sew front bottom edges to neckline.

PORTRAIT COLLAR (pullover): 4" (10 cm)

WIDE SQUARE COLLAR (cardigan): 8" (20.5 cm)

MOCK TURTLENECK: 4–8" (10-20.5 cm)

TURTLENECK: 7–10" (18-25.5 cm)

COWL: 8–14" (20.5–35.5 cm)

I'm making the size and gauge shown in the sample, so 34 stitches are removed in the neckline—17 per side. In a V-neck depth of 8"/20.5 cm at the specified row gauge, there are 64 rows. 64 / 17 = 3.76, so I'll decrease one stitch at the neck edge every 3 rows 17 times on each side of my neckline.

A **rounded neckline** can either be shallow (crew neck) or deep (scoop neck). It is shaped in the same fashion no matter what the depth: Around 40-50 percent of the stitches are bound off at the bottom of the neckline. Half of the remaining stitches are removed via one rate of shaping, and the remainder are removed via a different rate. The rate of shaping used depends on the depth of the neckline:

- **Crew necklines** are typically just 2-3" (5-7.5 cm) deep and remove stitches via every row decreases plus every RS row decreases.
- **Round necklines** are typically 3-5" (7.5-12.5 cm) deep and remove stitches as for crew necks (for a straight-sided shape) or as for scoop necks (for a round-sided shape).
- **Scoop necklines** are typically 5-8" (12.5-20.5 cm) deep, and remove stitches via every RS row decreases plus every other RS row decreases.

A **boat neckline** is typically quite shallow, at 2-3" (5-7.5 cm) deep. Nearly all of the stitches are removed within the neckline at once, working just 2 or 3 decrease rows after the initial bind-off.

ADDING NECKLINE EMBELLISHMENT

All of the basic neckline shapes can be added to in various ways to achieve something you might recognize as "a neckline." Here are some of the most common:

V necklines form the basis for shawl collars. On a cardigan, a shawl collar is formed by picking up stitches as normal and working short rows on the neckline stitches until the back neck edge is twice the depth of the front neck edge. On a pullover, the procedure is the same—but in addition to the short rows, stitches must be bound off at the bottom of the V to provide a place to seam the

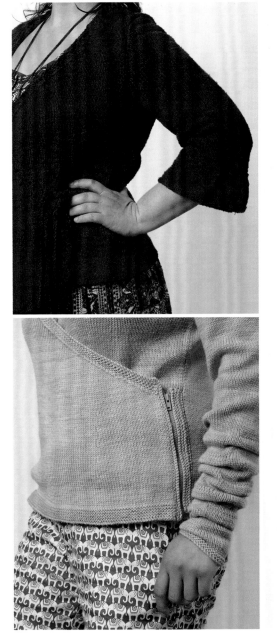

DIFFERENT SLEEVE SHAPES AND TREATMENTS (clockwise from top left): three-quarter-length and pleated, long and belled, long and ruched,

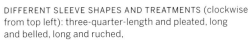

neckline stitches. Typically, a 2" (5 cm) bind-off is appropriate.

Round necklines form the basis for tons of different neckline embellishments.

- **Crew necklines** form the base for hoods, turtle-necks, mock turtlenecks, portrait necklines, and wide square collars. For all neckline edgings, pick up stitches around the neckline. Then, for a:

  Turtleneck, work in the round for 7-10" (18-25.5 cm) in desired edging, then BO. You may wish to switch to a larger needle size half-way through.

  Mock turtleneck, work in the round for 4-8" (10-20.5 cm) in desired edging, then BO.

  Portrait collars (on cardigans or pullovers), work flat in desired edging for approximately 4" (10 cm), optionally decreasing one stitch at each end of every RS row for the last inch. BO all sts.

  Wide square collars (on cardigans or pullovers), work flat in desired edging for approximately 8" (20.5 cm) or even more, then BO all sts.

- **Round necklines** form the base for henleys. Approximately 2-5" (5-12.5 cm) below the main BOs for the neck, BO around 1" (2.5 cm) of stitches. Continue straight until the traditional round neck shaping. The plackets will need to be trimmed, in addition to the existing neckline trim. (For an example, see the Sporty Tunic on page 117.)

- **Scoop necklines** form the base for cowls of all heights. To work a cowl, work in the round for a whopping 8-14" (20.5-35.5 cm). The longer the cowl, the more luscious! Check out the appearance of different cowl lengths in the cowl chapter, pages 94-111.

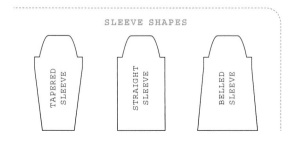

SLEEVE SHAPES

TAPERED SLEEVE   STRAIGHT SLEEVE   BELLED SLEEVE

SLEEVE ADJUSTMENTS

Sleeves are also an easy place to adjust a written pattern to suit your style. As with necklines, there are relatively few options for the basic sleeve shape. Each shape might be matched with any length, from a cozy extra-long sleeve to a short one.

Tapered sleeves are those whose cuff edge are smaller than the sleeve's upper arm. Shorter sleeves typically have zero ease at the cast-on (meaning that the width of the sleeve is the same as the width of the arm at that point); long sleeves typically have some positive ease in the wrist (meaning they measure larger than the wrist). Positive ease in the wrist gives a more gradual shape to the sleeve and a more uniform appearance to the shape of the arm.

Straight sleeves have no shaping: The cast-on stitches are worked straight to the sleeve cap shaping. Short sleeves and elbow sleeves are often straight. On a ¾-length sleeve, a straight shape will give a cute and slightly kicky look. Straight long sleeves appear slightly belled since the fit in the wrist is so generous.

Belled sleeves have a cast-on that is larger than the bicep. Elbow-length belled sleeves have an adorable flutter look; long belled sleeves are dramatic and call the eye to the hip area as with the Bohemian Cowl, opposite and on page 96. Typical belled sleeves have a cast-on that's 1-5" (2.5-12.5 cm) wider than the upper arm.

Phew! That's a ton of information. But, trust me, it will all become clear once you get going on your next project. So are you ready to play around with some yarn and knit that sweater you've been dreaming of? Let's go!

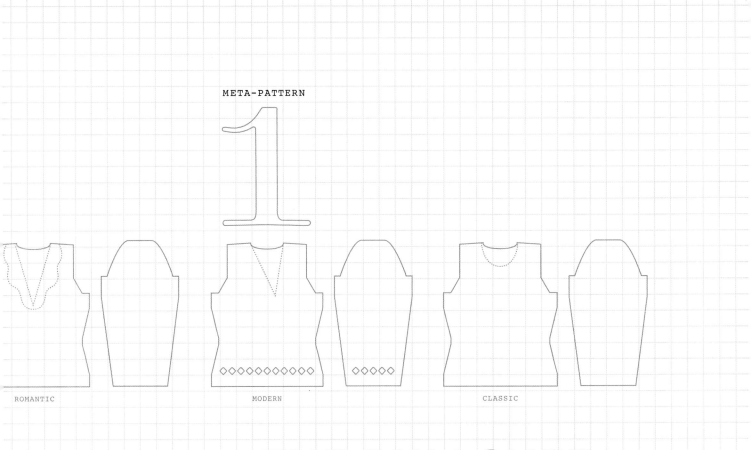

ROMANTIC   MODERN   CLASSIC

THE PULLOVER

I don't think there's anything more essentially "sweater" than a pullover, so that's where I'm starting us off on our sweater journey. A good pullover has you covered in any situation, and I've shown this one in three very different styles: a sport-weight romantic style with a deep V, lace, and ruffle; a DK-weight modern take on the V-neck classic with funky colorwork and an asymmetrical neckline; and a full-on classic preppy pullover in Aran-weight yarn and yummy texture.

All of the gauges and customization options can be mixed and matched for flexibility, so don't let these examples limit your imagination. Begin with the exercises you completed in Chapter One, and let your needles run wild!

Make this sweater suit your own style!

Classic crew
neckline.

META-PATTERN #1

CLASSIC
—
The Pullover

Neutral,
shaded-solid
color.

Texture
gives subtle
interest.

Traditional
ribbed trims.

» Courtney is wearing
size 34" (86.5 cm)
in Aran gauge.

<p>

The Pullover

FINISHED BUST

FINGERING/SPORT: 30 (32, 34, 36, 38, 40, 42, 44, 46, 48, 50, 54)" [76 (81.5, 86.5, 91.5, 96.5, 101.5, 106.5, 112, 117, 122, 127, 137) cm]

DK: 30½ (32, 34¼, 36¼, 38½, 40, 42¼, 44¼, 46½, 48, 50¼, 54½)" [77.5 (81.5, 87, 92.5, 98, 101.5, 107, 112.5, 118, 122, 127.5, 138.5) cm]

ARAN: 30¼ (32, 34¾, 36½, 38¼, 40, 42¾, 44½, 46¼, 48, 50¾, 54¼)" [77 (81.5, 88, 92.5, 97, 101.5, 108.5, 113, 117.5, 122, 128.5, 137.5) cm]

(Note: For ease in reading, the precise finished bust measurements have been rounded in the instructions below to 30 (32, 34, 36, 38, 40, 42, 44, 46, 48, 50, 54)" [76 (81.5, 86.5, 91.5, 96.5, 101.5, 106.5, 112, 117, 122, 127, 137) cm]. Your finished measurements will be as given above.

MATERIALS

See page 190 for fiber content.

FINGERING/SPORT: Quince and Co. Tern in Oyster, 5 (6, 6, 6, 7, 7, 8, 8, 9, 9, 10, 10) hanks

DK: Blue Sky Alpacas Sport Weight in #508 Medium Gray (MC) with #511 Red (CC1), #539 Capri (CC2), and Melange in #809 Toasted Almond (CC3) accents, 8 (9, 9, 10, 10, 11, 12, 13, 13, 14, 15, 16) hanks MC with 1 hank each of CC1, CC2, CC3 for all sizes

ARAN: Swans Island Organic Washable Wool Aran Weight in Sienna, 10 (10, 11, 12, 13, 14, 15, 15, 16, 17, 18, 20) hanks

GAUGE

FINGERING/SPORT: 24 sts and 36 rows = 4" (10 cm) in Stockinette st
DK: 22 sts and 30 rows = 4" (10 cm) in Stockinette st
ARAN: 18 sts and 28 rows = 4" (10 cm) in Stockinette st

NEEDLES

Change needle size if necessary to obtain correct gauge:
FINGERING/SPORT: US 3 / 3.25 mm
DK: US 5 / 3.75 mm
ARAN: US 8 / 5 mm

BACK

Using long-tail cast-on method (or a different one, if you prefer), CO

	30"	32	34	36	38	40	42	44	46	48	50	54
SPORT	90	96	102	108	114	120	126	132	138	144	150	162
DK	84	88	94	100	106	110	116	122	128	132	138	150
ARAN	68	72	78	82	86	90	96	100	104	108	114	122

sts. Work even in trim of your choice, as follows:

ROMANTIC STYLE: Beginning with a WS row, work 3 rows even in Garter st.
Switch to English Lace pattern (page 52) and work until piece measures 3½" (9 cm).
Switch to Stockinette st.

MODERN STYLE: Using MC, work even in 2x2 rib for 1" (2.5 cm). Work 2 rows in Stockinette st.
Beginning with Row 1, work Funky Dots—Body chart (page 54) until chart is complete.
Switch to Stockinette st in MC.

THE PULLOVER / **43**

CLASSIC STYLE: Work even in 2x2 rib until piece measures 2½" (6.5 cm). Switch to Stockinette st and work even.

When piece measures approximately 4" (10 cm) from CO edge, ending with a WS row, place two waist shaping markers, one on either side of the center section so that there are

	30"	32	34	36	38	40	42	44	46	48	50	54
SPORT	30	32	34	36	38	40	42	44	46	48	50	54
DK	28	30	32	34	36	36	38	40	42	44	46	50
ARAN	22	24	26	28	28	30	32	34	34	36	38	40

sts between waist shaping markers.

DECREASE ROW (RS): Work to 2 sts before first marker, ssk, sm, work to next marker, sm, k2tog, work to end. 2 sts decreased.

Work a decrease row every

SPORT: 6 / **DK:** 4 / **ARAN:** 6 rows

SPORT: 5 / **DK:** 5 / **ARAN:** 4 times total.

When all decreases are complete,

	30"	32	34	36	38	40	42	44	46	48	50	54
SPORT	80	86	92	98	104	110	116	122	128	134	140	152
DK	74	78	84	90	96	100	106	112	118	122	128	140
ARAN	60	64	70	74	78	82	88	92	96	100	106	114

sts remain. Work even until piece measures 8" (20.5 cm) from CO edge, ending with a WS row.

INCREASE ROW (RS): Work to first marker, M1-r, sm, work to next marker, sm, M1-l, work to end. 2 sts increased.

Work an increase row every

SPORT: 10 / **DK:** 8 / **ARAN:** 10 rows

SPORT: 5 / **DK:** 5 / **ARAN:** 4 times total.

When all increases are complete,

	30"	32	34	36	38	40	42	44	46	48	50	54
SPORT	90	96	102	108	114	120	126	132	138	144	150	162
DK	84	88	94	100	106	110	116	122	128	132	138	150
ARAN	68	72	78	82	86	90	96	100	104	108	114	122

sts total. Work even until piece measures 14½ (14¾, 15, 15¼, 15½, 15¾, 16, 16, 16½, 16½, 16½, 16½)" [37 (37.5, 38, 38.5, 39.5, 40, 40.5, 40.5, 42, 42, 42, 42) cm] from CO edge, ending with a WS row.

SHAPE ARMHOLES

BO

	30"	32	34	36	38	40	42	44	46	48	50	54
SPORT	6	6	6	6	6	6	6	8	8	10	10	12
DK	6	6	6	6	6	6	6	8	8	10	10	12
ARAN	6	6	6	6	6	6	6	6	8	8	8	10

sts at the beginning of the next 2 rows. BO

	30"	32	34	36	38	40	42	44	46	48	50	54
SPORT	2	2	2	2	2	2	4	4	6	6	8	10
DK	2	2	2	2	2	2	4	4	6	6	8	10
ARAN	0	0	2	2	2	2	2	4	4	4	6	6

sts at the beginning of the following 2 rows.

META-PATTERN #1

MODERN

The Pullover

Neutral base
with bright
pops of color.

Unusual
asymmetrical
neckline.

Geometric
color motif
on edges.

» Jackie is
wearing size
38" (96.5 cm)
in DK gauge.

Decrease 1 st at each end of every RS row

	30"	32	34	36	38	40	42	44	46	48	50	54
SPORT	2	4	5	7	7	8	8	8	8	8	9	8
DK	2	3	4	6	6	7	6	7	7	6	6	6
ARAN	2	3	2	3	3	4	6	5	5	6	6	6

times:

	30"	32	34	36	38	40	42	44	46	48	50	54
SPORT	70	72	76	78	84	88	90	92	94	96	96	102
DK	64	66	70	72	78	80	84	84	86	88	90	94
ARAN	52	54	58	60	64	66	68	70	70	72	74	78

sts remain. Work even until armhole measures 5½ (6, 6¼, 6½, 7, 7¼, 7½, 8, 8¼, 8¾, 9, 9½)" [14 (15, 16, 16.5, 18, 18.5, 19, 20.5, 21, 22, 23, 24) cm] and piece measures 20 (20¾, 21¼, 21¾, 22½, 23, 23½, 24, 24¾, 25¼, 25½, 26)" [51 (52.5, 54, 55, 57, 58.5, 59.5, 61, 63, 64, 65, 66) cm] from CO edge, ending with a WS row.

SHAPE NECK

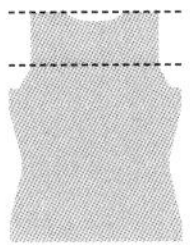

NEXT ROW (RS): Work

	30"	32	34	36	38	40	42	44	46	48	50	54
SPORT	22	22	23	24	26	27	27	28	28	29	29	31
DK	20	21	22	22	24	24	26	26	26	27	27	28
ARAN	17	17	18	19	20	21	21	22	22	22	23	24

sts, attach a new ball of yarn and BO center

	30"	32	34	36	38	40	42	44	46	48	50	54
SPORT	26	28	30	30	32	34	36	36	38	38	38	40
DK	24	24	26	28	30	32	32	32	34	34	36	38
ARAN	18	20	22	22	24	24	26	26	26	28	28	30

sts, work to end. *You will now work both sides of the neckline at the same time.*
Decrease 1 st at neck edge of every RS row twice:

	30"	32	34	36	38	40	42	44	46	48	50	54
SPORT	20	20	21	22	24	25	25	26	26	27	27	29
DK	18	19	20	20	22	22	24	24	24	25	25	26
ARAN	15	15	16	17	18	19	19	20	20	20	21	22

sts remain for each shoulder. Work even until armhole measures 6½ (7, 7¼, 7½, 8, 8¼, 8½, 9, 9¼, 9¾, 10, 10½)" [16.5 (18, 18.5, 19, 20.5, 21, 21.5, 23, 23.5, 25, 25.5, 26.5) cm] and piece measures 21 (21¾, 22¼, 22¾, 23½, 24, 24½, 25, 25¾, 26¼, 26½, 27)" [53.5 (55, 56.5, 58, 59.5, 61, 62, 63.5, 65.5, 66.5, 67.5, 68.5) cm] from CO edge, ending at the armhole edge for each side.
NEXT ROW: BO

	30"	32	34	36	38	40	42	44	46	48	50	54
SPORT	10	10	11	11	12	13	13	13	13	14	14	15
DK	9	10	10	10	11	11	12	12	12	13	13	13
ARAN	8	8	8	9	9	10	10	10	10	10	11	11

sts, work to end. Work 1 row even. BO remaining sts.

FRONT

CLASSIC STYLE: You will work the front as for the back, except front should be worked in Purl Texture pattern (page 54) after finishing the rib, and waist shaping markers should be placed around the center sts as below. *(Note: While working waist shaping, maintain established Purl Texture pattern on either side of the decreases and increases.)*

ALL OTHER STYLES: Aside from neck shaping, you will work the front as for the back, except place waist shaping markers around the center sts so that there are

	30"	32	34	36	38	40	42	44	46	48	50	54
SPORT	44	48	50	54	56	60	62	66	68	72	74	80
DK	42	44	46	50	52	54	58	60	64	66	68	74
ARAN	34	36	38	40	42	44	48	50	52	54	56	60

sts between waist shaping markers.

SHAPE NECK

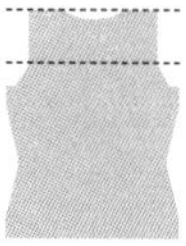

When piece measures

ROMANTIC: 12½ (12¾, 13, 13¼, 13½, 13¾, 14, 14, 14½, 14½, 14½, 14½)" [32 (32.5, 33, 33.5, 34.5, 35, 35.5, 35.5, 37, 37, 37, 37) cm]

MODERN: 13 (13¾, 14¼, 14¾, 15½, 16, 16½, 17, 17¾, 18¼, 18½, 19)" [33 (35, 36, 37.5, 39.5, 40.5, 42, 43, 45, 46.5, 47, 48.5) cm]

CLASSIC: 17½ (18¼, 18¾, 19¼, 20, 20½, 21, 21½, 22¼, 22¾, 23, 23½)" [44.5 (46.5, 47.5, 49, 51, 52, 53.5, 54.5, 56.5, 58, 58.5, 59.5) cm]

from CO edge, *shape neckline* according to instructions for your style. *Note: For the Romantic neckline and some Modern necklines, this shaping begins before armhole shaping begins.*

ROMANTIC NECKLINE: Mark the center of sts.
DECREASE ROW (RS): Work to 3 sts before center marker, k2tog, k1, remove marker and join a new ball of yarn, k1, ssk, work to end. You will now work both sides of neckline at the same time. *Note: Armhole shaping will begin before neck shaping is complete.*
Decrease 1 stitch at neck edge every 4 rows until a total of

	30"	32	34	36	38	40	42	44	46	48	50	54
SPORT	15	16	17	17	18	19	20	20	21	21	21	22
DK	14	14	15	16	17	18	18	18	19	19	20	21
ARAN	11	12	13	13	14	14	15	15	15	16	16	17

decreases have been worked.

MODERN NECKLINE: Before beginning armhole shaping, place marker for neck shaping on a RS row as follows:
Work

	30"	32	34	36	38	40	42	44	46	48	50	54
SPORT	39	41	44	47	49	52	55	58	60	63	66	72
DK	36	38	41	43	46	47	50	53	56	58	61	66
ARAN	29	31	33	35	37	39	42	44	46	47	50	54

sts, pm, work to end.

NECK SHAPING ROW (RS): Work to 3 sts before marker, k2tog, k1, remove marker and join a new ball of yarn, k1, ssk, work to end.

Working both sides of neck at the same time and continuing armhole shaping if necessary, work a Neck Shaping Row on the LEFT shoulder every

	30"	32	34	36	38	40	42	44	46	48	50	54
SPORT	7	7	6	6	6	6	5	5	5	5	5	5
DK	6	6	6	6	5	5	5	5	4	4	4	4
ARAN	8	7	7	7	6	6	5	5	5	5	5	5

rows

	30"	32	34	36	38	40	42	44	46	48	50	54
SPORT	9	9	10	10	10	11	12	12	12	12	12	13
DK	8	8	9	9	10	10	10	10	11	11	12	12
ARAN	6	7	7	7	8	8	9	9	9	9	9	10

times, and on the RIGHT shoulder every

	30"	32	34	36	38	40	42	44	46	48	50	54
SPORT	3	2	2	2	2	2	2	2	2	2	2	2
DK	2	2	2	2	2	2	2	2	2	2	2	2
ARAN	3	3	2	2	2	2	2	2	2	2	2	2

rows

	30"	32	34	36	38	40	42	44	46	48	50	54
SPORT	21	23	24	24	26	27	28	28	30	30	30	31
DK	20	20	21	23	24	26	26	26	27	27	28	30
ARAN	16	17	19	19	20	20	21	21	21	23	23	24

times.

CLASSIC NECKLINE: **NEXT ROW (RS):** Work

	30"	32	34	36	38	40	42	44	46	48	50	54
SPORT	27	28	29	30	33	34	35	36	36	37	37	40
DK	25	26	27	28	30	31	33	33	33	34	35	36
ARAN	20	21	22	23	25	26	26	27	27	28	29	30

sts, attach a new ball of yarn and BO center

	30"	32	34	36	38	40	42	44	46	48	50	54
SPORT	16	16	18	18	18	20	20	20	22	22	22	22
DK	14	14	16	16	18	18	18	18	20	20	20	22
ARAN	12	12	14	14	14	14	16	16	16	16	16	18

sts, work to end. Working both sides of the neck at the same time, decrease 1 st at neck edge *every row*

	30"	32	34	36	38	40	42	44	46	48	50	54
SPORT	4	4	4	4	5	5	6	6	6	6	6	6
DK	4	4	4	4	4	5	5	5	5	5	6	6
ARAN	3	3	3	3	4	4	4	4	4	4	4	4

times,

META-PATTERN #1

ROMANTIC
The Pullover

V neckline
is softened
by a wide
ruffle.

Light color
and silk/wool
blend.

Lace edging
on hem and
sleeves.

›› Morgan is wearing
size 40" (101.5 cm)
in sport gauge.

then every RS row

	30"	32	34	36	38	40	42	44	46	48	50	54
SPORT	3	4	4	4	4	4	4	4	4	4	4	5
DK	3	3	3	4	4	4	4	4	4	4	4	4
ARAN	2	3	3	3	3	3	3	3	3	4	4	4

times.

ALL STYLES, ALL SIZES: When all neck and armhole shaping is complete

	30"	32	34	36	38	40	42	44	46	48	50	54
SPORT	20	20	21	22	24	25	25	26	26	27	27	29
DK	18	19	20	20	22	22	24	24	24	25	25	26
ARAN	15	15	16	17	18	19	19	20	20	20	21	22

sts remain for each shoulder. Complete shoulder shaping as for back.

SLEEVE

Using long-tail cast-on method (or a different one, if you prefer), CO

	30"	32	34	36	38	40	42	44	46	48	50	54
SPORT	52	52	54	54	54	58	58	60	60	60	66	66
DK	48	48	50	50	50	54	54	56	56	56	62	62
ARAN	40	40	42	42	42	44	44	46	46	46	50	50

sts. Work even in trim of your choice, as follows:

ROMANTIC STYLE: Beginning with a WS row, work 3 rows even in Garter st.
Switch to English Lace pattern (page 52) and work until chart is complete.

MODERN STYLE: Using MC, work even in 2x2 rib for 1" (2.5 cm). Work 2 rows in Stockinette st.
Beginning with Row 1, work Funky Dots—Sleeve pattern (page 54) until chart is complete.

CLASSIC STYLE: Work even in 2x2 rib until piece measures 3½" (9 cm).
Switch to Stockinette st and work 1 row. Work the 8 rows of Purl Texture pattern (page 54) once.

Switch to Stockinette st.
When sleeve measures 5" (12.5 cm) from CO edge, beginning with a RS row, work shaping:
INCREASE ROW (RS): K1, M1-r, knit to last st, M1-l, k1.
Repeat increase row every

	30"	32	34	36	38	40	42	44	46	48	50	54
SPORT	16	12	12	12	10	10	10	8	6	6	6	4
DK	16	12	12	10	8	8	8	8	6	4	4	4
ARAN	16	14	14	12	10	10	10	8	8	6	6	4

rows until a total of

	30"	32	34	36	38	40	42	44	46	48	50	54
SPORT	7	9	9	10	12	12	13	15	18	21	21	24
DK	6	8	8	9	11	11	12	13	16	19	19	22
ARAN	5	6	6	7	9	9	10	11	13	15	15	18

increase rows have been worked:

	30"	32	34	36	38	40	42	44	46	48	50	54
SPORT	66	70	72	74	78	82	84	90	96	102	108	114
DK	60	64	66	68	72	76	78	82	88	94	100	106
ARAN	50	52	54	56	60	62	64	68	72	76	80	86

sts total.

Work even until sleeve measures 18 (18, 18, 18½, 18½, 18½, 19, 19, 19, 19, 19½, 19½)" [45.5 (45.5, 45.5, 47, 47, 47, 48.5, 48.5, 48.5, 48.5, 49.5, 49.5) cm] from CO edge, ending with a WS row.

SHAPE SLEEVE CAP

BO

	30"	32	34	36	38	40	42	44	46	48	50	54
SPORT	6	6	6	6	6	6	6	8	8	10	10	12
DK	6	6	6	6	6	6	6	8	8	10	10	12
ARAN	6	6	6	6	6	6	6	6	8	8	8	10

sts at the beginning of the next 2 rows. BO

	30"	32	34	36	38	40	42	44	46	48	50	54
SPORT	2	2	2	2	2	2	4	4	6	6	8	9
DK	2	2	2	2	2	2	4	4	6	6	8	8
ARAN	0	0	2	2	2	2	2	4	4	4	6	6

sts at the beginning of the following 2 rows. Decrease 1 st at each end of every 3rd RS row

	30"	32	34	36	38	40	42	44	46	48	50	54
SPORT	2	2	2	2	2	2	3	3	5	5	5	7
DK	1	1	1	1	1	0	1	2	4	4	4	5
ARAN	1	2	3	2	2	2	2	3	4	4	5	5

time(s), then every other RS row

	30"	32	34	36	38	40	42	44	46	48	50	54
SPORT	0	1	1	1	1	0	0	1	0	1	1	0
DK	0	0	0	0	0	0	0	1	0	1	1	1
ARAN	1	0	0	1	1	1	1	0	1	1	0	0

time(s), then every RS row

	30"	32	34	36	38	40	42	44	46	48	50	54
SPORT	9	10	11	12	14	17	15	15	10	10	11	10
DK	10	12	13	14	16	19	17	15	8	8	9	9
ARAN	7	8	6	7	9	10	11	11	5	7	7	8

times. BO

	30"	32	34	36	38	40	42	44	46	48	50	54
SPORT	3	3	3	3	3	3	3	3	4	4	4	4
DK	2	2	2	2	2	2	2	2	4	4	4	4
ARAN	2	2	2	2	2	2	2	2	3	3	3	3

sts at the beginning of the next 4 rows. BO remaining

	30"	32	34	36	38	40	42	44	46	48	50	54
SPORT	16	16	16	16	16	16	16	16	22	22	22	22
DK	14	14	14	14	14	14	14	14	20	20	20	20
ARAN	12	12	12	12	12	12	12	12	16	16	16	16

sts.

FINISHING

Wet-block all pieces to finished measurements. Sew shoulder seams using mattress stitch. Set in sleeves and sew side and sleeve seams using Mattress st.

ROMANTIC PULLOVER: Beginning at right shoulder seam, pick up and knit sts around neckline at the rate of 1 st for every bound-off st, 3 sts for every 4 rows along diagonal edges, and 2 sts for every 3 rows along vertical edges. (The exact number is not important, but it should be a multiple of 3.) Join to work in the round.

Knit 2 rounds even.
RUFFLE INCREASE ROUND: *K3, M1-r; repeat from * around.
Knit 1" (2.5 cm) even. Repeat Ruffle increase round.
Knit 2" (5 cm) even. Work 3 rounds in Garter St. BO all sts.

MODERN PULLOVER: With MC, beginning at right shoulder seam, pick up and knit sts around neckline at the rate of 1 st for every bound-off st, 3 sts for every 4 rows along diagonal edges, and 2 sts for every 3 rows along vertical edges. (The exact number is not important, but it should be a multiple of 4.) Join to work in the round.

Work even in 2x2 rib and MC, decreasing 2 sts at center of neckline every RS row, until neck trim measures ¾" (1.5 cm). BO in CC1.

CLASSIC PULLOVER: Beginning at right shoulder seam, pick up and knit sts around neckline at the rate of 1 st for every bound-off st, 3 sts for every 4 rows along diagonal edges, and 2 sts for every 3 rows along vertical edges. (The exact number is not important, but it should be a multiple of 4.)

Join to work in the round and work even in 2x2 rib until rib measures 1" (2.5 cm). BO all sts.

SPECIAL STITCHES

ENGLISH LACE (multiple of 8 sts + 1)
ROW 1 (RS): K1, *k2, yo, sl 1, k2tog, psso, yo, k3; repeat from * to end.
ROW 2: *P2, yo, p2tog, p1, ssp, yo, p1; repeat from * to last st, p1.
ROW 3: K1, *yo, ssk, yo, sl 1, k2tog, psso, yo, k2tog, yo, k1; repeat from * to end.
ROW 4: Repeat Row 2.
ROW 5: Repeat Row 1.
ROW 6: Purl.
ROW 7: K2tog, *yo, k5, yo, sl 1, k2tog, psso; repeat from * to last 7 sts, yo, k5, yo, ssk.
ROW 8: *P1, ssp, yo, p3, yo, p2tog; repeat from * to last st, p1.
ROW 9: K2tog, *yo, k2tog, yo, k1, yo, ssk, yo, sl 1, k2tog, psso; repeat from * to last 7 sts, yo, k2tog, yo, k1, [yo, ssk] twice.
ROW 10: Repeat Row 8.
ROW 11: Repeat Row 9.
ROW 12: Purl.
Repeat Rows 1–12 for English Lace.

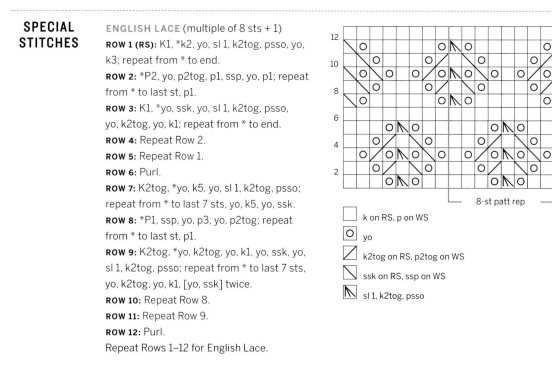

8-st patt rep

☐ k on RS, p on WS

O yo

╱ k2tog on RS, p2tog on WS

╲ ssk on RS, ssp on WS

Ⱳ sl 1, k2tog, psso

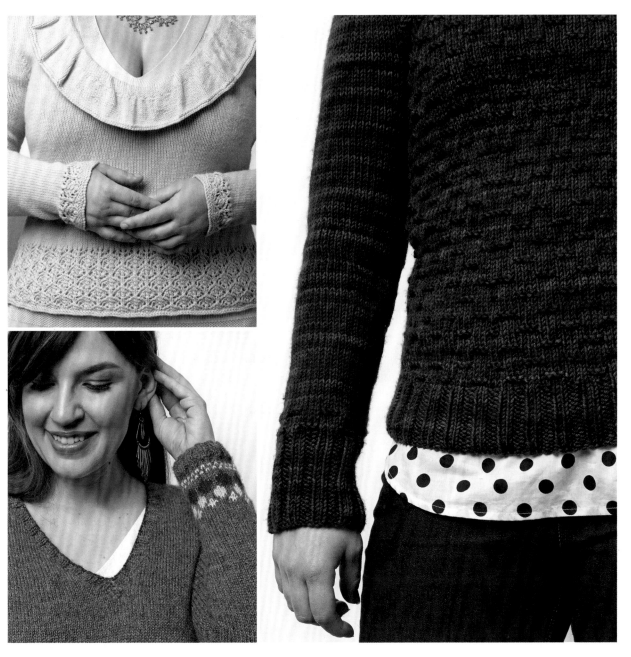

THREE STYLE OPTIONS (clockwise from top left):
romantic lace, classic texture, modern colorwork.

PURL TEXTURE PATTERN (multiple of 6 sts)

ROW 1 (RS): *K3, p3; repeat from * to end.

ROW 2 AND ALL WS ROWS: Purl.

ROWS 3 AND 7: Knit.

ROW 5: *P3, k3; repeat from * to end.

ROW 8: Purl.

Repeat Row 1–8 for Purl Texture Pattern.

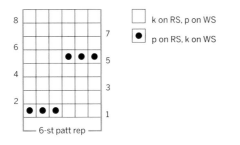

☐ k on RS, p on WS

● p on RS, k on WS

— 6-st patt rep —

FUNKY DOTS–BODY **SLEEVE**

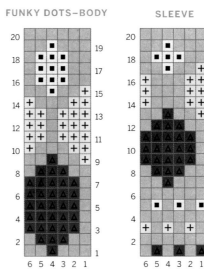

K1 MC RS, p1 MC WS

K1 CC1 RS, p1 CC1 WS

K1 CC2 RS, p1 CC2 WS

K1 CC3 RS, p1 CC3 WS

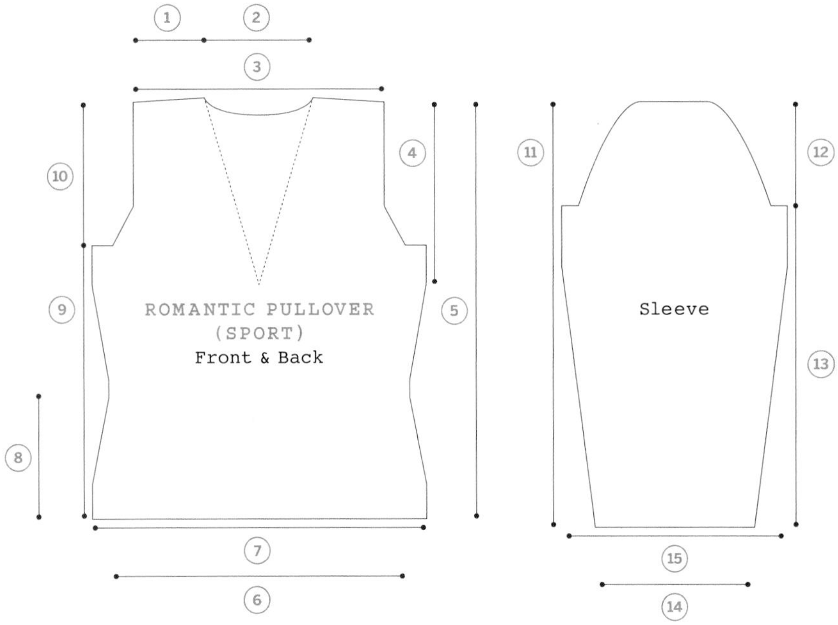

ROMANTIC PULLOVER
(SPORT)
Front & Back

Sleeve

1 3¼ (3¼, 3½, 3¾, 4, 4¼, 4¼, 4¼, 4¼, 4½, 4½, 4¾)"
   8.5 (8.5, 9, 9.5, 10, 10.5, 10.5, 11, 11, 11.5, 11.5, 12.5) cm

2 5 (5¼, 5¾, 5¾, 6, 6¼, 6¾, 6¾, 7, 7, 7, 7¼)"
   12.5 (13.5, 14.5, 14.5, 15, 16, 17, 18, 18, 18, 18.5) cm

3 11¾ (12, 12¾, 13, 14, 14¾, 15, 15¼, 15¾, 16, 16, 17)"
   29.5 (30.5, 32, 33, 35.5, 37.5, 38, 39, 40, 40.5, 40.5, 43) cm

4 8½ (9, 9¼, 9½, 10, 10¼, 10½, 11, 11¼, 11¾, 12, 12½)"
   21.5 (23, 23.5, 24, 25.5, 26, 26.5, 28, 28.5, 30, 30.5, 32) cm

5 21 (21¾, 22¼, 22¾, 23½, 24, 24½, 25, 25¾, 26¼, 26½, 27)"
   53.5 (55, 56.5, 58, 59.5, 61, 62, 63.5, 65.5, 66.5, 67.5, 68.5) cm

6 13¼ (14¼, 15¼, 16¼, 17¼, 18¼, 19¼, 20¼, 21¼, 22¼, 23¼, 25¼)"
   34 (36.5, 39, 41.5, 44, 46.5, 49, 51.5, 54, 56.5, 59.5, 64.5) cm

7 15 (16, 17, 18, 19, 20, 21, 22, 23, 24, 25, 27)"
   38 (40.5, 43, 45.5, 48.5, 51, 53.5, 56, 58.5, 61, 63.5, 68.5) cm

8 7½"/19 cm

9 14½ (14¾, 15, 15¼, 15½, 15¾, 16, 16, 16½, 16½, 16½, 16½)"
   37 (37.5, 38, 38.5, 39.5, 40, 40.5, 40.5, 42, 42, 42, 42) cm

10 6½ (7, 7¼, 7½, 8, 8¼, 8½, 9, 9¼, 9¾, 10, 10½)"
    16.5 (18, 18.5, 19, 20.5, 21, 21.5, 23, 23.5, 25, 25.5, 26.5) cm

11 22¼ (23, 23, 23¾, 24¼, 24½, 25¼, 25¾, 25½, 26, 26½, 27)"
    56.5 (58, 58.5, 60.5, 61.5, 62, 64, 65, 64.5, 66, 67.5, 69) cm

12 4¼ (5, 5, 5¼, 5¾, 6, 6¼, 6¾, 6½, 7, 7, 7¾)"
    10.5 (12.5, 13, 13.5, 14.5, 15, 16, 17, 16.5, 17.5, 18, 20) cm

13 18 (18, 18, 18½, 18½, 18½, 19, 19, 19, 19, 19½, 19½)"
    45.5 (45.5, 45.5, 47, 47, 47, 48.5, 48.5, 48.5, 48.5, 49.5, 49.5) cm

14 8¾ (8¾, 9, 9, 9, 9¾, 9¾, 10, 10, 10, 11, 11)"
    22 (22, 23, 23, 23, 24.5, 24.5, 25.5, 25.5, 25.5, 28, 28) cm

15 11 (11¾, 12, 12¼, 13, 13¾, 14, 15, 16, 17, 18, 19)"
    28 (29.5, 30.5, 31.5, 33, 34.5, 35.5, 38, 40.5, 43, 45.5, 48.5) cm

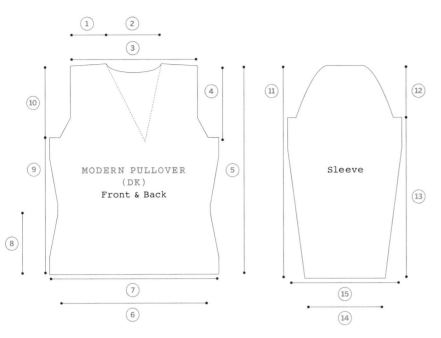

MODERN PULLOVER
(DK)
Front & Back

Sleeve

1 3¼ (3½, 3¾, 3¾, 4, 4, 4¼, 4¼, 4¼, 4½, 4½, 4¾)"
   8.5 (9, 9, 9, 10, 10, 11, 11, 11, 11.5, 11.5, 12) cm

2 5 (5, 5½, 5¾, 6¼, 6½, 6½, 6½, 7, 7, 7¼, 7¾)"
   13 (13, 14, 15, 15.5, 16.5, 16.5, 16.5, 17.5, 17.5, 18.5, 19.5) cm

3 11¾ (12, 12¾, 13, 14¼, 14½, 15¼, 15¼, 15¾, 16, 16¼, 17)"
   29.5 (30.5, 32.5, 33.5, 36, 37, 39, 39, 39.5, 40.5, 41.5, 43.5) cm

4 8"/20.5 cm

5 21 (21¾, 22¼, 22¾, 23½, 24, 24½, 25, 25¾, 26¼, 26½, 27)"
   53.5 (55, 56.5, 58, 59.5, 61, 62, 63.5, 65.5, 66.5, 67.5, 68.5) cm

6 13½ (14¼, 15¼, 16¼, 17½, 18¼, 19¼, 20¼, 21½, 22¼, 23¼, 25½)"
   34 (36, 39, 41.5, 44.5, 46, 49, 51.5, 54.5, 56.5, 59, 64.5) cm

7 15¼ (16, 17, 18¼, 19¼, 20, 21, 22¼, 23¼, 24, 25, 27¼)"
   39 (40.5, 43.5, 46, 49, 51, 53.5, 56.5, 59, 61, 63.5, 69.5) cm

8 7½"/19 cm

9 14½ (14¾, 15, 15¼, 15½, 15¾, 16, 16, 16½, 16½, 16½, 16½)"
   37 (37.5, 38, 38.5, 39.5, 40, 40.5, 40.5, 42, 42, 42, 42) cm

10 6½ (7, 7¼, 7½, 8, 8¼, 8½, 9, 9¼, 9¾, 10, 10½)"
   16.5 (18, 18.5, 19, 20.5, 21, 21.5, 23, 23.5, 25, 25.5, 26.5) cm

11 22½ (23, 23¼, 24, 24¾, 24¾, 25½, 26¼, 25½, 26, 26¾, 27)"
   57 (58.5, 59.5, 61, 62.5, 62.5, 64.5, 66.5, 64.5, 66, 68, 69) cm

12 4½ (5, 5¼, 5½, 6¼, 6¼, 6½, 7¼, 6½, 7, 7¼, 8)"
   11.5 (13, 13.5, 14, 15.5, 15.5, 16.5, 18.5, 16.5, 17.5, 18.5, 20.5) cm

13 18 (18, 18, 18½, 18½, 18½, 19, 19, 19, 19, 19½, 19½)"
   45.5 (45.5, 45.5, 47, 47, 47, 48.5, 48.5, 48.5, 48.5, 49.5, 49.5) cm

14 8¾ (8¾, 9, 9, 9, 9¾, 9¾, 10¼, 10¼, 10¼, 11¼, 11¼)"
   22 (22, 23, 23, 23, 25, 25, 26, 26, 26, 28.5, 28.5) cm

15 11 (11¾, 12, 12¼, 13, 13¾, 14¼, 15, 16, 17, 18¼, 19¼)"
   27.5 (29.5, 30.5, 31.5, 33.5, 35, 36, 38, 40.5, 43.5, 46, 49) cm

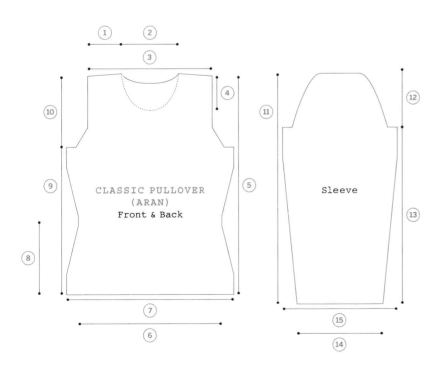

CLASSIC PULLOVER
(ARAN)
Front & Back

Sleeve

1 3¼ (3¼, 3½, 3¾, 4, 4¼, 4¼, 4½, 4½, 4½, 4¾, 5)"
   8.5 (8.5, 9, 9.5, 10, 10.5, 10.5, 11.5, 11.5, 11.5, 12, 12.5) cm

2 5 (5¼, 5¾, 5¾, 6¼, 6¼, 6¾, 6¾, 6¾, 7, 7, 7½)"
   12.5 (13.5, 14.5, 14.5, 16, 16, 17, 17, 17, 18, 18, 19) cm

3 11½ (12, 13, 13¼, 14¼, 14¾, 15, 15½, 15½, 16, 16½, 17¼)"
   29.5 (30.5, 32.5, 34, 36, 37.5, 38.5, 39.5, 39.5, 40.5, 42, 44) cm

4 3½"/9 cm

5 21 (21¾, 22¼, 22¾, 23½, 24, 24½, 25, 25¾, 26¼, 26½, 27)"
   53.5 (55, 56.5, 58, 59.5, 61, 62, 63.5, 65.5, 66.5, 67.5, 68.5) cm

6 13¼ (14¼, 15½, 16½, 17¼, 18¼, 19½, 20½, 21¼, 22¼, 23½, 25¼)"
   34 (36, 39.5, 42, 44, 46.5, 49.5, 52, 54, 56.5, 60, 64.5) cm

7 15 (16, 17¼, 18¼, 19, 20, 21¼, 22¼, 23, 24, 25¼, 27)"
   38.5 (40.5, 44, 46.5, 48.5, 51, 54, 56.5, 58.5, 61, 64.5, 69) cm

8 7½"/19 cm

9 14½ (14¾, 15, 15¼, 15½, 15¾, 16, 16, 16½, 16½, 16½, 16½)"
   37 (37.5, 38, 38.5, 39.5, 40, 40.5, 40.5, 42, 42, 42, 42) cm

10 6½ (7, 7¼, 7½, 8, 8¼, 8½, 9, 9¼, 9¾, 10, 10½)"
   16.5 (18, 18.5, 19, 20.5, 21, 21.5, 23, 23.5, 25, 25.5, 26.5) cm

11 22½ (23¼, 23½, 24, 24½, 24¾, 25½, 25¾, 25½, 26¼, 27, 27)"
   57.5 (59, 59.5, 61, 62, 63, 65, 65.5, 65, 66.5, 68.5, 69) cm

12 4½ (5¼, 5½, 5½, 6, 6¼, 6½, 6¾, 6½, 7¼, 7½, 7¾)"
   11.5 (13, 14, 14, 15, 16, 16.5, 17.5, 16.5, 18, 19, 19.5) cm

13 18 (18, 18, 18½, 18½, 18½, 19, 19, 19, 19, 19½, 19½)"
   45.5 (45.5, 45.5, 47, 47, 47, 48.5, 48.5, 48.5, 48.5, 49.5, 49.5) cm

14 11 (11½, 12, 12½, 13¼, 13¾, 14¼, 15, 16, 17, 17¾, 19)"
   28 (29.5, 30.5, 31.5, 34, 35, 36, 38.5, 40.5, 43, 45, 48.5) cm

15 9 (9, 9¼, 9¼, 9¼, 9¾, 9¾, 10¼, 10¼, 10¼, 11, 11)"
   22.5 (22.5, 23.5, 23.5, 23.5, 25, 25, 26, 26, 26, 28, 28) cm

THE PULLOVER

Use this worksheet as a handy way to get all of the numbers for each individual pullover you knit in one simple place. You can photocopy these pages or download a fresh copy any time you like at www.amyherzogdesigns.com/knitwearlove.

BACK

Using long-tail cast-on method (or a different one, if you prefer), CO _____ sts.

EDGING: Work even in _____ until piece measures _____ from CO edge, ending with a WS row.

Switch to _____ and work even until piece measures _____ from CO edge, ending with a WS row.

On your last row, place markers on each side of center _____ sts.

DECREASE ROW (RS): Work to 2 sts before marker, ssk, sm, work to next marker, sm, k2tog, work to end.

Work decrease row every _____ rows _____ times total: _____ sts remain. Work even until piece measures _____ from CO edge, ending with a WS row.

INCREASE ROW (RS): Work to marker, M1-r, sm, work to next marker, sm, M1-l, work to end.

Work increase row every _____ rows _____ times total: _____ sts total. Work even until piece measures _____ from CO edge, ending with a WS row.

SHAPE ARMHOLES: BO _____ sts at the beginning of the next 2 rows. BO _____ sts at the beginning of the following 2 rows. Decrease 1 st at each end of every RS row _____ times: _____ sts remain.

Work even until piece measures _____ from CO edge, ending with a WS row.

SHAPE NECK:

NEXT ROW (RS): Work _____ sts, attach a new ball of yarn and BO center _____ sts, work to end.

Working both sides of the neckline at the same time, decrease 1 st at neck edge of every RS row twice. _____ shoulder sts remain. Work even until piece measures _____ from CO edge, ending at the armhole edge.

NEXT ROW: BO _____ sts, work to end. Work 1 row even. BO rem sts.

FRONT

Using long-tail cast-on method (or a different one, if you prefer), CO _____ sts.

EDGING: Work even in _____ until piece measures _____ from CO edge, ending with a WS row.

Switch to _____ and work even until piece measures _____ from CO edge, ending with a WS row.

On your last row, place markers on each side of center _____ sts.

DECREASE ROW (RS): Work to 2 sts before marker, ssk, sm, work to next marker, sm, k2tog, work to end.

Work decrease row every _____ rows _____ times total: _____ sts remain. Work even until piece measures _____ from CO edge, ending with a WS row.

INCREASE ROW (RS): Work to marker, M1-r, sm, work to next marker, sm, M1-l, work to end.

Work increase row every _____ rows _____ times total: _____ sts remain. Work even until piece measures _____ from CO edge, ending with a WS row.

Note: For some styles, neck shaping begins before armhole shaping.

ROMANTIC NECKLINE: Mark center of stitches.

MODERN V NECKLINE: Work _____ sts, pm, work to end.

SHAPE ARMHOLES: BO _____ sts at the beginning of the next 2 rows. BO _____ sts at the beginning of the following 2 rows. Decrease 1 st at each end of every RS row _____ times: _____ sts remain.

SHAPE NECK: When piece measures _____ from CO edge, ending with a WS row, shape neckline:

ROMANTIC NECKLINE–BOTH SIDES: Decrease 1 st at neck edge every _____ rows _____ times.

MODERN V NECKLINE–RIGHT SIDE: Decrease 1 st at neck edge every _____ rows _____ times.

MODERN V NECKLINE–LEFT SIDE: Decrease 1 st at neck edge every _____ rows _____ times.

CREW NECKLINE: NEXT ROW (RS): Work _____ sts, attach a new ball of yarn and BO center _____ sts, work to end.

Decrease 1 st at neck edge every row _____ times, then every RS row _____ times.

ALL NECKLINES: When all neck and armhole shaping is complete, _____ shoulder sts remain. Work even until piece measures _____ from CO edge, ending at the armhole edge for each side.

NEXT ROW: BO _____ sts, work to end. Work 1 row even. BO rem sts.

SLEEVE

Using long-tail cast-on method (or a different one, if you prefer), CO _____ sts.

EDGING: Work even in _____ until piece measures _____ from CO edge, ending with a WS row.

Switch to _____ and work even until piece measures _____ from CO edge, ending with a WS row.

INCREASE ROW (RS): Knit 1, M1-r, work to last st, M1-l, knit 1.

Work increase row every _____ rows _____ times total: _____ sts total. Work even until sleeve measures _____ from CO edge, ending with a WS row.

SHAPE SLEEVE CAP: BO _____ sts at the beginning of the next 2 rows. BO _____ sts at the beginning of the following 2 rows. Decrease 1 st at each end of every 3rd RS row _____ times, then every 2nd RS row _____ times, then every RS row _____ times.

BO _____ sts at the beginning of the next 4 rows.

BO remaining _____ sts.

FINISHING

Follow instructions on page 52.

2

VINTAGE   CASUAL   CLASSIC

THE CARDIGAN

Change it up!

Gauges offered
Sport, bulky, worsted

Closures
Ties, none, buttons

Stitch patterns
Lacy ribbing, allover texture, bamboo ribbing

Cardigans probably win the award for most versatile sweater. They're at home in almost any wardrobe, almost any climate, and almost any yarn. They can be closed here or there, with this or that, and are a great showcase for stitch patterns and trims. I've shown three super-versatile styles here: a sweet vintage number with tie closures and a lacy rib accenting the waist; a comfortable casual cardigan with bamboo ribbing accents and an easy worn-open style; and a classic, office-appropriate version with elegant buttons and subtle textured stripes. (Want to know the best thing? All of these great options have the same V-neck shaping.)

Of course, all of the gauges and customization options can be mixed and matched. So ask yourself: What kind of cardigan have I been dreaming of?

Make this sweater suit your own style!

META-PATTERN #2

VINTAGE
The Cardigan

Tie closure works beautifully with shirts and dresses.

Lightweight yak/wool blend yarn.

Lace rib at waist.

Deep lace ribbing on sleeves.

» Francesca is wearing size 40" (101.5 cm) in sport gauge.

FINISHED BUST	**SPORT:** 30 (32, 34, 36, 38, 40, 42, 44, 46, 48, 50, 54)" [76 (81.5, 86.5, 91.5, 96.5, 101.5, 106.5, 112, 117, 122, 127, 137) cm]

SPORT: 30 (32, 34, 36, 38, 40, 42, 44, 46, 48, 50, 54)" [76 (81.5, 86.5, 91.5, 96.5, 101.5, 106.5, 112, 117, 122, 127, 137) cm]

WORSTED: 30½ (32, 34¼, 36¼, 38½, 40, 42¼, 44¼, 46½, 48, 50¼, 54½)" [77.5 (81.5, 87, 92.5, 98, 101.5, 107, 112.5, 118, 122, 127.5, 138.5) cm]

BULKY: 31 (32, 34¼, 36½, 38½, 40¾, 43, 44¼, 46¼, 48½, 50¾, 54)" [78.5 (81.5, 87, 92.5, 98, 103.5, 109.5, 112, 117.5, 123.5, 129, 137.5) cm]

(Note: For ease in reading, the precise finished bust measurements have been rounded in the instructions below to 30 (32, 34, 36, 38, 40, 42, 44, 46, 48, 50, 54)" [76 (81.5, 86.5, 91.5, 96.5, 101.5, 106.5, 112, 117, 122, 127, 137) cm]. Your finished measurements will be as given above.

MATERIALS

See page 190 for fiber content.
SPORT: Bijou Basin Ranch Bijouspun Sport Weight in Moss, 3 (3, 3, 4, 4, 4, 5, 5, 5, 5, 6) hanks
WORSTED: Rowan Lima Yarns in #885 Machu Picchu, 8 (8, 9, 10, 10, 11, 12, 12, 13, 14, 15, 16) balls
BULKY: Blue Sky Alpacas Techno in #1973 Rogue, 6 (6, 7, 7, 8, 8, 9, 9, 10, 11, 11, 12) hanks

GAUGE

SPORT: 24 sts and 32 rows = 4" (10 cm) in Stockinette st
WORSTED: 22 sts and 30 rows = 4" (10 cm) in Stockinette st
BULKY: 14.5 sts and 22 rows = 4" (10 cm) in Stockinette st

NEEDLES

Change needle size if necessary to obtain correct gauge:
SPORT: US 4 / 3.5 mm
WORSTED: US 7 / 4.5 mm
BULKY: US 9 / 5.5 mm

NOTIONS

CLASSIC STYLE: Six ¾" (19mm) buttons

BACK

Using long-tail cast-on method (or a different one, if you prefer), CO

	30"	32	34	36	38	40	42	44	46	48	50	54
SPORT	90	96	102	108	114	120	126	132	138	144	150	162
WORSTED	84	88	94	100	106	110	116	122	128	132	138	150
BULKY	56	58	62	66	70	74	78	80	84	88	92	98

sts. Work even in trim of your choice, as follows:
VINTAGE STYLE: Work even in 1x1 rib for 1" (2.5 cm), then switch to Stockinette stitch.
CASUAL STYLE: Work even in 2x2 rib for 2½" (6.5 cm), then switch to Stockinette stitch.
CLASSIC STYLE: Work even in 1x1 rib for 1" (2.5 cm), then switch to Stockinette stitch.

Continue until piece measures 2½" (6.5 cm) from CO edge, ending with a WS row, place two waist shaping markers, one on either side of the center section so that there are

	30"	32	34	36	38	40	42	44	46	48	50	54
SPORT	30	32	34	36	38	40	42	44	46	48	50	54
WORSTED	28	30	32	34	36	36	38	40	42	44	46	50
BULKY	18	20	20	22	24	24	26	26	28	30	30	32

sts between waist shaping markers.

DECREASE ROW (RS): Work to 2 sts before first marker, ssk, sm, work to next marker, sm, k2tog, work to end. 2 sts decreased.

Work a decrease row every

SPORT: 8 / **WORSTED:** 8 / **BULKY:** 12 rows

SPORT: 5 / **WORSTED:** 5 / **BULKY:** 3 times total.

When all decreases are complete,

	30"	32	34	36	38	40	42	44	46	48	50	54
SPORT	80	86	92	98	104	110	116	122	128	134	140	152
WORSTED	74	78	84	90	96	100	106	112	118	122	128	140
BULKY	50	52	56	60	64	68	72	74	78	82	86	92

sts remain.

ADDING THE VINTAGE LACE DETAIL AT WAIST: Form the Vintage Lace waist detail by switching all sts to Single Eyelet Rib (page 72) immediately after the last decrease row, and continuing in Single Eyelet Rib until the first increase row. Switch all sts to Stockinette st and proceed.

Work even until piece measures 8" (20.5 cm) from CO edge, ending with a WS row.

INCREASE ROW (RS): Work to first marker, M1-r, sm, work to next marker, sm, M1-l, work to end. 2 sts increased.

Work an increase row every

SPORT: 8 / **WORSTED:** 8 / **BULKY:** 10 rows

SPORT: 5 / **WORSTED:** 5 / **BULKY:** 3 times total.

When all increases are complete,

	30"	32	34	36	38	40	42	44	46	48	50	54
SPORT	90	96	102	108	114	120	126	132	138	144	150	162
WORSTED	84	88	94	100	106	110	116	122	128	132	138	150
BULKY	56	58	62	66	70	74	78	80	84	88	92	98

sts total. Work even until piece measures 13½ (13¾, 14, 14¼, 14½, 14¾, 15, 15, 15½, 15½, 15½, 15½)" [34.5 (35, 35.5, 36, 37, 37.5, 38, 38, 39.5, 39.5, 39.5, 39.5) cm] from CO edge, ending with a WS row.

SHAPE ARMHOLES

BO

	30"	32	34	36	38	40	42	44	46	48	50	54
SPORT	6	6	6	6	6	6	8	8	10	10	12	14
WORSTED	6	6	6	6	6	6	6	8	8	10	10	12
BULKY	4	4	4	4	4	4	6	6	6	8	8	8

sts at the beginning of the next 2 rows. BO

	30"	32	34	36	38	40	42	44	46	48	50	54
SPORT	2	2	2	2	2	4	4	6	6	8	8	10
WORSTED	2	2	2	2	2	2	4	4	6	6	8	10
BULKY	0	0	2	2	2	2	2	2	4	4	6	6

sts at the beginning of the following 2 rows. Decrease 1 st at each end of every RS row

	30"	32	34	36	38	40	42	44	46	48	50	54
SPORT	2	4	5	7	7	6	6	6	6	6	7	6
WORSTED	2	3	4	6	6	7	6	7	7	6	6	6
BULKY	3	3	2	3	3	4	3	4	3	3	3	4

times:

META-PATTERN #2

CLASSIC
The Cardigan

Yarn is large gauge, but lofty and light.

Traditional V-neck shape with buttons.

Allover texture adds understated interest.

Long, simple sleeves.

» Courtney is wearing size 34" (86.5 cm) in bulky gauge.

	30"	32	34	36	38	40	42	44	46	48	50	54
SPORT	70	72	76	78	84	88	90	92	94	96	96	102
WORSTED	64	66	70	72	78	80	84	84	86	88	90	94
BULKY	42	44	46	48	52	54	56	56	58	58	58	62

sts remain. Work even until armhole measures 5½ (6, 6¼, 6½, 7, 7¼, 7½, 8, 8¼, 8¾, 9, 9½)" [14 (15, 16, 16.5, 18, 18.5, 19, 20.5, 21, 22, 23, 24) cm] and piece measures 19 (19¾, 20¼, 20¾, 21½, 22, 22½, 23, 23¾, 24¼, 24½, 25)" [48.5 (50, 51.5, 52.5, 54.5, 56, 57, 58.5, 60.5, 61.5, 62, 63.5) cm], ending with a WS row.

SHAPE NECK

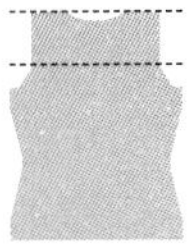

NEXT ROW (RS): Work

	30"	32	34	36	38	40	42	44	46	48	50	54
SPORT	20	20	22	22	23	25	25	25	26	26	26	28
WORSTED	18	19	20	20	22	22	23	23	24	24	25	26
BULKY	13	13	14	14	15	16	17	17	17	17	17	18

sts, attach a new ball of yarn and BO center

	30"	32	34	36	38	40	42	44	46	48	50	54
SPORT	30	32	32	34	38	38	40	42	42	44	44	46
WORSTED	28	28	30	32	34	36	38	38	38	40	40	42
BULKY	16	18	18	20	22	22	22	22	24	24	24	26

sts, work to end. *You will now work both sides of the neckline at the same time.*
Decrease 1 st at neck edge of every RS row twice:

	30"	32	34	36	38	40	42	44	46	48	50	54
SPORT	18	18	20	20	21	23	23	23	24	24	24	26
WORSTED	16	17	18	18	20	20	21	21	22	22	23	24
BULKY	11	11	12	12	13	14	15	15	15	15	15	16

sts remain for each shoulder. Work even until armhole measures 6½ (7, 7¼, 7½, 8, 8¼, 8½, 9, 9¼, 9¾, 10, 10½)" [16.5 (18, 18.5, 19, 20.5, 21, 21.5, 23, 23.5, 25, 25.5, 26.5) cm] and piece measures 20 (20¾, 21¼, 21¾, 22½, 23, 23½, 24, 24¾, 25¼, 25½, 26)" [51 (52.5, 54, 55, 57, 58.5, 59.5, 61, 63, 64, 65, 66) cm] from CO edge, ending at the armhole edge for each side.
NEXT ROW: BO

	30"	32	34	36	38	40	42	44	46	48	50	54
SPORT	9	9	10	10	11	12	12	12	12	12	12	13
WORSTED	8	9	9	9	10	10	11	11	11	11	12	12
BULKY	6	6	6	6	7	7	8	8	8	8	8	8

sts, work to end. Work 1 row even. BO remaining sts.

FRONTS

Using long-tail cast-on method (or a different one, if you prefer), CO

	30"	32	34	36	38	40	42	44	46	48	50	54
SPORT	42	46	48	52	54	58	60	64	66	70	72	78
WORSTED	38	42	44	48	50	52	56	58	60	64	66	72
BULKY	26	28	30	32	34	34	36	38	40	42	44	48

sts. Set up and work trim pattern as follows:

VINTAGE STYLE: Work even in 1x1 rib for 1" (2.5 cm), then switch to Stockinette St.

CASUAL STYLE: Set up 2x2 rib and Bamboo Rib (page 72): Mark the 15 sts on the neck edge of the front.

RIGHT FRONT FIRST ROW (RS): K1, work next 14 sts in Bamboo Rib, pm, work remainder in 2x2 rib starting with k2.

LEFT FRONT FIRST ROW (RS): Work in 2x2 rib to last 15 sts, ending with k2, pm, work next 14 sts in Bamboo Rib, k1.

Work even in 2x2 rib and Bamboo Rib for 2½" (6.5 cm), then switch to Stockinette st and preserve Bamboo Rib throughout front.

Note: All neck shaping should be worked at the edge of the Stockinette st section, leaving the Bamboo Rib panel intact. For the smaller sizes worked at Bulky gauge, the front neck shaping will eventually remove some of the Bamboo Rib.

CLASSIC STYLE: Work even in 1x1 rib for 1" (2.5 cm), then switch to Roman Stripes pattern (page 70).

Continue until piece measures 2½" (6.5 cm) from CO edge, ending with a WS row. Place waist shaping marker

	30"	32	34	36	38	40	42	44	46	48	50	54
SPORT	21	23	24	26	27	29	30	32	33	35	36	39
WORSTED	19	21	22	24	25	26	28	29	30	32	33	36
BULKY	10	11	14	16	17	17	18	19	20	21	22	24

sts from armhole edge on each front. Armhole edge is beginning of RS rows for left front and end of RS rows for right front

DECREASE ROW–RIGHT FRONT (RS): Work to marker, sm, k2tog, work to end. 1 st decreased.

DECREASE ROW–LEFT FRONT (RS): Work to 2 sts before marker, ssk, sm, work to end. 1 st decreased.

Work a decrease row every

SPORT: 8 / **WORSTED:** 8 / **BULKY:** 12 rows

SPORT: 5 / **WORSTED:** 5 / **BULKY:** 3 times total.

When all decreases are complete,

	30"	32	34	36	38	40	42	44	46	48	50	54
SPORT	37	41	43	47	49	53	55	59	61	65	67	73
WORSTED	33	37	39	43	45	47	51	53	55	59	61	67
BULKY	23	25	27	29	31	31	33	35	37	39	41	45

sts remain.

ADDING THE VINTAGE LACE DETAIL AT WAIST: Form the Vintage Lace waist detail by switching all sts to Single Eyelet Rib (page 72) immediately after the last decrease row, and continuing in Single Eyelet Rib until the first increase row. Switch all sts to Stockinette st and proceed.

Work even until piece measures 8" (20.5 cm) from CO edge, ending with a WS row.

INCREASE ROW–RIGHT FRONT (RS): Work to marker, sm, M1-l, work to end. 1 st increased.

INCREASE ROW–LEFT FRONT (RS): Work to marker, M1-r, sm, work to end. 1 st increased.

Work an increase row every

SPORT: 8 / **WORSTED:** 8 / **BULKY:** 10 rows

SPORT: 5 / **WORSTED:** 5 / **BULKY:** 3 times total.

When all increases are complete,

	30"	32	34	36	38	40	42	44	46	48	50	54
SPORT	42	46	48	52	54	58	60	64	66	70	72	78
WORSTED	38	42	44	48	50	52	56	58	60	64	66	72
BULKY	26	28	30	32	34	34	36	38	40	42	44	48

sts total.

SHAPE NECK

When piece measures 12½ (12¾, 13, 13¼, 13½, 13¾, 14, 14, 14½, 14½, 14½, 14½)" [32 (32.5, 33, 33.5, 34.5, 35, 35.5, 35.5, 37, 37, 37, 37) cm], shape neck.

Note: Armhole shaping starts 1" (2.5 cm) after neck shaping begins.

DECREASE ROW (RS): Decrease 1 st at neck edge every

	30"	32	34	36	38	40	42	44	46	48	50	54
SPORT	3	3	3	3	3	3	3	3	3	3	3	3
WORSTED	4	3	3	3	3	3	3	3	4	3	3	3
BULKY	4	3	3	3	3	4	4	4	4	4	4	4

rows

	30"	32	34	36	38	40	42	44	46	48	50	54
SPORT	14	16	15	17	18	19	19	21	20	22	21	22
WORSTED	12	14	14	16	16	17	19	18	17	20	19	20
BULKY	8	10	10	11	12	10	10	11	12	12	12	14

times.

At the same time, when piece measures 13½ (13¾, 14, 14¼, 14½, 14¾, 15, 15, 15½, 15½, 15½, 15½)" [34.5 (35, 35.5, 36, 37, 37.5, 38, 38, 39.5, 39.5, 39.5, 39.5) cm] from CO edge, ending with a WS row for the left front and a RS row for the right front, *shape armholes.*

SHAPE ARMHOLES

BO

	30"	32	34	36	38	40	42	44	46	48	50	54
SPORT	6	6	6	6	6	6	8	8	10	10	12	14
WORSTED	6	6	6	6	6	6	6	8	8	10	10	12
BULKY	4	4	4	4	4	4	6	6	6	8	8	8

sts at the beginning of the next row. Work 1 row even. BO

	30"	32	34	36	38	40	42	44	46	48	50	54
SPORT	2	2	2	2	2	4	4	6	6	8	8	10
WORSTED	2	2	2	2	2	2	4	4	6	6	8	10
BULKY	0	0	2	2	2	2	2	2	4	4	6	6

sts at the beginning of the following row.

Decrease 1 st at armhole edge of every RS row

	30"	32	34	36	38	40	42	44	46	48	50	54
SPORT	2	4	5	7	7	6	6	6	6	6	7	6
WORSTED	2	3	4	6	6	7	6	7	7	6	6	6
BULKY	3	3	2	3	3	4	3	4	3	3	3	4

times.

META-PATTERN #2

CASUAL
The Cardigan

Two ribbing variations.

Soft, slightly heathered alpaca.

Casual worn-open style.

Comfy sleeves trimmed with bamboo rib.

Francesca is wearing size 38" (91.5 cm) in worsted gauge.

When all neck and armhole shaping is complete

	30"	32	34	36	38	40	42	44	46	48	50	54
SPORT	18	18	20	20	21	23	23	23	24	24	24	26
WORSTED	16	17	18	18	20	20	21	21	22	22	23	24
BULKY	11	11	12	12	13	14	15	15	15	15	15	16

sts remain for shoulders. Work even and complete shoulder shaping as for back.

SLEEVES

Using long-tail cast-on method (or a different one, if you prefer), CO

	30"	32	34	36	38	40	42	44	46	48	50	54
SPORT	48	48	52	52	54	54	58	58	60	60	66	72
WORSTED	44	44	48	48	50	50	54	54	56	56	62	66
BULKY	30	30	32	32	34	34	36	36	38	38	40	44

sts.
Set up and work sleeve trims as follows.

VINTAGE STYLE: Work even in Single Eyelet Rib (page 72) for 6" (15 cm) and then switch to Stockinette st, *starting shaping as described below when sleeve measures 2½" (6.5 cm).*

CASUAL STYLE: Work even in 2x2 rib for 1" (2.5 cm), then work 2 rows in Stockinette st.
Work 2" (5 cm) in Bamboo Rib (page 72) then switch to Stockinette st, *starting shaping as described below when sleeve measures 2½" (6.5 cm).*

CLASSIC STYLE: Work even in 1x1 rib for 1" (2.5 cm), then switch to Stockinette st.

When sleeve measures 2½" (6.5 cm), beginning with a RS row, *shape sleeve:*
INCREASE ROW (RS): Work 1, M1-r, work to last st, M1-l, work 1.
Repeat increase row every

	30"	32	34	36	38	40	42	44	46	48	50	54
SPORT	12	10	10	10	10	8	8	8	6	6	6	4
WORSTED	12	12	12	10	10	8	10	8	6	6	6	4
BULKY	14	12	12	10	10	10	10	8	8	6	6	6

rows until a total of

	30"	32	34	36	38	40	42	44	46	48	50	54
SPORT	9	10	10	12	12	13	13	16	18	21	22	24
WORSTED	8	9	9	11	11	12	12	15	16	19	20	22
BULKY	5	6	6	7	7	8	8	9	10	12	13	14

increase rows have been worked:

	30"	32	34	36	38	40	42	44	46	48	50	54
SPORT	66	68	72	76	78	80	84	90	96	102	110	120
WORSTED	60	62	66	70	72	74	78	84	88	94	102	110
BULKY	40	42	44	46	48	50	52	54	58	62	66	72

sts total.
Work even until sleeve measures 18 (18, 18, 18½, 18½, 18½, 19, 19, 19, 19½, 19½, 19½)" [45.5 (45.5, 45.5, 47, 47, 47, 48.5, 48.5, 48.5, 49.5, 49.5, 49.5) cm] from CO edge, ending with a WS row.

SHAPE SLEEVE CAP

BO

	30"	32	34	36	38	40	42	44	46	48	50	54
SPORT	6	6	6	6	6	6	8	8	10	10	12	14
WORSTED	6	6	6	6	6	6	6	8	8	10	10	12
BULKY	4	4	4	4	4	4	6	6	6	8	8	8

sts at the beginning of the next 2 rows. BO

	30"	32	34	36	38	40	42	44	46	48	50	54
SPORT	2	2	2	2	2	4	4	6	6	8	8	9
WORSTED	2	2	2	2	2	2	4	4	6	6	8	8
BULKY	0	0	2	2	2	2	2	2	4	4	5	5

sts at the beginning of the following 2 rows. Decrease 1 st at each end of every 3rd RS row

	30"	32	34	36	38	40	42	44	46	48	50	54
SPORT	1	2	1	0	1	2	2	3	4	5	4	4
WORSTED	1	1	1	0	1	0	1	1	4	4	3	4
BULKY	0	0	1	1	1	1	2	2	3	4	4	3

time(s), then every other RS row

	30"	32	34	36	38	40	42	44	46	48	50	54
SPORT	0	0	0	1	0	0	1	0	1	0	1	1
WORSTED	0	1	0	1	0	1	0	1	0	1	1	0
BULKY	0	0	0	0	0	0	0	0	1	0	0	0

time(s), then every RS row

	30"	32	34	36	38	40	42	44	46	48	50	54
SPORT	10	10	13	15	16	14	13	14	8	9	11	13
WORSTED	10	10	13	15	16	17	17	17	8	8	11	13
BULKY	9	10	8	9	10	11	9	10	4	4	5	9

times. BO

	30"	32	34	36	38	40	42	44	46	48	50	54
SPORT	3	3	3	3	3	3	3	3	4	4	4	4
WORSTED	2	2	2	2	2	2	2	2	4	4	4	4
BULKY	1	1	1	1	1	1	1	1	2	2	2	2

st(s) at the beginning of the next 4 rows. BO final

	30"	32	34	36	38	40	42	44	46	48	50	54
SPORT	16	16	16	16	16	16	16	16	22	22	22	22
WORSTED	14	14	14	14	14	14	14	14	20	20	20	20
BULKY	10	10	10	10	10	10	10	10	14	14	14	14

sts.

FINISHING

Wet-block all pieces to finished measurements. Sew shoulder seams using mattress stitch. Set in sleeves and sew side and sleeve seams using mattress stitch.

VINTAGE STYLE: Pm at beginning of neck shaping on each front edge.

With RS facing and beginning at lower edge of right front, pick up and knit 3 sts for every 4 rows along right front edge to neck shaping marker. Count sts and adjust if necessary to make total a multiple of 5 sts plus 2. Work in Single Eyelet Rib until trim measures 1¼" (3 cm). BO all sts.

Repeat for left front between neck shaping and lower edge.

CO 75 sts, then pick up and knit sts around neck edge starting at right neck shaping marker and ending at left neck shaping marker, at the rate of 4 sts for every 5 rows along diagonal edges, 3 sts for every 4 rows along vertical edges, and 1 st for every bound-off st, then CO 75 additional sts. Count sts and adjust if necessary to make total a multiple of 5 sts plus 2. Work in Single Eyelet Rib (page 72) until trim and ties measure 1¼" (3 cm). BO all sts.

Sew top edge of front trim to underside of ties.

CASUAL STYLE: With RS facing and beginning at lower edge of right front, pick up and knit sts along front and neck edges at the rate of 3 sts for every 4 rows along vertical edges, 4 sts for every 5 rows along diagonal edges, and 1 st for every bound-off st. Count sts and adjust if necessary to make total a multiple of 4 sts plus 2.

Work even in 2x2 rib until neck trim measures 2" (5 cm). BO all sts.

CLASSIC STYLE: With RS facing and beginning at lower edge of right front, pick up and knit sts along front and neck edges at the rate of 3 sts for every 4 rows along vertical edges, 4 sts for every 5 rows along diagonal edges, and 1 st for every bound-off st. Count sts and adjust if necessary to make total an odd number of sts.

Work even in 1x1 rib for ½" (1.5 cm), ending with a WS row.
Place 6 markers for buttonholes evenly along right front placket between lower edge and beginning of neck shaping.

BUTTONHOLE ROW 1 (RS): *Work as established to first (next) marker; remove marker and BO 2 sts; rep from * for additional markers.

BUTTONHOLE ROW 2 (WS): Work as established, casting on 2 sts at each buttonhole BO. You are back to your original number of sts.

Continue in 1x1 rib until trim measures 1½" (4 cm). BO all sts.

SPECIAL STITCHES

ROMAN STRIPES (over an even number of sts)
ROWS 1 AND 3 (RS): Knit
ROWS 2 AND 4: Purl.
ROW 5: *K1, p1; repeat from * to end.
ROW 6: *P1, k1; repeat from * to end.
Repeat Rows 1–6 for Roman Stripes.

THREE STITCH PATTERNS (clockwise from top left):
classic Roman Stripes, vintage lace rib, casual
bamboo rib.

SINGLE EYELET RIB (multiple of 5 sts + 2)

ROWS 1 AND 5 (RS): P2, *k3, p2; repeat from * to end.

ROW 2–AND ALL WS ROWS: K2, *p3, k2; repeat from * to end.

ROW 3: P2, *k2tog, yo, k1, p2; repeat from * to end.

ROW 7: P2, *k1, yo, ssk, p2; repeat from * to end

ROW 8: Repeat row 2.

Repeat Rows 1–8 for Single Eyelet Rib.

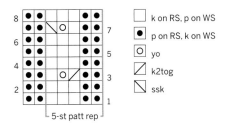

8
7
6
5
4
3
2
1
5-st patt rep
k on RS, p on WS
p on RS, k on WS
yo
k2tog
ssk

BAMBOO RIB (multiple of 12 sts + 2)

ROWS 1, 3, 7, AND 9 (RS): *P2, k4; repeat from * to last 2 sts, p2.

ROWS 2, 4, 8, AND 10: K2, *p4, k2; repeat from * to end.

ROW 5: *P8, k4; repeat from * to last 2 sts, p2.

ROW 6: K2, *p4, k8; repeat from * to end.

ROW 11: P2, *k4, p8; repeat from * to end.

ROW 12: *K8, p4; repeat from * to last 2 sts, k2.

Repeat Rows 1–12 for Bamboo Rib.

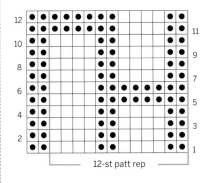

12
11
10
9
8
7
6
5
4
3
2
1
12-st patt rep

VINTAGE CARDIGAN
(SPORT)
Front & Back

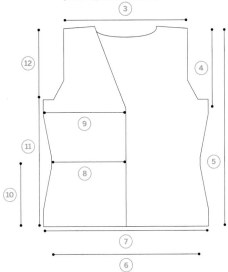

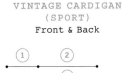

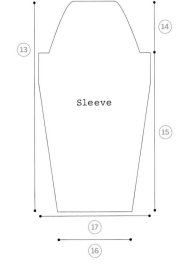

1
2
3
4
5
6
7
8
9
10
11
12
13
14
15
16
17
Sleeve

1 3 (3, 3¼, 3¼, 3½, 3¾, 3¾, 3¾, 4, 4, 4, 4¼)"
7.5 (7.5, 8.5, 8.5, 9, 9.5, 9.5, 9.5, 10, 10, 10, 11) cm

2 5¾ (6, 6, 6¼, 7, 7, 7¼, 7¾, 7¾, 8, 8, 8¼)"
14.5 (15, 15, 16, 18, 18, 18.5, 19.5, 19.5, 20.5, 20.5, 21) cm

3 11¾ (12, 12¾, 13, 14, 14¾, 15, 15¼, 15¾, 16, 16, 17)"
29.5 (30.5, 32, 33, 35.5, 37.5, 38, 39, 40, 40.5, 40.5, 43) cm

4 7½ (8, 8¼, 8½, 9, 9¼, 9½, 10, 10¼, 10¾, 11, 11½)"
19 (20.5, 21, 21.5, 23, 23.5, 24, 25.5, 26, 27.5, 28, 29) cm

5 20 (20¾, 21¼, 21¾, 22½, 23, 23½, 24, 24¾, 25¼, 25½, 26)"
51 (52.5, 54, 55, 57, 58.5, 59.5, 61, 63, 64, 65, 66) cm

6 13¼ (14¼, 15¼, 16¼, 17¼, 18¼, 19¼, 20¼, 21¼, 22¼, 23¼, 25¼)"
34 (36.5, 39, 41.5, 44, 46.5, 49, 51.5, 54, 56.5, 59.5, 64.5) cm

7 15 (16, 17, 18, 19, 20, 21, 22, 23, 24, 25, 27)"
38 (40.5, 43, 45.5, 48.5, 51, 53.5, 56, 58.5, 61, 63.5, 68.5) cm

8 6¼ (6¾, 7¼, 7¾, 8¼, 8¾, 9¼, 9¾, 10¼, 10¾, 11¼, 12¼)"
15.5 (17.5, 18, 20, 20.5, 22.5, 23.5, 25, 26, 27.5, 28.5, 31) cm

9 7 (7¾, 8, 8¾, 9, 9¾, 10, 10¾, 11, 11¾, 12, 13)"
18 (19.5, 20.5, 22, 23, 24.5, 25.5, 27, 28, 29.5, 30.5, 33) cm

10 7½"/19 cm

11 13½ (13¾, 14, 14¼, 14½, 14¾, 15, 15, 15½, 15½, 15½, 15½)"
34.5 (35, 35.5, 36, 37, 37.5, 38, 38, 39.5, 39.5, 39.5, 39.5) cm

12 6½ (7, 7¼, 7½, 8, 8¼, 8½, 9, 9¼, 9¾, 10, 10½)"
16.5 (18, 18.5, 19, 20.5, 21, 21.5, 23, 23.5, 25, 25.5, 26.5) cm

13 22¼ (23, 23, 23¾, 24¼, 24½, 25¼, 25¾, 25½, 26½, 26¾, 27¼)"
56.5 (58.5, 58.5, 60.5, 61.5, 62, 64, 65.5, 65, 67.5, 68, 69) cm

14 4¼ (5, 5, 5¼, 5¾, 6, 6¼, 6¾, 6½, 7, 7¼, 7¾)"
11 (12.5, 12.5, 13.5, 14.5, 15, 16, 17, 16.5, 18, 18.5, 19.5) cm

15 18 (18, 18, 18½, 18½, 18½, 19, 19, 19, 19½, 19½, 19½)"
45.5 (45.5, 45.5, 47, 47, 47, 48.5, 48.5, 48.5, 49.5, 49.5, 49.5) cm

16 8 (8, 8¾, 8¾, 9, 9, 9¾, 9¾, 10, 10, 11, 12)"
20.5 (20.5, 22, 22, 23, 23, 24.5, 24.5, 25.5, 25.5, 28, 30.5) cm

17 11 (11¼, 12, 12¾, 13, 13¼, 14, 15, 16, 17, 18¼, 20)"
28 (29, 30.5, 32, 33, 34, 35.5, 38, 40.5, 43, 46.5, 51) cm

CASUAL CARDIGAN (WORSTED)

Front & Back

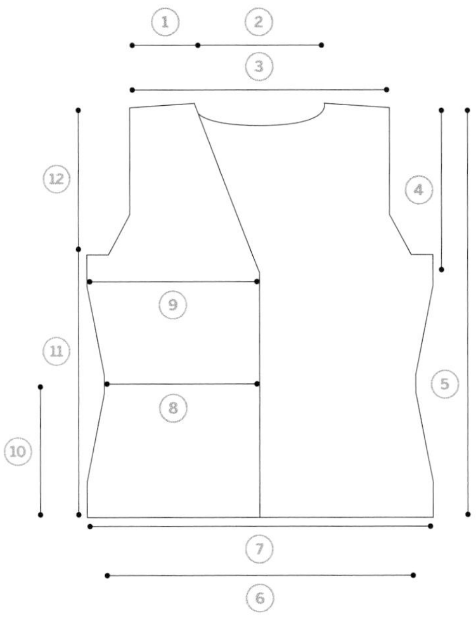

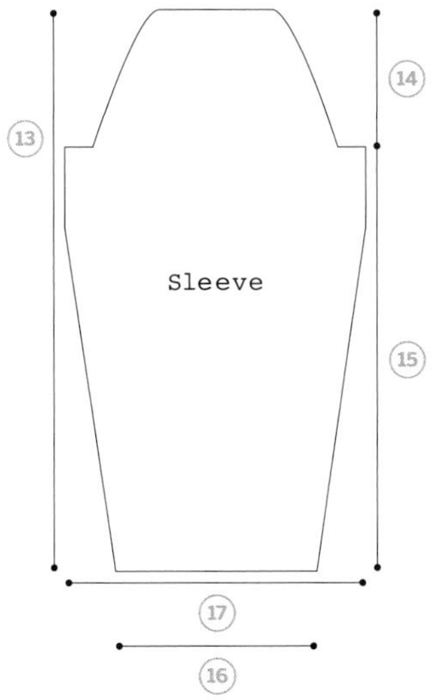

1 3 (3, 3¼, 3¼, 3¾, 3¾, 3¾, 3¾, 4, 4, 4¼, 4¼)"
7.5 (8, 8.5, 8.5, 9, 9, 9.5, 9.5, 10, 10, 10.5, 11) cm

2 5¾ (5¾, 6¼, 6½, 7, 7¼, 7¾, 7¾, 7¾, 8, 8, 8¼)"
15 (15, 15.5, 16.5, 17.5, 18.5, 19.5, 19.5, 19.5, 20.5, 20.5, 21) cm

3 11¾ (12, 12¾, 13, 14¼, 14½, 15¼, 15¼, 15¾, 16, 16¼, 17)"
29.5 (30.5, 32.5, 33.5, 36, 37, 39, 39, 39.5, 40.5, 41.5, 43.5) cm

4 7½ (8, 8¼, 8½, 9, 9¼, 9½, 10, 10¼, 10¾, 11, 11½)"
19 (20.5, 21, 21.5, 23, 23.5, 24, 25.5, 26, 27.5, 28, 29) cm

5 20 (20¾, 21¼, 21¾, 22½, 23, 23½, 24, 24¾, 25¼, 25½, 26)"
51 (52.5, 54, 55, 57, 58.5, 59.5, 61, 63, 64, 65, 66) cm

6 13½ (14¼, 15¼, 16¼, 17½, 18¼, 19¼, 20¼, 21½, 22¼, 23¼, 25½)"
34 (36, 39, 41.5, 44.5, 46, 49, 51.5, 54.5, 56.5, 59, 64.5) cm

7 15¼ (16, 17, 18¼, 19¼, 20, 21, 22¼, 23¼, 24, 25, 27¼)"
39 (40.5, 43.5, 46, 49, 51, 53.5, 56.5, 59, 61, 63.5, 69.5) cm

8 6 (6¾, 7, 7¾, 8¼, 8½, 9¼, 9¾, 10, 10¾, 11, 12¼)"
15 (17, 18, 20, 21, 21.5, 23.5, 24.5, 25.5, 27, 28, 31) cm

9 7 (7¾, 8, 8¾, 9, 9½, 10¼, 10½, 11, 11¾, 12, 13)"
17.5 (19.5, 20.5, 22, 23, 24, 26, 27, 27.5, 29.5, 30.5, 33.5) cm

10 7½"/19 cm

11 13½ (13¾, 14, 14¼, 14½, 14¾, 15, 15, 15½, 15½, 15½, 15½)"
34.5 (35, 35.5, 36, 37, 37.5, 38, 38, 39.5, 39.5, 39.5, 39.5) cm

12 6½ (7, 7¼, 7½, 8, 8¼, 8½, 9, 9¼, 9¾, 10, 10½)"
16.5 (18, 18.5, 19, 20.5, 21, 21.5, 23, 23.5, 25, 25.5, 26.5) cm

13 22½ (23, 23¼, 24, 24¾, 24¾, 25½, 26, 25½, 26½, 26½, 27¼)"
57 (58.5, 59.5, 61, 62.5, 62.5, 64.5, 66, 64.5, 67, 67, 69) cm

14 4½ (5, 5¼, 5½, 6¼, 6¼, 6½, 7, 6½, 7, 7, 7¾)"
11.5 (13, 13.5, 14, 15.5, 15.5, 16.5, 17.5, 16.5, 17.5, 17.5, 19.5) cm

15 18 (18, 18, 18½, 18½, 18½, 19, 19, 19, 19½, 19½, 19½)"
45.5 (45.5, 45.5, 47, 47, 47, 48.5, 48.5, 48.5, 49.5, 49.5, 49.5) cm

16 8 (8, 8¾, 8¾, 9, 9, 9¾, 9¾, 10¼, 10¼, 11¼, 12)"
20.5 (20.5, 22, 22, 23, 23, 25, 25, 26, 26, 28.5, 30.5) cm

17 11 (11¼, 12, 12¾, 13, 13½, 14¼, 15¼, 16, 17, 18½, 20)"
27.5 (28.5, 30.5, 32.5, 33.5, 34, 36, 39, 40.5, 43.5, 47, 51) cm

---

CLASSIC CARDIGAN (BULKY)

Front & Back

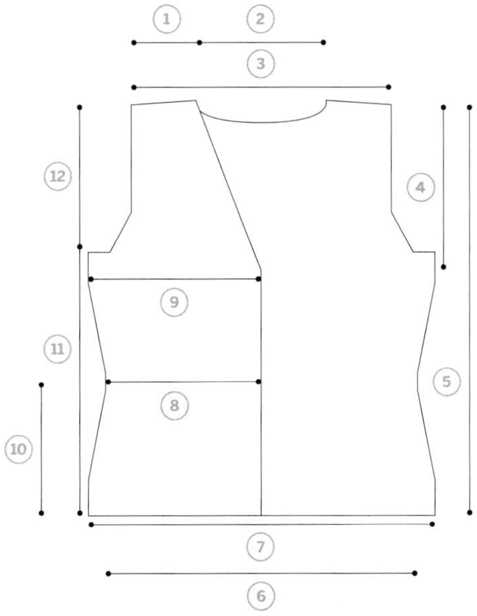

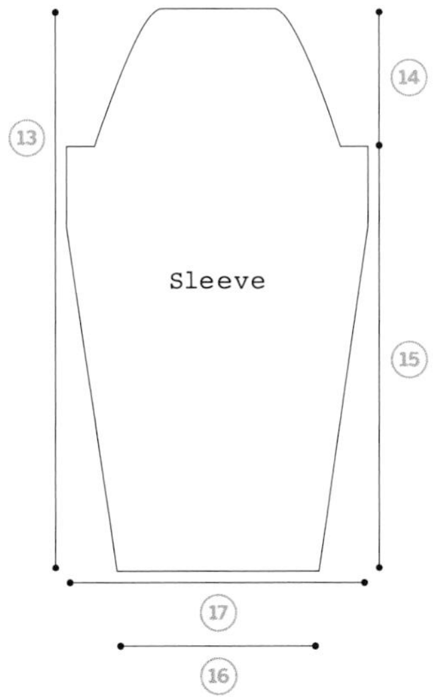

1 3 (3, 3¼, 3¼, 3½, 3¾, 4¼, 4¼, 4¼, 4¼, 4¼, 4½)"
7.5 (7.5, 8.5, 8.5, 9, 10, 10.5, 10.5, 10.5, 10.5, 10.5, 11) cm

2 5½ (6, 6, 6½, 7¼, 7¼, 7¼, 7¼, 7¾, 7¾, 7¾, 8¼)"
14 (15.5, 15.5, 17, 18, 18, 18, 18, 19.5, 19.5, 19.5, 21) cm

3 11½ (12¼, 12¾, 13¼, 14¼, 15, 15½, 15½, 16, 16, 16, 17)"
29.5 (31, 32, 33.5, 36.5, 38, 39, 39, 40.5, 40.5, 40.5, 43.5) cm

4 7½ (8, 8¼, 8½, 9, 9¼, 9½, 10, 10¼, 10¾, 11, 11½)"
19 (20.5, 21, 21.5, 23, 23.5, 24, 25.5, 26, 27.5, 28, 29) cm

5 20 (20¾, 21¼, 21¾, 22½, 23, 23½, 24, 24¾, 25¼, 25½, 26)"
51 (52.5, 54, 55, 57, 58.5, 59.5, 61, 63, 64, 65, 66) cm

6 13¾ (14¼, 15½, 16½, 17¾, 18¾, 19¾, 20½, 21½, 22½, 23¾, 25½)"
35 (36.5, 39, 42, 45, 47.5, 50.5, 52, 54.5, 57.5, 60.5, 64.5) cm

7 15½ (16, 17, 18¼, 19¼, 20½, 21½, 22, 23¼, 24¼, 25½, 27)"
39 (40.5, 43.5, 46, 49, 52, 54.5, 56, 59, 61.5, 64.5, 68.5) cm

8 6¼ (7, 7½, 8, 8½, 8½, 9, 9¾, 10¼, 10¾, 11¼, 12½)"
16 (17.5, 19, 20.5, 21.5, 21.5, 23, 24.5, 26, 27.5, 28.5, 31.5) cm

9 7¼ (7¾, 8¼, 8¾, 9½, 9½, 10, 10½, 11, 11½, 12¼, 13¼)"
18 (19.5, 21, 22.5, 24, 24, 25, 26.5, 28, 29.5, 31, 33.5) cm

10 7½"/19 cm

11 13½ (13¾, 14, 14¼, 14½, 14¾, 15, 15, 15½, 15½, 15½, 15½)"
34.5 (35, 35.5, 36, 37, 37.5, 38, 38, 39.5, 39.5, 39.5, 39.5) cm

12 6½ (7, 7¼, 7½, 8, 8¼, 8½, 9, 9¼, 9¾, 10, 10½)"
16.5 (18, 18.5, 19, 20.5, 21, 21.5, 23, 23.5, 25, 25.5, 26.5) cm

13 22¾ (23, 23½, 24¼, 24¾, 25, 26, 26¼, 26, 26¾, 27¼, 27½)"
57.5 (58.5, 59.5, 62, 62.5, 63.5, 66, 66.5, 66, 68, 69, 70) cm

14 4¼ (4¾, 5½, 5¾, 6¼, 6½, 7, 7¼, 7, 7¼, 7¾, 8)"
11 (12, 14, 15, 15.5, 16.5, 17.5, 18.5, 17.5, 18.5, 19.5, 20.5) cm

15 18 (18, 18, 18½, 18½, 18½, 19, 19, 19, 19½, 19½, 19½)"
45.5 (45.5, 45.5, 47, 47, 47, 48.5, 48.5, 48.5, 49.5, 49.5, 49.5) cm

16 8¼ (8¼, 8¾, 8¾, 9½, 9½, 10, 10, 10½, 10½, 11, 12¼)"
21 (21, 22.5, 22.5, 24, 24, 25, 25, 26.5, 26.5, 28, 31) cm

17 11 (11½, 12¼, 12¾, 13¼, 13¾, 14¼, 15, 16, 17, 18¼, 19¾)"
28 (29.5, 31, 32, 33.5, 35, 36.5, 38, 40.5, 43.5, 46, 50.5) cm

META-PATTERN #2

THE CARDIGAN

Use this worksheet as a handy way to get all of the numbers for each individual cardigan you knit in one simple place. You can photocopy these pages or download a fresh copy any time you like at www.amyherzogdesigns.com/knitwearlove.

BACK

Using long-tail cast-on method (or a different one, if you prefer), CO _____ sts.

EDGING: Work even in _____ until piece measures _____ from CO edge, ending with a WS row.

Switch to _____ and work even until piece measures _____ from CO edge, ending with a WS row.

On your last row, place markers on each side of center _____ sts.

DECREASE ROW (RS): Work to 2 sts before marker, ssk, sm, work to next marker, sm, k2tog, work to end.

Work decrease row every _____ rows _____ times total: _____ sts remain. Work even until piece measures _____ from CO edge, ending with a WS row.

Form the Vintage Lace waist detail by switching all sts to Single Eyelet Rib immediately after the last decrease row, continuing until the 1st increase row. Switch all sts to Stockinette st and proceed.

INCREASE ROW (RS): Work to marker, M1-r, sm, work to next marker, sm, M1-l, work to end.

Work increase row every _____ rows _____ times total: _____ sts total. Work even until piece measures _____ from CO edge, ending with a WS row.

SHAPE ARMHOLES: BO _____ sts at the beginning of the next 2 rows. BO _____ sts at the beginning of the following 2 rows. Decrease 1 st at each end of every RS row _____ times: _____ sts remain.

Work even until piece measures _____ from CO edge, ending with a WS row.

NEXT ROW (RS): Work _____ sts. Attach a new ball of yarn and BO center _____ sts, work to end.

Working both sides of neckline at the same time, decrease 1 st at neck edge of every RS row twice. _____ shoulder sts remain. Work even until piece measures _____ from CO edge, ending at the armhole edge.

NEXT ROW: BO _____ sts, work to end. Work 1 row even. BO rem sts.

FRONTS

Using long-tail cast-on method (or a different one, if you prefer), CO _____ sts.

EDGING: Work even in _____ until piece measures _____ from CO edge, ending with a WS row.

Switch to _____ and work even until piece measures _____ from CO edge, ending with a WS row.

On your last row, place marker _____ sts from armhole edge.

DECREASE ROW—RIGHT FRONT (RS): Work to marker, sm, k2tog, work to end.

DECREASE ROW—LEFT FRONT (RS): Work to 2 sts before marker, ssk, sm, work to end.

Work decrease row every _____ rows _____ times total: _____ sts remain. Work even until piece measures _____ from CO edge, ending with a WS row. Repeat Vintage Lace Detail as for back, if desired.

INCREASE ROW–RIGHT FRONT (RS): Work to marker, sm, M1-l, work to end.

INCREASE ROW–LEFT FRONT (RS): Work to marker, M1-r, M1-l, work to end.

Work increase row every _____ rows _____ times total: _____ sts total. Work even until piece measures _____ from CO edge, ending with a WS row.

Note: Armhole shaping begins before neck shaping is complete—please read ahead.

SHAPE NECK: Decrease 1 st at neck edge every _____ rows _____ times total.

When neck shaping measures 1" (2.5 cm), shape armholes:

BO _____ sts at the beginning of the next armhole edge. Work 1 row even.

BO _____ sts at the beginning of the following armhole edge.

Decrease 1 st at armhole edge of every RS row _____ times.

ALL: When all neck and armhole shaping is complete, _____ shoulder sts remain. Work even until piece measures _____ from CO edge, ending at the armhole edge.

NEXT ROW: BO _____ sts, work to end. Work 1 row even. BO rem sts.

SLEEVES

Using long-tail cast-on method (or a different one, if you prefer), CO _____ sts.

EDGING: Work even in _____ until piece measures _____ from CO edge, ending with a WS row.

Switch to _____ and work even until piece measures _____ from CO edge, ending with a WS row.

INCREASE ROW (RS): Work 1, M1-r, work to last st, M1-l, work 1.

Work increase row every _____ rows _____ times total: _____ sts total. Work even until sleeve measures _____ from CO edge, ending with a WS row.

SHAPE SLEEVE CAP: BO _____ sts at the beginning of the next 2 rows. BO _____ sts at the beginning of the following 2 rows. Decrease 1 st at each end of every 3rd RS row _____ times total, then every other RS row _____ times, then every RS row _____ times.

BO _____ sts at the beginning of the next 4 rows.

BO final _____ sts.

FINISHING

Follow instructions on page 70.

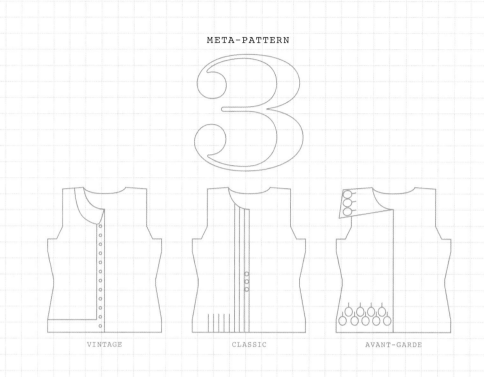

VINTAGE   CLASSIC   AVANT-GARDE

THE VEST

Sometimes overlooked, vests are versatile in the wardrobe and a great place to start if you're a newbie to sweater knitting. They're light on yarn, generally quicker to knit than sleeved sweaters, and only require minimal finishing.

I've given you three different takes on the classic crewneck vest by playing around with the gauge, finishing, and stitch patterning. All of these options can be mixed and matched, so don't limit yourself to the exact versions shown here! I've created a vintage feel by pairing lots of small buttons with a small-scale texture and portrait collar; a classic feel through the use of crisp ribbing and buttons on the middle of the button band only (imagine it under a tweedy blazer!), and an attention-getting avant-garde style with a huge collar, geometric 3-D stitch pattern, and a zipper.

Change it up!

Gauges offered
Sport, worsted, Aran

Closures/Finishing
Buttons, portrait collar, wide collar, zipper

Stitch patterns
Texture, geometric, ribbing

Make this sweater suit your own style!

META-PATTERN #3

CLASSIC
The Vest

Simple
ribbed trim
on armholes.

Ribbing panel
adds interest.

Stockinette
for easy
shaping.

Buttons at the
waist only.

» Courtney is wearing
size 34" (86.5 cm)
in worsted gauge.

FINISHED BUST	**SPORT:** 30 (32, 34, 36, 38, 40, 42, 44, 46, 48, 50, 54)" [76 (81.5, 86.5, 91.5, 96.5, 101.5, 106.5, 112, 117, 122, 127, 137) cm]

SPORT: 30 (32, 34, 36, 38, 40, 42, 44, 46, 48, 50, 54)" [76 (81.5, 86.5, 91.5, 96.5, 101.5, 106.5, 112, 117, 122, 127, 137) cm]

WORSTED: 30½ (32, 34¼, 36½, 38, 40½, 42¼, 44¼, 46½, 48, 50¼, 54)" [77.5 (81.5, 87, 92.5, 96.5, 103, 108.5, 112.5, 118, 122, 125, 137) cm]

ARAN: 30 (32, 34, 36, 38, 40, 42, 44, 46, 48, 50, 54)" [76 (81.5, 86.5, 91.5, 96.5, 101.5, 106.5, 112, 117, 122, 127, 137) cm]

(Note: For ease in reading, the precise finished bust measurements have been rounded in the instructions below to 30 (32, 34, 36, 38, 40, 42, 44, 46, 48, 50, 54)" [76 (81.5, 86.5, 91.5, 96.5, 101.5, 106.5, 112, 117, 122, 127, 137) cm]. Your finished measurements will be as given above.

MATERIALS

See page 190 for fiber content.

SPORT: Imperial Yarns Tracie Too in Quail, 2 (2, 2, 3, 3, 3, 3, 4, 4, 4, 4) hanks

WORSTED: Stonehedge Fiber Mill Shepherd's Wool Worsted Weight in Pewter, 3 (3, 3, 3, 4, 4, 4, 4, 5, 5, 5, 5) hanks

ARAN: Quince and Co. Osprey in Pea Coat, 4 (4, 4, 5, 5, 5, 6, 6, 6, 7, 7, 8) hanks

GAUGE

SPORT: 24 sts and 36 rows = 4" (10 cm) in Stockinette st
WORSTED: 21 sts and 32 rows = 4" (10 cm) in Stockinette st
ARAN: 16 sts and 24 rows = 4" (10 cm) in Stockinette st

NEEDLES

Change needle size if necessary to obtain correct gauge:
SPORT: US 4 / 3.5 mm
WORSTED: US 7 / 4.5 mm
ARAN: US 8 / 5 mm

NOTIONS

VINTAGE STYLE: 8–10 ½" (18 mm) buttons
CLASSIC STYLE: Five ¾" (20 mm) buttons
AVANT-GARDE STYLE: 20" (50 cm) separating zipper

BACK

Using long-tail cast-on method (or a different one, if you prefer), CO

	30"	32	34	36	38	40	42	44	46	48	50	54
SPORT	90	96	102	108	114	120	126	132	138	144	150	162
WORSTED	80	84	90	96	100	106	112	116	122	126	132	142
ARAN	60	64	68	72	76	80	84	88	92	96	100	108

sts. Work even in trim of your choice, as follows:

VINTAGE STYLE: Work 3 rows of Garter st, then work even in Woven Pattern (page 88) until piece measures 2" (5 cm) from CO edge. Switch to Stockinette st.

CLASSIC STYLE: Work even in 2x2 rib until piece measures 4" (10 cm), then switch to Stockinette st.

AVANT-GARDE STYLE: Work even in 2x2 rib until piece measures 1" (2.5 cm), then work 2 rows even in Reverse Stockinette st.

Switch to Cherry Stitch (page 89). Work 32 rows of pattern. *Note: Shaping begins before Cherry Stitch is complete. Work shaping on WS rows.*

Switch to Reverse Stockinette st.

Continue until piece measures 4" (10 cm) from CO edge, ending with a WS row.

On your last row, place two waist shaping markers, one on either side of the center section so that there are:

	30"	32	34	36	38	40	42	44	46	48	50	54
SPORT	32	34	36	38	40	42	44	46	48	50	52	56
WORSTED	26	28	30	32	34	36	38	38	40	42	44	48
ARAN	20	22	22	24	26	26	28	30	30	32	34	36

sts between waist shaping markers.

DECREASE ROW (RS): Work to 2 sts before first marker, ssk, sm, work to next marker, sm, k2tog, work to end. 2 sts decreased.

Work a decrease row every

SPORT: 8 / **WORSTED:** 8 / **ARAN:** 8 rows

SPORT: 5 / **WORSTED:** 4 / **ARAN:** 3 times total.

When all decreases are complete,

	30"	32	34	36	38	40	42	44	46	48	50	54
SPORT	80	86	92	98	104	110	116	122	128	134	140	152
WORSTED	72	76	82	88	92	98	104	108	114	118	124	134
ARAN	54	58	62	66	70	74	78	82	86	90	94	102

sts remain. Work even until piece measures 8½" (21.5 cm) from CO edge, ending with a WS row.

INCREASE ROW (RS): Work to first marker, M1-r, sm, work to next marker, sm, M1-l, work to end. 2 sts increased.

Work an increase row every

SPORT: 8 / **WORSTED:** 10 / **ARAN:** 10 rows

SPORT: 5 / **WORSTED:** 4 / **ARAN:** 3 times total.

When all increases are complete,

	30"	32	34	36	38	40	42	44	46	48	50	54
SPORT	90	96	102	108	114	120	126	132	138	144	150	162
WORSTED	80	84	90	96	100	106	112	116	122	126	132	142
ARAN	60	64	68	72	76	80	84	88	92	96	100	108

sts total. Work even until piece measures 14 (14¼, 14½, 14¾, 15, 15¼, 15½, 15½, 16, 16, 16, 16)" [35.5 (36, 37, 37.5, 38, 38.5, 39.5, 39.5, 40.5, 40.5, 40.5, 40.5) cm] from CO edge, ending with a WS row.

SHAPE ARMHOLES

BO

	30"	32	34	36	38	40	42	44	46	48	50	54
SPORT	6	6	6	6	6	6	6	8	8	10	10	12
WORSTED	6	6	6	6	6	6	6	6	8	8	10	12
ARAN	4	4	4	4	4	4	6	6	6	8	8	10

sts at the beginning of the next 2 rows. BO

META-PATTERN #3

AVANT-GARDE
The Vest

Oversized
collar.

Dark, bold
color.

Clean zipper
closure.

Large-scale
stitch pattern.

» Francesca is
wearing size
38" (96.5 cm) in
Aran gauge.

	30"	32	34	36	38	40	42	44	46	48	50	54
SPORT	2	2	2	2	2	2	4	4	6	6	8	10
WORSTED	0	2	2	2	2	2	4	4	6	6	8	8
ARAN	0	2	2	2	2	2	2	2	4	4	6	6

sts at the beginning of the following 2 rows. Decrease 1 st at each end of every RS row

	30"	32	34	36	38	40	42	44	46	48	50	54
SPORT	2	4	5	7	7	8	8	8	8	8	9	8
WORSTED	3	2	4	5	5	6	6	7	6	7	6	6
ARAN	3	2	3	4	4	5	4	5	5	4	4	4

times:

	30"	32	34	36	38	40	42	44	46	48	50	54
SPORT	70	72	76	78	84	88	90	92	94	96	96	102
WORSTED	62	64	66	70	74	78	80	82	82	84	84	90
ARAN	46	48	50	52	56	58	60	62	62	64	64	68

sts remain. Work even until armhole measures 5½ (6, 6¼, 6½, 7, 7¼, 7½, 8, 8¼, 8¾, 9, 9½)" [14 (15, 16, 16.5, 18, 18.5, 19, 20.5, 21, 22, 23, 24) cm] and piece measures 19½ (20¼, 20¾, 21¼, 22, 22½, 23, 23½, 24¼, 24¾, 25, 25½)" [49.5 (51.5, 52.5, 54, 56, 57, 58.5, 59.5, 61.5, 63, 63.5, 65) cm], ending with a WS row.

SHAPE NECK

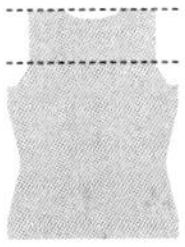

NEXT ROW (RS): Work

	30"	32	34	36	38	40	42	44	46	48	50	54
SPORT	20	20	22	22	23	25	25	25	26	26	26	28
WORSTED	18	18	19	20	21	22	23	23	23	23	23	25
ARAN	14	14	15	15	16	17	17	18	18	18	18	19

sts, attach a new ball of yarn and BO center

	30"	32	34	36	38	40	42	44	46	48	50	54
SPORT	30	32	32	34	38	38	40	42	42	44	44	46
WORSTED	26	28	28	30	32	34	34	36	36	38	38	40
ARAN	18	20	20	22	24	24	26	26	26	28	28	30

sts, work to end. *You will now work both sides of the neckline at the same time.*
Decrease 1 st at neck edges of every RS row twice:

	30"	32	34	36	38	40	42	44	46	48	50	54
SPORT	18	18	20	20	21	23	23	23	24	24	24	26
WORSTED	16	16	17	18	19	20	21	21	21	21	21	23
ARAN	12	12	13	13	14	15	15	16	16	16	16	17

sts remain for each shoulder. Work even until armhole measures 6½ (7, 7¼, 7½, 8, 8¼, 8½, 9, 9¼, 9¾, 10, 10½)" [16.5 (18, 18.5, 19, 20.5, 21, 21.5, 23, 23.5, 25, 25.5, 26.5) cm] and piece measures 20½ (21¼, 21¾, 22¼, 23, 23½, 24, 24½, 25¼, 25¾, 26, 26½)" [52 (54, 55, 56.5, 58.5, 59.5, 61, 62, 64, 65.5, 66, 67.5) cm] from CO edge, ending at the armhole edge for each side.

NEXT ROW: BO

	30"	32	34	36	38	40	42	44	46	48	50	54
SPORT	9	9	10	10	11	12	12	12	12	12	12	13
WORSTED	8	8	9	9	10	10	11	11	11	11	11	12
ARAN	6	6	7	7	7	8	8	8	8	8	8	9

sts, work to end. Work 1 row even. BO remaining sts.

FRONTS Using long-tail cast-on method (or a different one, if you prefer), CO

	30"	32	34	36	38	40	42	44	46	48	50	54
SPORT	46	48	52	54	58	60	64	66	70	72	76	82
WORSTED	40	42	46	48	50	54	56	58	62	64	66	72
ARAN	30	32	34	36	38	40	42	44	46	48	50	54

sts. Set up and work trim pattern as follows:

VINTAGE STYLE: Work 3 rows of Garter Stitch, then work even in Woven Pattern (page 88) until piece measures 2" (5 cm) from CO edge.
Switch to Stockinette st.

CLASSIC STYLE: Work even in 2x2 rib until piece measures 4" (10 cm).

Place a marker 20 sts in from the neck edge for Sport gauges, 16 sts in from edge for Worsted gauges, and 12 sts in from edge for Aran gauges. Neck edge is at beginning of RS row for the right front, and at the end of the RS row for the left front.

Keeping marked sts at neck edge in 2x2 rib, switch to Stockinette st on remaining sts.

AVANT-GARDE STYLE: Work even in 2x2 rib until piece measures 1" (2.5 cm). Work 2 rows even in Reverse Stockinette.
Switch to Cherry Stitch (page 89). Work 32 rows of pattern. *Note: Shaping begins before Cherry Stitch is complete. Work shaping on WS rows.*
Switch to Reverse Stockinette st.

Continue until piece measures 4" (10 cm) from CO edge, ending with a WS row.
On your last row, place a waist shaping marker in the center of your sts. If you have an odd number of sts, place the marker to the left of the center st for the left front, to the right of the center st for the right front.
DECREASE ROW–RIGHT FRONT (RS): Work to marker, sm, k2tog, work to end. 1 st decreased.
DECREASE ROW–LEFT FRONT (RS): Work 2 sts before marker, ssk, sm, work to end. 1 st decreased.
Work a decrease row every
SPORT: 8 / **WORSTED:** 8 / **ARAN:** 8 rows
SPORT: 5 / **WORSTED:** 4 / **ARAN:** 3 times total.
When all decreases are complete,

	30"	32	34	36	38	40	42	44	46	48	50	54
SPORT	41	43	47	49	53	55	59	61	65	67	71	77
WORSTED	36	38	42	44	46	50	52	54	58	60	62	68
ARAN	27	29	31	33	35	37	39	41	43	45	47	51

sts remain. Work even until piece measures 8½" (21.5 cm) from CO edge, ending with a WS row.
INCREASE ROW–RIGHT FRONT (RS): Work to marker, sm, M1-l, work to end. 1 st increased.
INCREASE ROW–LEFT FRONT (RS): Work to marker, M1-r, sm, work to end. 1 st increased.
Work an increase row every
SPORT: 8 / **WORSTED:** 10 / **ARAN:** 10 rows
SPORT: 5 / **WORSTED:** 4 / **ARAN:** 3 times total.

META-PATTERN #3

VINTAGE
The Vest

Fine wool
in neutral
palette.

Portrait
collar.

Small-scale
texture.

Tailored
waist
shaping.

» Kiki is
wearing size
34" (86.5 cm) in
sport gauge.

When all increases are complete,

	30"	32	34	36	38	40	42	44	46	48	50	54
SPORT	46	48	52	54	58	60	64	66	70	72	76	82
WORSTED	40	42	46	48	50	54	56	58	62	64	66	72
ARAN	30	32	34	36	38	40	42	44	46	48	50	54

sts total. Work even until piece measures 14 (14¼, 14½, 14¾, 15, 15¼, 15½, 15½, 16, 16, 16, 16)" [35.5 (36, 37, 37.5, 38, 38.5, 39.5, 39.5, 40.5, 40.5, 40.5, 40.5) cm] from CO edge, ending with a WS row for the left front and a RS row for the right front.

SHAPE ARMHOLES

BO

	30"	32	34	36	38	40	42	44	46	48	50	54
SPORT	6	6	6	6	6	6	6	8	8	10	10	12
WORSTED	6	6	6	6	6	6	6	6	8	8	10	12
ARAN	4	4	4	4	4	4	6	6	6	8	8	10

sts at the beginning of the next row. Work 1 row even. BO

	30"	32	34	36	38	40	42	44	46	48	50	54
SPORT	2	2	2	2	2	2	4	4	6	6	8	10
WORSTED	0	2	2	2	2	2	4	4	6	6	8	8
ARAN	0	2	2	2	2	2	2	2	4	4	6	6

sts at the beginning of the following row. Work 1 row even.
Decrease 1 st at armhole edge of every RS row

	30"	32	34	36	38	40	42	44	46	48	50	54
SPORT	2	4	5	7	7	8	8	8	8	8	9	8
WORSTED	3	2	4	5	5	6	6	7	6	7	6	6
ARAN	3	2	3	4	4	5	4	5	5	4	4	4

times:

	30"	32	34	36	38	40	42	44	46	48	50	54
SPORT	36	36	39	39	43	44	46	46	48	48	49	52
WORSTED	31	32	34	35	37	40	40	41	42	43	42	46
ARAN	23	24	25	26	28	29	30	31	31	32	32	34

sts remain. Work even until armhole measures 3½ (4, 4¼, 4½, 5, 5¼, 5½, 6, 6¼, 6¾, 7, 7½)" [9 (10, 11, 11.5, 12.5, 13.5, 14, 15, 16, 17, 18, 19) cm], and piece measures 17½ (8¼, 18¾, 19¼, 20, 20½, 21, 21½, 22¼, 22¾, 23, 23½)" [44.5 (46.5, 47.5, 49, 51, 52, 53.5, 54.5, 56.5, 58, 58.5, 59.5) cm], ending with a RS row for left front and with a WS row for right front.

SHAPE NECK

BIND-OFF ROW (NECK SIDE): BO

	30"	32	34	36	38	40	42	44	46	48	50	54
SPORT	8	8	8	8	9	9	10	10	10	10	10	11
WORSTED	6	7	7	7	8	8	8	8	9	9	9	10
ARAN	5	5	5	6	6	6	6	6	6	7	7	7

sts at the beginning of the next neck-edge row, then decrease 1 st at neck edge every row

	30"	32	34	36	38	40	42	44	46	48	50	54
SPORT	5	5	5	5	6	6	6	6	7	7	7	7
WORSTED	4	4	5	5	5	6	5	6	6	6	6	6
ARAN	3	3	3	3	4	4	4	4	4	4	4	5

times and then every RS row

	30"	32	34	36	38	40	42	44	46	48	50	54
SPORT	5	5	6	6	7	6	7	7	7	7	8	8
WORSTED	5	5	5	5	5	6	6	6	6	7	6	7
ARAN	3	4	4	4	4	4	5	5	5	5	5	5

times.

ALL STYLES, ALL SIZES: When all neck and armhole shaping is complete

	30"	32	34	36	38	40	42	44	46	48	50	54
SPORT	18	18	20	20	21	23	23	23	24	24	24	26
WORSTED	16	16	17	18	19	20	21	21	21	21	21	23
ARAN	12	12	13	13	14	15	15	16	16	16	16	17

sts remain. Work even and complete shoulder shaping as for back.

FINISHING

Wet-block all pieces to finished measurements. Sew shoulder seams using mattress stitch. Sew side seams using mattress stitch.

VINTAGE STYLE: *Trim armholes in applied i-cord as follows:*
With RS facing and circular needle, beginning at underarm seam, pick up and knit sts around armhole at the rate of 1 st for every bound-off st and 1 st for each row. Using double-pointed needle, CO 3 sts. You will now work an applied i-cord around the armhole edge. K2 on dpns, sl 1 knitwise, knit first st from circular needle onto dpn, psso. Slide sts to the right-hand end of the dpn.

Using the other dpn, k2, sl 1 knitwise, knit second st from circular needle onto dpn, psso. Slide sts to the right-hand end of the dpn. Continue in this manner until all armhole sts have been worked and you have a nice edge on your armhole. Bind off 3 remaining i-cord sts. Cut yarn and sew ends of cord together.
Repeat for other armhole.
Weave in ends.

RIGHT FRONT PLACKET: With RS facing and starting at lower right front corner, pick up and knit 3 sts for every 4 rows along right front edge to neck edge. Work 3 rows even in Woven Pattern (page 88). Count sts and adjust if necessary to make a multiple of 4 sts.
Place markers for buttonholes every 2" (5 cm) along edge.
BUTTONHOLE ROW (RS): Work to marker, remove marker, yo, k2tog; repeat to end.
Work 3 more rows in Woven Pattern. Work 3 rows in Garter st. BO all sts.

LEFT FRONT PLACKET: Work as for right front placket, omitting buttonholes.

PORTRAIT COLLAR: With RS facing and starting at right neck edge, pick up and knit sts around neckline at the rate of 1 st for every bound-off st, 4 sts for every 5 rows along diagonal edges, and 3 sts for every 4 rows along vertical edges.

Work even in Woven Pattern until collar measures 2" (5 cm), then decrease 1 st at each end of every row 6 times.
BO all sts.

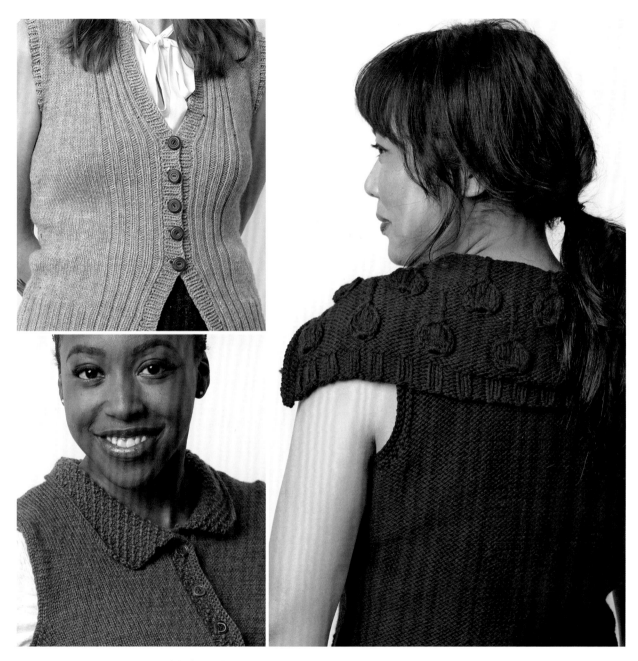

STITCH PATTERNS AND CLOSURES (clockwise from top left): Classic waist-only buttons with ribbing, avant-garde collar, vintage texture and tiny buttons.

CLASSIC STYLE

ARMHOLES: With RS facing and circular needle, beginning at underarm seam, pick up and knit sts around armhole at the rate of 1 st for every bound-off st, 4 sts for every 5 rows along diagonal edges, and 3 sts for every 4 rows along vertical edges. Join for working in the round. Work even in 1x1 rib until armhole trim measures ½" (1.5 cm). BO all sts.

PLACKET: With RS facing and starting at lower right front corner, pick up and knit 3 sts for every 4 rows along right front edge to neck edge. Work 2 rows even in 2x2 rib.

Place markers for 5 buttonholes evenly spaced over the center third of your sts.
BUTTONHOLE ROW (RS): Work to marker, remove marker, yo, k2tog; repeat to end.
Work 3 more rows in 1x1 rib. BO all sts.

LEFT FRONT PLACKET: Work as for right front placket, omitting buttonholes.

NECK EDGE: With RS facing and starting at right neck edge, pick up and knit sts around neckline at the rate of 1 st for every bound-off st, 4 sts for every 5 rows along diagonal edges, and 3 sts for every 4 rows along vertical edges. Count sts and adjust if needed to a multiple of 4 sts. Work even in 2x2 rib until neck trim measures ½" (1.5 cm). BO all sts.

AVANT-GARDE STYLE

ARMHOLES: Beginning at side seam, pick up sts around armholes at the rate of 3 sts for every 4 rows along vertical edges, 4 sts for every 5 rows along diagonal edges, and 1 st for every bound-off st. Join for working in the round and work 2 rounds even in Garter st, starting with a purl round. BO all sts.

COLLAR: CO

	30"	32	34	36	38	40	42	44	46	48	50	54
SPORT	114	116	116	118	126	126	130	132	134	136	136	140
WORSTED	90	94	94	96	100	104	104	106	108	112	110	116
ARAN	68	70	70	74	78	78	80	80	80	84	84	88

sts.
Work even in 2x2 rib until piece measures 1" (2.5 cm), then work 2 rows even in Reverse Stockinette st. Work 32 rows of Cherry Stitch, then continue in Reverse Stockinette st until collar measures 8" (20 cm) from CO edge. BO all sts.

Seam bound-off edge of collar to neck edge of vest, making sure RS of collar shows when collar is folded.

PLACKET: With RS facing, beginning at lower front edge, pick up and knit sts along right front edge at the rate of 3 sts for every 4 rows. Work 3 rows even in Garter st. BO all sts.
Repeat for left front.
Hand-sew zipper to WS of front opening.

SPECIAL STITCHES

WOVEN PATTERN (multiple of 4 sts)
PURL TWIST (PT): P2tog, leaving sts on left-hand needle, insert right-hand needle from back between sts just worked and purl the 2nd st again, slip both sts from needle together.
ROW 1 (RS): *K2, PT; repeat from * to end.
ROWS 2 AND 4: Purl.
ROW 3: *PT, k2; repeat from * to end.
Repeat Rows 1–4 for Woven Pattern.

CHERRY STITCH (multiple of 10 sts)

INCREASE 5 (INC 5): [K1, p1, k1, p1, k1] in one st.

ROW 1 (RS): *P2, inc 5, p7; repeat from * to end.

ROW 2: *K7, p5, k2; repeat from * to end.

ROW 3: *P2, k1, M1-r, k3, M1-l, k1, p7; repeat from * to end.

ROW 4: *K7, p7, k2; repeat from * to end.

ROW 5: *P2, k1, M1-r, k5, M1-l, k1, p7; repeat from * to end.

ROW 6: *K7, p9, k2; repeat from * to end.

ROW 7: *P2, ssk, k5, k2tog, p7; repeat from * to end.

ROW 8: *K7, p2tog, p3, p2tog tbl, k2; repeat from * to end.

ROW 9: *P2, ssk, k1, k2tog, p7; repeat from * to end.

ROW 10: *K7, p3tog, k2; repeat from * to end.

ROW 11: *P2, k1 tbl, p7; repeat from * to end.

ROW 12: *K7, p1 tbl, k2; repeat from * to end.

ROWS 13 AND 14: Repeat Rows 11 and 12.

ROW 15: *P2, k1 tbl, p4, inc 5, p2; repeat from * to end.

ROW 16: *K2, p5, k4, p1 tbl, k2; repeat from * to end.

ROW 17: *P2, k1 tbl, p4, k1, M1-r, k3, M1-l, k1, p2; repeat from * to end.

ROW 18: *K2, p7, k4, p1 tbl, k2; repeat from * to end.

ROW 19: *P7, k1, M1-r, k5, M1-l, k1, p2; repeat from * to end.

ROW 20: *K2, p9, k7; repeat from * to end.

ROW 21: *P7, ssk, k5, k2tog, p2; repeat from * to end.

ROW 22: *K2, p2tog, p3, p2tog tbl, k7; repeat from * to end.

ROW 23: *P7, ssk, k1, k2tog, p2; repeat from * to end.

ROW 24: *K2, p3tog, k7; repeat from * to end.

ROW 25: *P7, k1 tbl, p2; repeat from * to end.

ROW 26: *K2, p1 tbl, k7; repeat from * to end.

ROWS 27-32: Repeat rows 25 and 26 three more times.

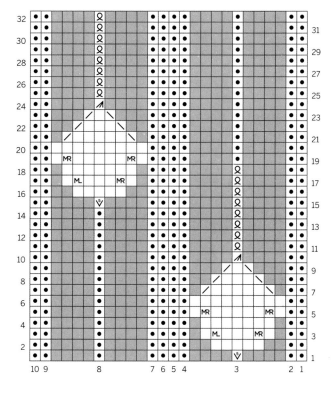

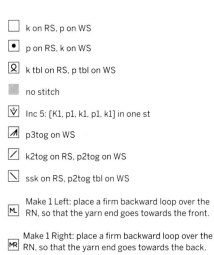

☐ k on RS, p on WS

• p on RS, k on WS

Ω k tbl on RS, p tbl on WS

▨ no stitch

⋁ Inc 5: [K1, p1, k1, p1, k1] in one st

◪ p3tog on WS

◿ k2tog on RS, p2tog on WS

◺ ssk on RS, p2tog tbl on WS

ML Make 1 Left: place a firm backward loop over the RN, so that the yarn end goes towards the front.

MR Make 1 Right: place a firm backward loop over the RN, so that the yarn end goes towards the back.

VINTAGE VEST (SPORT)
Front & Back

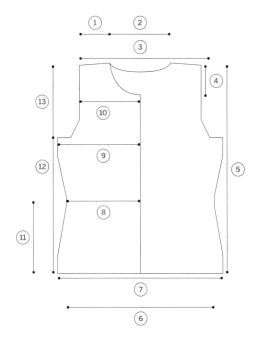

1 3 (3, 3¼, 3¼, 3½, 3¾, 3¾, 3¾, 4, 4, 4¼)"
   7.5 (7.5, 8.5, 8.5, 9, 9.5, 9.5, 9.5, 10, 10, 10, 11) cm

2 5¾ (6, 6, 6¼, 7, 7, 7¼, 7¾, 7¾, 8, 8, 8¼)"
   14.5 (15, 15, 16, 18, 18, 18.5, 19.5, 19.5, 20.5, 20.5, 21) cm

3 11¾ (12, 12¾, 13, 14, 14¾, 15, 15¼, 15¾, 16, 16, 17)"
   29.5 (30.5, 32, 33, 35.5, 37.5, 38, 39, 40, 40.5, 40.5, 43) cm

4 3"/7.5 cm

5 20½ (21¼, 21¾, 22¼, 23, 23½, 24, 24½, 25¼, 25¾, 26, 26½)"
   52 (54, 55, 56.5, 58.5, 59.5, 61, 62, 64, 65.5, 66, 67.5) cm

6 13¼ (14¼, 15¼, 16¼, 17¼, 18¼, 19¼, 20¼, 21¼, 22¼, 23¼, 25¼)"
   34 (36.5, 39, 41.5, 44, 46.5, 49, 51.5, 54, 56.5, 59.5, 64.5) cm

7 15 (16, 17, 18, 19, 20, 21, 22, 23, 24, 25, 27)"
   38 (40.5, 43, 45.5, 48.5, 51, 53.5, 56, 58.5, 61, 63.5, 68.5) cm

8 6¾ (7¼, 7¾, 8¼, 8¾, 9¼, 9¾, 10¼, 10¾, 11¼, 11¾, 12¾)"
   17.5 (18, 20, 20.5, 22.5, 23.5, 25, 26, 27.5, 28.5, 30, 32.5) cm

9 7¾ (8, 8¾, 9, 9¾, 10, 10¾, 11, 11¾, 12, 12¾, 13¾)"
   19.5 (20.5, 22, 23, 24.5, 25.5, 27, 28, 29.5, 30.5, 32, 34.5) cm

10 6 (6, 6½, 6½, 7¼, 7¼, 7¾, 7¾, 8, 8, 8¼, 8¾)"
   15 (15, 16.5, 16.5, 18, 18.5, 19.5, 19.5, 20.5, 20.5, 20.5, 22) cm

11 8"/20.5 cm

12 14 (14¼, 14½, 14¾, 15, 15¼, 15½, 15½, 16, 16, 16, 16)"
   35.5 (36, 37, 37.5, 38, 38.5, 39.5, 39.5, 40.5, 40.5, 40.5, 40.5) cm

13 6½ (7, 7¼, 7½, 8, 8¼, 8½, 9, 9¼, 9¾, 10, 10½)"
   16.5 (18, 18.5, 19, 20.5, 21, 21.5, 23, 23.5, 25, 25.5, 26.5) cm

CLASSIC VEST (WORSTED)
Front & Back

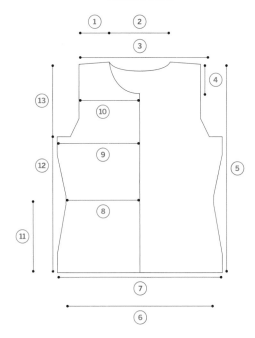

1 3 (3, 3¼, 3½, 3½, 3¾, 4, 4, 4, 4, 4, 4½)"
   7.5 (7.5, 8, 8.5, 9, 9.5, 10, 10, 10, 10, 10, 11) cm

2 5¾ (6, 6, 6½, 6¾, 7¼, 7¼, 7½, 7½, 8, 8, 8½)"
   14.5 (15.5, 15.5, 16.5, 17.5, 18.5, 18.5, 19.5, 19.5, 20.5, 20.5, 21.5) cm

3 11¾ (12¼, 12½, 13¼, 14, 14¾, 15¼, 15½, 15½, 16, 16, 17¼)"
   30 (31, 32, 34, 36, 37.5, 38.5, 39.5, 39.5, 40.5, 40.5, 43.5) cm

4 3"/7.5 cm

5 20½ (21¼, 21¾, 22¼, 23, 23½, 24, 24½, 25¼, 25¾, 26, 26½)"
   52 (54, 55, 56.5, 58.5, 59.5, 61, 62, 64, 65.5, 66, 67.5) cm

6 13¾ (14½, 15½, 16¾, 17½, 18¾, 19¾, 20½, 21¾, 22½, 23½, 25½)"
   35 (37, 39.5, 42.5, 44.5, 47.5, 50.5, 52.5, 55, 57, 60, 65) cm

7 15¼ (16, 17¼, 18¼, 19, 20¼, 21¼, 22, 23¼, 24, 25¼, 27)"
   38.5 (40.5, 43.5, 46.5, 48.5, 51.5, 54, 56, 59, 61, 64, 68.5) cm

8 6¾ (7¼, 8, 8½, 8¾, 9½, 10, 10¼, 11, 11½, 11¾, 13)"
   17.5 (18.5, 20.5, 21.5, 22.5, 24, 25, 26, 28, 29, 30, 33) cm

9 7½ (8, 8¾, 9¼, 9½, 10¼, 10¾, 11, 11¾, 12¼, 12½, 13¾)"
   19.5 (20.5, 22.5, 23, 24, 26, 27, 28, 30, 31, 32, 35) cm

10 6 (6, 6½, 6¾, 7, 7½, 7½, 7¾, 8, 8¼, 8, 8¾)"
   15 (15.5, 16.5, 17, 18, 19.5, 19.5, 20, 20.5, 21, 20.5, 22.5) cm

11 8"/20.5 cm

12 14 (14¼, 14½, 14¾, 15, 15¼, 15½, 15½, 16, 16, 16, 16)"
   35.5 (36, 37, 37.5, 38, 38.5, 39.5, 39.5, 40.5, 40.5, 40.5, 40.5) cm

13 6½ (7, 7¼, 7½, 8, 8¼, 8½, 9, 9¼, 9¾, 10, 10½)"
   16.5 (18, 18.5, 19, 20.5, 21, 21.5, 23, 23.5, 25, 25.5, 26.5) cm

AVANT-GARDE VEST (ARAN)
Front & Back

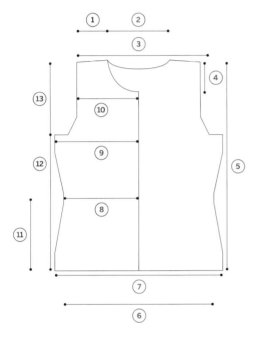

1   3 (3, 3¼, 3¼, 3½, 3¾, 3¾, 4, 4, 4, 4, 4¼)"
7.5 (7.5, 8.5, 8.5, 9, 9.5, 9.5, 10, 10, 10, 10, 11) cm

2   5½ (6, 6, 6½, 7, 7, 7½, 7½, 7½, 8, 8, 8½)"
14 (15, 15, 16.5, 18, 18, 19, 19, 19, 20.5, 20.5, 21.5) cm

3   11½ (12, 12½, 13, 14, 14½, 15, 15½, 15½, 16, 16, 17)"
29 (30.5, 32, 33, 35.5, 37, 38, 39.5, 39.5, 40.5, 40.5, 43) cm

4   3"/7.5 cm

5   20½ (21¼, 21¾, 22¼, 23, 23½, 24, 24½, 25¼, 25¾, 26, 26½)"
52 (54, 55, 56.5, 58.5, 59.5, 61, 62, 64, 65.5, 66, 67.5) cm

6   13½ (14½, 15½, 16½, 17½, 18½, 19½, 20½, 21½, 22½, 23½, 25½)"
34.5 (37, 39.5, 42, 44.5, 47, 49.5, 52, 54.5, 57, 59.5, 65) cm

7   15 (16, 17, 18, 19, 20, 21, 22, 23, 24, 25, 27)"
38 (40.5, 43, 45.5, 48.5, 51, 53.5, 56, 58.5, 61, 63.5, 68.5) cm

8   6¾ (7¼, 7¾, 8¼, 8¾, 9¼, 9¾, 10¼, 10¾, 11¼, 11¾, 12¾)"
17 (18.5, 19.5, 21, 22, 23.5, 25, 26, 27.5, 28.5, 30, 32.5) cm

9   7½ (8, 8½, 9, 9½, 10, 10½, 11, 11½, 12, 12½, 13½)"
19 (20.5, 21.5, 23, 24, 25.5, 26.5, 28, 29, 30.5, 32, 34.5) cm

10   5¾ (6, 6¼, 6½, 7, 7¼, 7½, 7¾, 7¾, 8, 8, 8½)"
14.5 (15, 16, 16.5, 18, 18.5, 19, 19.5, 19.5, 20.5, 20.5, 21.5) cm

11   8"/20.5 cm

12   14 (14¼, 14½, 14¾, 15, 15¼, 15½, 15½, 16, 16, 16, 16)"
35.5 (36, 37, 37.5, 38, 38.5, 39.5, 39.5, 40.5, 40.5, 40.5, 40.5) cm

13   6½ (7, 7¼, 7½, 8, 8¼, 8½, 9, 9¼, 9¾, 10, 10½)"
16.5 (18, 18.5, 19, 20.5, 21, 21.5, 23, 23.5, 25, 25.5, 26.5) cm

Pattern Worksheet

META-PATTERN #3
THE VEST

Use this worksheet as a handy way to get all of the numbers for each individual vest you knit in one simple place. You can photocopy these pages or download a fresh copy any time you like at www.amyherzogdesigns.com/knitwearlove.

BACK

Using long-tail cast-on method (or a different one, if you prefer), CO _____ sts.

EDGING: Work even in _____ until piece measures _____ from CO edge, ending with a WS row.

Switch to _____ and work even until piece measures _____ from CO edge, ending with a WS row.

On your last row, place markers on each side of center _____ sts.

DECREASE ROW (RS): Work to 2 sts before marker, ssk, sm, work to next marker, sm, k2tog, work to end.

Work decrease row every _____ rows _____ times total: _____ sts remain. Work even until piece measures _____ from CO edge, ending with a WS row.

INCREASE ROW (RS): Work to marker, M1-r, sm, work to next marker, sm, M1-l, work to end.

Work increase row every _____ rows _____ times total: _____ sts total. Work even until piece measures _____ from CO edge, ending with a WS row.

SHAPE ARMHOLES: BO _____ sts at the beginning of the next 2 rows. BO _____ sts at the beginning of the following 2 rows. Decrease 1 st at each end of every RS row _____ times: _____ sts remain.

Work even until piece measures _____ from CO edge, ending with a WS row.

NEXT ROW (RS): Work _____ sts, attach a new ball of yarn and BO center _____ sts, work to end.

Working both sides of neckline at same time, decrease 1 st at neck edge of every RS row twice. _____ shoulder sts remain. Work even until piece measures _____ from CO edge, ending at the armhole edge for each side.

NEXT ROW: BO _____ sts, work to end. Work 1 row even. BO rem sts.

FRONTS

Using long-tail cast on (or a different one, if you prefer), CO _____ sts.

EDGING: Work even in _____ until piece measures _____ from CO edge, ending with a WS row.

Switch to _____ and work even until piece measures _____ from CO edge, ending with a WS row.

On your last row, place marker at center of your sts. If you have an odd number of sts, place the marker to the left of the center st for the left front and to the right of the center st for the right front.

DECREASE ROW–RIGHT FRONT (RS): Work to marker, sm, k2tog, work to end.

DECREASE ROW–LEFT FRONT (RS): Work to 2 sts before marker, ssk, sm, work to end.

Work decrease row every _____ rows _____ times total: _____ sts remain. Work even until piece measures _____ from CO edge, ending with a WS row.

INCREASE ROW—RIGHT FRONT (RS): Work to marker, sm, M1-l, work to end.

INCREASE ROW—LEFT FRONT(RS): Work to marker, M1-r, sm, work to end.

Work increase row every _____ rows _____ times total: _____ sts remain. Work even until piece measures _____ from CO edge, ending with a WS row for left front and RS row for right front.

SHAPE ARMHOLES: BO _____ sts at the beginning of the next armhole edge. Work 1 row even.

BO _____ sts at the beginning of the following armhole edge.

Decrease 1 st at armhole edge of every RS row _____ times. _____ sts remain.

SHAPE NECK: When armhole measures _____, shape neck:

BO _____ sts at the beginning of the next neck-edge row, then decrease 1 st at neck edge every row _____ times, then every RS row _____ times.

When all neck and armhole shaping is complete, _____ shoulder sts remain. Work even until piece measures _____ from CO edge, ending at the armhole edge.

NEXT ROW: BO _____ sts, work to end. Work 1 row even. BO rem sts.

FINISHING

Follow instructions on page 86.

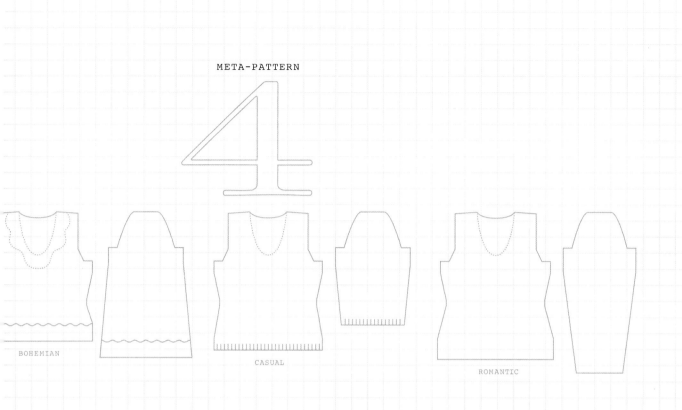

META-PATTERN

4

BOHEMIAN

CASUAL

ROMANTIC

THE COWL

Cowls are the sweater equivalent of a warm snuggle. They envelop you, they puddle enticingly around your neck, and they can keep you warm even on the coldest days. They're a great, and versatile, step up from a basic pullover.

I've offered you a few different directions here by working variations on both sleeves (shorter and longer, belled and snuggly) and cowl/sweater length. The bohemian option in a crunchy silk-wool blend has long belled sleeves and a shorter body length for a funky look. The casual cowl (my personal favorite) combines a luscious yarn blend with super-simple Stockinette stitch and ribbing. Finally, the romantic cowl includes longer sweater and sleeve lengths in yarn that's truly to die for.

Whatever your personal style, the gauge and customization options can be combined to produce the cowl of your dreams. I can't wait to see what you choose!

Change it up!

Gauges offered
DK, worsted, bulky

Sleeves
Long and belled,
three-quarter-
length,
long and tapered

Sweater & cowl
lengths
From short
to long and in
between

Make this sweater suit your own style!

META-PATTERN #4

BOHEMIAN

The Cowl

Shallow cowl with eyelets.

Textured, nubby yarn.

Shorter sweater length with intricate stitch pattern.

Long belled sleeves.

Jackie is wearing size 38" (96.5 cm) in DK gauge.

FINISHED BUST		**DK:** 30½ (32¾, 35, 37, 38½, 40¾, 43, 45, 46½, 48¾, 51, 54½)" [77.5 (83, 88.5, 94, 98, 103.5, 109, 114.5, 118, 124, 129.5, 138.5) cm]	

FINISHED BUST

DK: 30½ (32¾, 35, 37, 38½, 40¾, 43, 45, 46½, 48¾, 51, 54½)" [77.5 (83, 88.5, 94, 98, 103.5, 109, 114.5, 118, 124, 129.5, 138.5) cm]

WORSTED: 29½ (32, 33½, 36, 37½, 40, 41½, 44, 45½, 48, 49½, 53½)" [75 (81.5, 85.5, 91.5, 95.5, 101.5, 105.5, 112, 116, 122, 126, 136) cm]

BULKY: 30¾ (33¼, 34¾, 37¼, 38¾, 41¼, 42¾, 45¼, 46¾, 49¼, 50¾, 54¾)" [78 (84.5, 88, 95, 98, 105, 108.5, 115, 118.5, 125.5, 128.5, 139) cm]

(Note: For ease in reading, the precise finished bust measurements have been rounded in the instructions below to 30 (32, 34, 36, 38, 40, 42, 44, 46, 48, 50, 54)" [76 (81.5, 86.5, 91.5, 96.5, 101.5, 106.5, 112, 117, 122, 127, 137) cm]. Your finished measurements will be as given above.

MATERIALS

See page 190 for fiber content.

DK: Harrisville Designs Silk & Wool in Cappuccino, 6 (6, 7, 7, 8, 8, 9, 10, 10, 10, 11) hanks

WORSTED: Shibui Staccato in #2026 Brass, 4 (4, 4, 5, 5, 5, 6, 6, 6, 7, 7, 8) hanks, and Shibui Baby Alpaca in #2026 Brass, 4 (4, 4, 5, 5, 5, 6, 6, 6, 7, 7, 8) hanks. Worked with one strand of each yarn held together

BULKY: Blue Sky Alpacas Brushed Suri in #908 Snowcone, 4 (5, 5, 5, 5, 6, 6, 6, 7, 7, 8, 8) hanks

GAUGE

DK: 22 sts and 34 rows = 4" (10 cm) in Stockinette st
WORSTED: 20 sts and 28 rows = 4" (10 cm) in Stockinette st
BULKY: 12 sts and 20 rows = 4" (10 cm) in Stockinette st

NEEDLES

Change needle size if necessary to obtain correct gauge:
DK: US 5 / 3.75 mm
WORSTED: US 7 / 4.5 mm
BULKY: US 10½ / 6.5 mm

All gauges: Circular needles in main needle size, one size larger than main needle size, and two sizes larger than main needle size, to achieve correct cowl drape.

BACK

BOHEMIAN STYLE: Using long-tail cast-on method (or a different one, if you prefer), CO

	30"	32	34	36	38	40	42	44	46	48	50	54
DK	84	90	96	102	106	112	118	124	128	134	140	150
WORSTED	74	80	84	90	94	100	104	110	114	120	124	134
BULKY	46	50	52	56	58	62	64	68	70	74	76	82

sts. Work 5 rows even in Garter st.
Work 24 rows of Brocade Chevron (page 107) once.

DK: Work 4 rows of Ribbon Eyelet (page 106) once.
WORSTED: Work 4 rows of Ribbon Eyelet once.
BULKY: Switch to Stockinette st.

Piece measures between 3½" (9 cm) and 5" (12.5cm) from CO edge, depending on yarn gauge. Switch to Stockinette st and end with a WS row. On your last row, place two waist shaping markers, one on either side of the center section so that there are:

	30"	32	34	36	38	40	42	44	46	48	50	54
DK	28	30	32	34	36	36	38	40	42	44	46	50
WORSTED	26	26	28	30	32	34	36	36	38	40	42	46
BULKY	16	16	18	18	20	20	22	22	24	24	26	28

sts between waist shaping markers.

DECREASE ROW (RS): Work to 2 sts before first marker, ssk, sm, work to next marker, sm, k2tog, work to end. 2 sts decreased.

Work a decrease row every

DK: 4 / **WORSTED:** 4 / **BULKY:** 4 rows

DK: 5 / **WORSTED:** 4 / **BULKY:** 3 times total.

CASUAL STYLE: Using long-tail cast-on method (or a different one, if you prefer), CO

	30"	32	34	36	38	40	42	44	46	48	50	54
DK	84	90	96	102	106	112	118	124	128	134	140	150
WORSTED	74	80	84	90	94	100	104	110	114	120	124	134
BULKY	46	50	52	56	58	62	64	68	70	74	76	82

sts. Work even in 1x1 rib until piece measures 2" (5 cm) from CO edge, ending with a WS row. Switch to Stockinette st and work even until piece measures 2½" (6.5 cm) from CO edge, ending with a WS row. On your last row, place two waist shaping markers, one on either side of the center section so that there are:

	30"	32	34	36	38	40	42	44	46	48	50	54
DK	28	30	32	34	36	36	38	40	42	44	46	50
WORSTED	26	26	28	30	32	34	36	36	38	40	42	46
BULKY	16	16	18	18	20	20	22	22	24	24	26	28

sts between waist shaping markers.

DECREASE ROW (RS): Work to 2 sts before first marker, ssk, sm, work to next marker, sm, k2tog, work to end. 2 sts decreased.

Work a decrease row every

DK: 10 / **WORSTED:** 10 / **BULKY:** 12 rows

DK: 5 / **WORSTED:** 4 / **BULKY:** 3 times total.

ROMANTIC STYLE: Using long-tail cast-on method (or a different one, if you prefer), CO

	30"	32	34	36	38	40	42	44	46	48	50	54
DK	88	94	100	106	110	116	122	128	132	138	144	154
WORSTED	80	86	90	96	100	106	110	116	120	126	130	140
BULKY	48	52	54	58	60	64	66	70	72	76	78	84

sts. Work 5 rows even in Garter st. Switch to Stockinette st and work even until piece measures 5½" (14 cm) from CO edge, ending with a WS row. On your last row, place two waist shaping markers, one on either side of the center section so that there are:

	30"	32	34	36	38	40	42	44	46	48	50	54
DK	30	32	34	36	36	38	40	42	44	46	48	52
WORSTED	26	28	30	32	34	36	36	38	40	42	44	46
BULKY	16	18	18	20	20	22	22	24	24	26	26	28

sts between waist shaping markers.

DECREASE ROW (RS): Work to 2 sts before first marker, ssk, sm, work to next marker, sm, k2tog, work to end. 2 sts decreased.

Deep cowl
for snuggling.

Soft, luscious
yarn with a
great halo.

ROMANTIC

The Cowl

Long sweater
length and
sleeves.

» Kiki is
wearing size
34" (86.5 cm)
in bulky gauge.

Work a decrease row every

DK: 6 / **WORSTED:** 4 / **BULKY:** 6 rows
DK: 7 / **WORSTED:** 7 / **BULKY:** 4 times total.

ALL STYLES: When all decreases are complete,

	30"	32	34	36	38	40	42	44	46	48	50	54
DK	74	80	86	92	96	102	108	114	118	124	130	140
WORSTED	66	72	76	82	86	92	96	102	106	112	116	126
BULKY	40	44	46	50	52	56	58	62	64	68	70	76

sts total. Work even until piece measures

BOHEMIAN STYLE: 7" (18 cm)
CASUAL STYLE: 8½" (21.5 cm)
ROMANTIC STYLE: 10" (25.5 cm)
from CO edge, ending with a WS row.

INCREASE ROW (RS): Work to first marker, M1-r, sm, work to next marker, sm, M1-l, work to end. 2 sts increased.

Work an increase row every

DK: 8 / **WORSTED:** 8 / **BULKY:** 8 rows
DK: 5 / **WORSTED:** 4 / **BULKY:** 3 times total.

When all increases are complete,

	30"	32	34	36	38	40	42	44	46	48	50	54
DK	84	90	96	102	106	112	118	124	128	134	140	150
WORSTED	74	80	84	90	94	100	104	110	114	120	124	134
BULKY	46	50	52	56	58	62	64	68	70	74	76	82

sts total. Work even until piece measures

BOHEMIAN STYLE: 12½ (12¾, 13, 13¼, 13½, 13¾, 14, 14, 14½, 14½, 14½, 14½)" [32 (32.5, 33, 33.5, 34.5, 35, 35.5, 35.5, 37, 37, 37, 37) cm]

CASUAL STYLE: 14 (14¼, 14½, 14¾, 15, 15¼, 15½, 15½, 16, 16, 16, 16)" [35.5 (36, 37, 37.5, 38, 38.5, 39.5, 39.5, 40.5, 40.5, 40.5, 40.5) cm]

ROMANTIC STYLE: 15½ (15¾, 16, 16¼, 16½, 16¾, 17, 17, 17½, 17½, 17½, 17½)" [39.5 (40, 40.5, 41.5, 42, 42.5, 43, 43, 44.5, 44.5, 44.5, 44.5) cm]
from CO edge, ending with a WS row.

SHAPE ARMHOLES

BO

	30"	32	34	36	38	40	42	44	46	48	50	54
DK	6	6	6	6	6	6	6	8	8	10	10	12
WORSTED	6	6	6	6	6	6	6	6	8	8	10	10
BULKY	3	4	4	4	4	4	4	6	6	6	6	8

sts at the beginning of the next 2 rows. BO

	30"	32	34	36	38	40	42	44	46	48	50	54
DK	2	2	2	2	2	2	4	4	6	6	8	8
WORSTED	0	2	2	2	2	2	2	4	4	6	6	8
BULKY	0	0	0	2	0	2	2	2	2	4	4	4

sts at the beginning of the following 2 rows.
Decrease 1 st at each end of every RS row

	30"	32	34	36	38	40	42	44	46	48	50	54
DK	2	4	5	7	6	8	7	8	7	7	7	8
WORSTED	2	2	2	4	4	5	6	6	6	6	6	6
BULKY	2	3	3	2	3	3	3	3	3	3	3	3

times:

	30"	32	34	36	38	40	42	44	46	48	50	54
DK	64	66	70	72	78	80	84	84	86	88	90	94
WORSTED	58	60	64	66	70	74	76	78	78	80	80	86
BULKY	36	36	38	40	44	44	46	46	48	48	50	52

sts remain. Work even until armhole measures 5½ (6, 6¼, 6½, 7, 7¼, 7½, 8, 8¼, 8¾, 9, 9½)" [14 (15, 16, 16.5, 18, 18.5, 19, 20.5, 21, 22, 23, 24) cm], ending with a WS row.

SHAPE NECK

NEXT ROW (RS): Work

	30"	32	34	36	38	40	42	44	46	48	50	54
DK	18	19	20	20	22	22	23	23	24	24	25	26
WORSTED	17	17	18	19	20	21	21	22	22	22	22	24
BULKY	11	11	12	12	14	14	14	14	14	14	15	15

sts, attach a new ball of yarn, and BO center

	30"	32	34	36	38	40	42	44	46	48	50	54
DK	28	28	30	32	34	36	38	38	38	40	40	42
WORSTED	24	26	28	28	30	32	34	34	34	36	36	38
BULKY	14	14	14	16	16	16	18	18	20	20	20	22

sts, work to end. *You will now work both sides of the neckline at the same time.* Decrease 1 st at neck edge of every RS row twice:

	30"	32	34	36	38	40	42	44	46	48	50	54
DK	16	17	18	18	20	20	21	21	22	22	23	24
WORSTED	15	15	16	17	18	19	19	20	20	20	20	22
BULKY	9	9	10	10	12	12	12	12	12	12	13	13

sts remain for each shoulder. Work even until armhole measures 6½ (7, 7¼, 7½, 8, 8¼, 8½, 9, 9¼, 9¾, 10, 10½)" [16.5 (18, 18.5, 19, 20.5, 21, 21.5, 23, 23.5, 25, 25.5, 26.5) cm], ending at the armhole edge for each side.

NEXT ROW: BO

	30"	32	34	36	38	40	42	44	46	48	50	54
DK	8	9	9	9	10	10	11	11	11	11	12	12
WORSTED	8	8	8	9	9	10	10	10	10	10	10	11
BULKY	5	5	5	5	6	6	6	6	6	6	7	7

sts, work to end. Work 1 row even. BO remaining sts.

FRONTS

Work as for back through armhole shaping, except place waist shaping markers around the center sts so that there are:

	30"	32	34	36	38	40	42	44	46	48	50	54
DK	44	46	50	52	54	58	60	64	66	68	72	76
WORSTED	40	42	44	48	50	52	54	58	60	62	64	70
BULKY	24	26	26	28	30	32	32	34	36	38	38	42

sts between waist shaping markers.

Note: Neck shaping will begin before armhole shaping is complete.

SHAPE NECK

When armhole measures 1" (2.5 cm), *shape neck.*

NEXT ROW (RS): Mark your center

	30"	**32**	**34**	**36**	**38**	**40**	**42**	**44**	**46**	**48**	**50**	**54**
DK	14	14	14	18	18	18	20	20	20	20	20	22
WORSTED	12	12	14	16	16	18	18	18	18	18	18	20
BULKY	8	8	8	10	10	10	10	10	12	12	12	12

sts.

NEXT ROW: Work to marker, attach a new ball of yarn and BO marked stitches, work to end. *Shape both sides of neck at the same time.*

Decrease 1 st at neck edge every RS row

	30"	**32**	**34**	**36**	**38**	**40**	**42**	**44**	**46**	**48**	**50**	**54**
DK	5	5	5	5	5	6	6	6	6	6	6	6
WORSTED	4	5	5	4	5	5	5	5	5	6	6	6
BULKY	3	3	3	3	3	3	3	3	3	3	3	4

times, then every other RS row

	30"	**32**	**34**	**36**	**38**	**40**	**42**	**44**	**46**	**48**	**50**	**54**
DK	4	4	5	4	5	5	5	5	5	6	6	6
WORSTED	4	4	4	4	4	4	5	5	5	5	5	5
BULKY	2	2	2	2	2	2	3	3	3	3	3	3

times.

When all neck and armhole shaping is complete

	30"	**32**	**34**	**36**	**38**	**40**	**42**	**44**	**46**	**48**	**50**	**54**
DK	16	17	18	18	20	20	21	21	22	22	23	24
WORSTED	15	15	16	17	18	19	19	20	20	20	20	22
BULKY	9	9	10	10	12	12	12	12	12	12	13	13

sts remain for each shoulder. Complete shoulder shaping as for back.

SLEEVES

BOHEMIAN STYLE: Using long-tail cast-on method (or a different one, if you prefer), CO

	30"	**32**	**34**	**36**	**38**	**40**	**42**	**44**	**46**	**48**	**50**	**54**
DK	78	80	82	84	86	90	94	98	104	110	110	114
WORSTED	70	72	74	76	78	80	84	90	94	98	98	104
BULKY	42	42	44	46	46	48	50	54	56	60	60	62

sts. Work 5 rows even in Garter st.

Work 4 rows of Ribbon Eyelet (page 106), then 1" (2.5 cm) of Stockinette st, then work 4 rows of Ribbon Eyelet once more. Switch to Stockinette st.

At the same time, when sleeve measures 1" (2.5 cm) from CO edge, beginning with a RS row, work shaping:

DECREASE ROW (RS): Knit 1, ssk, work in pattern to last 3 sts, k2tog, knit 1.

Repeat decrease row every

DK: 8 / **WORSTED:** 6 / **BULKY:** 4 rows until a total of

META-PATTERN #4

CASUAL

The Cowl

Average
cowl length.

Simple stitch
pattern is
casual and
wearable.

Warm color
in a soft,
strong yarn.

Easy ribbed
trim.

» Jackie is wearing
size 38" (103.5 cm)
in worsted gauge.

	30"	32	34	36	38	40	42	44	46	48	50	54
DK	8	8	8	8	8	8	8	8	8	8	4	2
WORSTED	7	7	7	7	7	7	7	7	7	7	3	2
BULKY	4	4	4	4	4	4	4	4	4	4	2	1

decrease rows have been worked:

	30"	32	34	36	38	40	42	44	46	48	50	54
DK	62	64	66	68	70	74	78	82	88	94	102	110
WORSTED	56	58	60	62	64	66	70	76	80	84	92	100
BULKY	34	34	36	38	38	40	42	46	48	52	56	60

sts remain.

Work even until sleeve measures 18 (18, 18½, 18½, 18½, 19, 19, 19, 19, 19½, 19½, 19½)" [45.5 (45.5, 47, 47, 47, 48.5, 48.5, 48.5, 48.5, 49.5, 49.5, 49.5) cm] from CO edge, ending with a WS row.

- -

CASUAL STYLE: Using long-tail cast-on method (or a different one, if you prefer), CO

	30"	32	34	36	38	40	42	44	46	48	50	54
DK	58	60	62	60	62	64	68	70	72	76	78	84
WORSTED	52	54	56	56	58	56	60	64	66	68	70	62
BULKY	32	32	34	34	34	34	36	40	40	42	44	46

sts. Work even in 1x1 rib for 1½" (4 cm), then switch to Stockinette st and work 2 rows even.

INCREASE ROW (RS): K 1, M1-r, knit to last st, M1-l, k 1.

Repeat increase row every

DK: 8 / **WORSTED:** 6 / **BULKY:** 4 rows until a total of

	30"	32	34	36	38	40	42	44	46	48	50	54
DK	2	2	2	4	4	5	5	6	8	9	12	13
WORSTED	2	2	2	3	3	5	5	6	7	8	11	12
BULKY	1	1	1	2	2	3	3	3	4	5	6	7

increase rows have been worked:

	30"	32	34	36	38	40	42	44	46	48	50	54
DK	62	64	66	68	70	74	78	82	88	94	102	110
WORSTED	56	58	60	62	64	66	70	76	80	84	92	100
BULKY	34	34	36	38	38	40	42	46	48	52	56	60

sts total.

Work even until sleeve measures 12 (12, 12, 13, 13, 13, 13, 13, 14, 14, 14, 14)" [30.5 (30.5, 30.5, 33, 33, 33, 33, 33, 35.5, 35.5, 35.5, 35.5) cm] from CO edge, ending with a WS row.

- -

ROMANTIC STYLE: Using long-tail cast-on method (or a different one, if you prefer), CO

	30"	32	34	36	38	40	42	44	46	48	50	54
DK	40	40	42	42	44	44	48	50	50	54	54	56
WORSTED	36	36	38	38	40	40	44	46	46	48	48	50
BULKY	22	22	24	24	24	24	26	28	28	30	30	30

sts.

Work even in Garter st for 5 rows. Switch to Stockinette st and work even until piece measures 3" (7.5 cm) from CO edge, ending with a WS row.

INCREASE ROW (RS): K 1, M1-r, knit to last st, M1-l, k 1.

Repeat increase row every

	30"	32	34	36	38	40	42	44	46	48	50	54
DK	10	10	10	10	10	10	10	8	8	8	6	6
WORSTED	10	10	10	8	10	8	8	8	6	6	6	4
BULKY	12	12	12	10	12	10	10	8	8	8	6	6

rows until a total of

	30"	32	34	36	38	40	42	44	46	48	50	54
DK	11	12	12	13	13	15	15	16	19	20	24	27
WORSTED	10	11	11	12	12	13	13	15	17	18	22	25
BULKY	6	6	6	7	7	8	8	9	10	11	13	15

increase rows have been worked:

	30"	32	34	36	38	40	42	44	46	48	50	54
DK	62	64	66	68	70	74	78	82	88	94	102	110
WORSTED	56	58	60	62	64	66	70	76	80	84	92	100
BULKY	34	34	36	38	38	40	42	46	48	52	56	60

sts total.

Work even until sleeve measures 19 (20, 20, 20, 21, 21, 21, 21, 22, 22, 22)" [48.5 (51, 51, 51, 53.5, 53.5, 53.5, 53.5, 56, 56, 56) cm] from CO, ending with a WS row.

SHAPE SLEEVE CAP

ALL STYLES: BO

	30"	32	34	36	38	40	42	44	46	48	50	54
DK	6	6	6	6	6	6	6	8	8	10	10	12
WORSTED	6	6	6	6	6	6	6	6	8	8	10	10
BULKY	3	4	4	4	4	4	4	6	6	6	6	8

sts at the beginning of the next 2 rows. BO

	30"	32	34	36	38	40	42	44	46	48	50	54
DK	2	2	2	2	2	2	4	4	6	6	8	8
WORSTED	0	2	2	2	2	2	2	4	4	6	6	7
BULKY	0	0	0	2	0	2	2	2	2	4	4	4

sts at the beginning of the following 2 rows. Decrease 1 st at each end of every 3rd RS row

	30"	32	34	36	38	40	42	44	46	48	50	54
DK	1	2	2	2	3	2	3	6	6	6	5	6
WORSTED	0	2	1	2	2	2	1	3	3	4	4	7
BULKY	0	1	1	2	1	2	2	4	3	4	3	4

times, then every other RS row

	30"	32	34	36	38	40	42	44	46	48	50	54
DK	2	1	1	1	0	1	0	2	0	1	2	1
WORSTED	3	3	4	2	3	2	3	3	3	3	2	1
BULKY	2	1	1	1	2	2	1	1	2	1	1	1

times, then every RS row

	30"	32	34	36	38	40	42	44	46	48	50	54
DK	9	10	11	12	13	15	15	5	6	6	8	5
WORSTED	8	5	6	8	8	10	12	7	7	6	9	3
BULKY	4	5	6	4	6	4	6	0	1	1	4	1

times.

BO

	30"	32	34	36	38	40	42	44	46	48	50	54
DK	2	2	2	2	2	2	2	3	4	4	4	4
WORSTED	2	2	2	2	2	2	2	3	3	3	3	5
BULKY	2	1	1	1	1	1	1	2	2	2	2	3

sts at the beginning of the next 4 rows. BO final

	30"	32	34	36	38	40	42	44	46	48	50	54
DK	14	14	14	14	14	14	14	20	20	20	20	26
WORSTED	14	14	14	14	14	14	14	18	18	18	18	24
BULKY	8	8	8	8	8	8	8	12	12	12	12	12

sts.

FINISHING

Wet-block all pieces to finished measurements. Sew shoulder seams using mattress stitch. Set in sleeves and sew side seams using mattress stitch.

With RS facing using circular needle and beginning at right shoulder seam, pick up and knit approximately

	30"	32	34	36	38	40	42	44	46	48	50	54
DK	120	126	130	138	146	152	158	164	166	174	176	186
WORSTED	106	114	120	124	132	138	142	148	150	158	160	168
BULKY	64	66	68	74	76	78	82	84	90	92	94	100

sts around neckline at the rate of 1 st for every bound-off st, 3 sts for every 4 rows along diagonal edges, and 2 sts for every 3 rows along in vertical edges. (The exact number is not important, but it must be an even number of sts.) Join to work in the round.

BOHEMIAN STYLE: Work even in Stockinette st, working 4 rows of Ribbon Eyelet every 3" (7.5 cm), switching to progressively larger needles after second and third repeats of Ribbon Eyelet, until cowl measures 8" (20.5 cm). After working Ribbon Eyelet for the third time, work 5 rounds in Garter st, beginning with a purl round. BO all sts loosely.

CASUAL STYLE: Work even in Stockinette st, switching to progressively larger needles after cowl measures 4" (10 cm), and then again when cowl measures 8" (20 cm); work until cowl measures 10" (25.5 cm). Switch to 1x1 rib and continue until cowl measures 11½" (29 cm). BO all sts loosely.

ROMANTIC STYLE: Work even in Garter st, beginning with a purl round, and switching to progressively larger needles after cowl measures 4" (10 cm), and then again when cowl measures 8" (20 cm); work until cowl measures 14" (35.5 cm). BO all sts loosely.

SPECIAL STITCHES

RIBBON EYELET (even number of sts)
Worked in rows:
ROWS 1, 2 AND 4: Knit.
ROW 3 (RS): K1, *k2tog, yo; repeat from * to last st, k1.
Worked in the round:
RND 1: Knit.

RNDS 2 AND 4: Purl.
RND 3: *K2tog, yo; repeat from * to end.

Chart legend:
- □ k on RS, p on WS
- ● p on RS, k on WS
- ○ yo
- ╱ k2tog

2-st patt rep

BROCADE CHEVRON (multiple of 10 sts + 4)

ROW 1 (RS): K1, *RT, k8; repeat from * to last 3 sts, RT, k1.

ROW 2: P1, sl 2 wyif, *p8, sl 2 wyif; repeat from * to last st, p1.

ROW 3: K2, *LT, k6, RT; repeat from * to last 2 sts, k2.

ROW 4: K1, p1, *k1, sl 1 wyif, p6, sl 1 wyif, p1; repeat from * to last 2 sts, k1, p1.

ROW 5: P1, k1, *p1, LT, k4, RT, k1; repeat from * to last 2 sts, p1, k1.

ROW 6: *[K1, p1] twice, sl 1 wyif, p4, sl 1 wyif; repeat from * to last 4 sts, [k1, p1] twice.

ROW 7: *[P1, k1] twice, LT, k2, RT; repeat from * to last 4 sts, [p1, k1] twice.

ROW 8: K1, *[p1, k1] twice, sl 1 wyif, p2, sl 1 wyif, p1, k1; repeat from * to last 3 sts, p1, k1, p1.

ROW 9: P1, *[k1, p1] twice, LT, RT, k1, p1; repeat from * to last 3 sts, k1, p1, k1.

ROW 10: *[K1, p1] 3 times, sl 2 wyif, k1, p1; repeat from * to last 4 sts, [k1, p1] twice.

ROW 11: *[P1, k1] 3 times, RT, p1, k1; repeat from * to last 4 sts, [p1, k1] twice.

ROW 12: *K1, p1; repeat from * to end.

ROW 13: P1, *RT, [k1, p1] 4 times; repeat from * to last 3 sts, RT, k1.

ROW 14: K1, *sl 2 wyif, [p1, k1] 4 times; repeat from * to last 3 sts, sl 2 wyif, k1.

ROW 15: K2, *LT, [p1, k1] 3 times, RT; repeat from * to last 2 sts, k2.

ROW 16: P2, *p1, sl 1wyif, [k1, p1] 3 times, sl 1 wyif, p1; repeat from * to last 2 sts, p2.

ROW 17: K1, *k2, LT, [k1, p1] twice, RT; repeat from * to last 3 sts, k3.

ROW 18: *P4, sl 1 wyif, [p1, k1] twice, sl 1 wyif; repeat from * to last 4 sts, p4.

ROW 19: *K4, LT, p1, k1, RT; repeat from * to last 4 sts, k4.

ROW 20: P2, *p3, sl 1 wyif, k1, p1, sl 1 wyif, p3; repeat from * to last 2 sts, p2.

ROW 21: K2, *k3, LT, RT, k3; repeat from * to last 2 sts, k2.

ROW 22: P2, *p4, sl 2 wyif, p4; repeat from * last 2 sts, p2.

ROW 23: K2, *k4, RT, k4; repeat from * to last 2 sts, k2.

ROW 24: Purl.

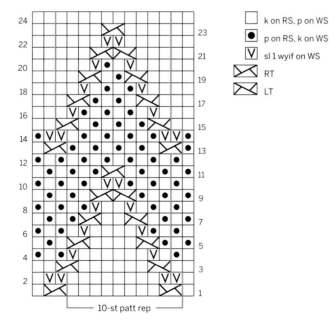

10-st patt rep

☐	k on RS, p on WS
●	p on RS, k on WS
V	sl 1 wyif on WS
✗	RT
✗	LT

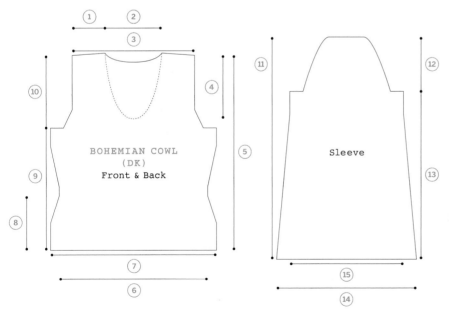

DIFFERENT FABRICS (left to right): Nubby bohemian silk/wool, soft casual alpaca/silk/wool.

1   3 (3, 3¼, 3¼, 3¾, 3¾, 3¾, 3¾, 4, 4, 4¼, 4¼)"
     7.5 (8, 8.5, 8.5, 9, 9, 9.5, 9.5, 10, 10, 10.5, 11) cm

2   5¾ (5¾, 6¼, 6½, 7, 7¼, 7¾, 7¾, 7¾, 8, 8, 8¼)"
     15 (15, 15.5, 16.5, 17.5, 18.5, 19.5, 19.5, 19.5, 20.5, 20.5, 21) cm

3   11¾ (12, 12¾, 13, 14¼, 14½, 15¼, 15¼, 15¾, 16, 16¼, 17)"
     29.5 (30.5, 32.5, 33.5, 36, 37, 39, 39, 39.5, 40.5, 41.5, 43.5) cm

4   5½ (6, 6¼, 6½, 7, 7¼, 7½, 8, 8¼, 8¾, 9, 9½)"
     14 (15, 16, 16.5, 18, 18.5, 19, 20.5, 21, 22, 23, 24) cm

5   19 (19¾, 20¼, 20¾, 21½, 22, 22½, 23, 23¾, 24¼, 24½, 25)"
     48.5 (50, 51.5, 52.5, 54.5, 56, 57, 58.5, 60.5, 61.5, 62, 63.5) cm

6   13½ (14¼, 15¼, 16¾, 17½, 18¼, 19¼, 20¾, 21½, 22¼, 23¾, 25½)"
     34 (36, 39, 42.5, 44.5, 46, 49, 52.5, 54.5, 56.5, 60, 64.5) cm

7   15¼ (16, 17½, 18¼, 19¼, 20, 21½, 22¼, 23¼, 24, 25½, 27¼)"
     39 (40.5, 44.5, 46, 49, 51, 54.5, 56.5, 59, 61, 64.5, 69.5) cm

8   6½"/16.5 cm

9   12½ (12¾, 13, 13¼, 13½, 13¾, 14, 14, 14½, 14½, 14½, 14½)"
     32 (32.5, 33, 33.5, 34.5, 35, 35.5, 35.5, 37, 37, 37, 37) cm

10   6½ (7, 7¼, 7½, 8, 8¼, 8½, 9, 9¼, 9¾, 10, 10½)"
     16.5 (18, 18.5, 19, 20.5, 21, 21.5, 23, 23.5, 25, 25.5, 26.5) cm

11   22½ (23, 23¾, 24, 24½, 25, 25¼, 26, 25¼, 26¼, 26½, 27)"
     57 (58.5, 60, 60.5, 62, 64, 64.5, 66, 64.5, 67, 67.5, 68.5) cm

12   4½ (5, 5¼, 5½, 6, 6, 6¼, 7, 6¼, 6¾, 7, 7½)"
     11.5 (12.5, 13, 13.5, 15, 15.5, 16, 18, 16, 17.5, 18, 19) cm

13   18 (18, 18½, 18½, 18½, 19, 19, 19, 19, 19½, 19½, 19½)"
     45.5 (45.5, 47, 47, 47, 48.5, 48.5, 48.5, 48.5, 49.5, 49.5, 49.5) cm

14   14¼ (14½, 15¼, 15¾, 16, 16¾, 17, 18¼, 19¼, 20, 20, 21)"
     36 (37, 39, 39.5, 40.5, 42.5, 43.5, 46, 49, 51, 51, 53.5) cm

15   11¼ (11¾, 12¼, 12¾, 13, 13¾, 14¼, 15¼, 16¼, 17, 18½, 20¼)"
     28.5 (29.5, 31.5, 32.5, 33.5, 35, 36, 39, 41.5, 43.5, 47, 51.5) cm

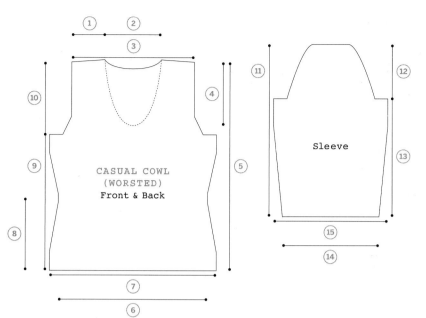

1 3 (3, 3¼, 3½, 3½, 3¾, 3¾, 4, 4, 4, 4, 4½)"
   7.5 (7.5, 8, 8.5, 9, 9.5, 9.5, 10, 10, 10, 10, 11) cm

2 5½ (6, 6½, 6½, 7¼, 7¼, 7½, 7½, 7½, 8, 8, 8½)"
   14 (15, 16.5, 16.5, 18.5, 18.5, 19.5, 19.5, 19.5, 20.5, 20.5, 21.5) cm

3 11½ (12, 12¾, 13¼, 14½, 14¾, 15¼, 15½, 15½, 16, 16, 17¼)"
   29.5 (30.5, 32.5, 33.5, 36.5, 37.5, 38.5, 39.5, 39.5, 40.5, 40.5, 43.5) cm

4 5½ (6, 6¼, 6½, 7, 7¼, 7½, 8, 8¼, 8¾, 9, 9½)''
   14 (15, 16, 16.5, 18, 18.5, 19, 20.5, 21, 22, 23, 24) cm

5 20½ (21¼, 21¾, 22¼, 23, 23½, 24, 24½, 25¼, 25¾, 26, 27½)"
   52 (54, 55, 56.5, 58.5, 59.5, 61, 62, 64, 65.5, 66, 70) cm

6 13½ (14½, 15½, 16½, 17½, 18½, 19½, 20½, 21½, 22½, 23½, 25½)"
   34.5 (36.5, 39.5, 41.5, 44.5, 46.5, 50, 52, 55, 57, 60, 65) cm

7 15¼ (16, 17¼, 18, 19¼, 20, 21¼, 22, 23¼, 24, 25¼, 27¼)
   38.5 (40.5, 43.5, 45.5, 49, 51, 54, 56, 59, 61, 64, 69) cm

8 8"/20.5 cm

9 14 (14¼, 14½, 14¾, 15, 15¼, 15½, 15½, 16, 16, 16, 16)"
   35.5 (36, 37, 37.5, 38, 38.5, 39.5, 39.5, 40.5, 40.5, 40.5, 40.5) cm

10 6½ (7, 7¼, 7½, 8, 8¼, 8½, 9, 9¼, 9¾, 10, 11½)"
    16.5 (18, 18.5, 19, 20.5, 21, 21.5, 23, 23.5, 25, 25.5, 29) cm

11 16½ (17¼, 17¼, 18½, 19¼, 19¼, 19½, 19¾, 20¾, 21¼, 21½, 21¾)"
    42 (44, 44, 47, 48.5, 48.5, 49.5, 50, 52.5, 54, 54.5, 55) cm

12 4½ (5¼, 5¼, 5½, 6, 6, 6½, 6¾, 6¾, 7¼, 7½, 8¾)"
    11.5 (13, 13, 14, 15, 15, 16.5, 17.5, 17.5, 18, 19, 22.5) cm

13 12 (12, 12, 13, 13, 13, 13, 13, 14, 14, 14, 14)"
    30.5 (30.5, 30.5, 33, 33, 33, 33, 33, 35.5, 35.5, 35.5, 35.5) cm

14 10 (10¾, 11¼, 11¼, 11½, 11½, 12, 12¾, 13¼, 13½, 14, 15¼)"
    25.5 (27.5, 28.5, 28.5, 29.5, 29.5, 30.5, 32.5, 33.5, 34.5, 35.5, 38.5) cm

15 10¾ (11½, 12, 12½, 12¾, 13½, 14, 15¼, 16, 16¾, 18½, 20)"
    27.5 (29.5, 30.5, 31.5, 32.5, 34.5, 35.5, 38.5, 40.5, 42.5, 46.5, 51) cm

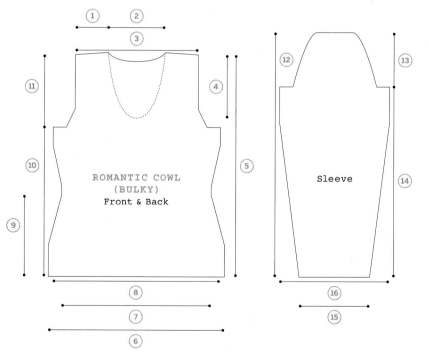

1 3 (3, 3¼, 3¼, 4, 4, 4, 4, 4, 4¼, 4¼)"
   7.5 (7.5, 8.5, 8.5, 10, 10, 10, 10, 10, 11, 11) cm

2 6 (6, 6, 6¾, 6¾, 6¾, 7¼, 7¼, 8, 8, 8¾)"
   15 (15, 15, 17, 17, 17, 18.5, 18.5, 20.5, 20.5, 22) cm

3 12 (12, 12¾, 13¼, 14¾, 14¾, 15¼, 15¼, 16, 16, 16¾, 17¼)"
   30.5 (30.5, 32, 34, 37.5, 37.5, 39, 39, 40.5, 40.5, 42.5, 44) cm

4 5½ (6, 6¼, 6½, 7, 7¼, 7½, 8, 8¼, 8¾, 9, 9½)''
   14 (15, 16, 16.5, 18, 18.5, 19, 20.5, 21, 22, 23, 24) cm

5 22 (22¾, 23¼, 23¾, 24½, 25, 25½, 26, 26¾, 27¼, 27½, 28)"
   56 (58, 59, 60.5, 62, 63.5, 65, 66, 68, 69, 70, 71) cm

6 16 (17¼, 18, 19¼, 20, 21¼, 22, 23¼, 24, 25¼, 26, 28)"
   40.5 (44, 45.5, 49, 51, 54, 56, 59.5, 61, 64.5, 66, 71) cm

7 13¼ (14¾, 15¼, 16¾, 17¼, 18¾, 19¼, 20¾, 21¼, 22¾, 23¼, 25¼)"
   34 (37.5, 39, 42.5, 44, 47.5, 49, 52.5, 54, 57.5, 59.5, 64.5) cm

8 15¼ (16¾, 17¼, 18¾, 19¼, 20¾, 21¼, 22¾, 23¼, 24¾, 25¼, 27¼)"
   39 (42.5, 44, 47.5, 49, 52.5, 54, 57.5, 59.5, 62.5, 64.5, 69.5) cm

9 9½"/24 cm

10 15½ (15¾, 16, 16¼, 16½, 16¾, 17, 17, 17½, 17½, 17½, 17½)"
    39.5 (40, 40.5, 41.5, 42, 42.5, 43, 43, 44.5, 44.5, 44.5, 44.5) cm

11 6½ (7, 7¼, 7½, 8, 8¼, 8½, 9, 9¼, 9¾, 10, 10½)"
    16.5 (18, 18.5, 19, 20.5, 21, 21.5, 23, 23.5, 25, 25.5, 26.5) cm

12 23½ (25¼, 25½, 26, 27½, 27¾, 27¾, 27¾, 27¾, 29¼, 29¼, 29¼)"
    59.5 (64, 65, 66, 69.5, 70.5, 70.5, 70.5, 70.5, 74, 74, 74) cm

13 4½ (5¼, 5½, 6, 6½, 6¾, 6¾, 6¾, 6¾, 7¼, 7¼, 7¼)"
    11 (13, 14, 15, 16.5, 17.5, 17.5, 17.5, 17.5, 18.5, 18.5, 18.5) cm

14 19 (20, 20, 20, 21, 21, 21, 21, 21, 22, 22, 22)"
    48.5 (51, 51, 51, 53.5, 53.5, 53.5, 53.5, 53.5, 56, 56, 56) cm

15 7¼ (7¼, 8, 8, 8, 8, 8¾, 9¼, 9¼, 10, 10, 10)"
    18.5 (18.5, 20.5, 20.5, 20.5, 20.5, 22, 23.5, 23.5, 25.5, 25.5, 25.5) cm

16 11¼ (11¼, 12, 12¾, 12¾, 13¼, 14, 15¼, 16, 17¼, 18¾, 20)"
    29 (29, 30.5, 32, 32, 34, 35.5, 39, 40.5, 44, 47.5, 51) cm

META-PATTERN #4
THE COWL

Use this worksheet as a handy way to get all of the numbers for each individual cowl you knit in one simple place. You can photocopy these pages or download a fresh copy any time you like at www.amyherzogdesigns.com/knitwearlove.

BACK

Using long-tail cast-on method (or a different one, if you prefer), CO _____ sts. Work even in _____

until piece measures _____ from CO edge, ending with a WS row.

Switch to _____ and work even until piece measures _____ from CO edge, ending with a WS row.

On your last row, place markers on each side of center _____ sts.

DECREASE ROW (RS): Work to 2 sts before marker, ssk, sm, work to next marker, sm, k2tog, work to end.

Work a decrease row every _____ rows _____ times total: _____ sts remain. Work even until piece measures _____ from CO edge, ending with a WS row.

INCREASE ROW (RS): Work to marker, M1-r, sm, work to next marker, sm, M1-l, work to end.

Work an increase row every _____ rows _____ times total: _____ sts remain. Work even until piece measures _____ from CO edge, ending with a WS row.

SHAPE ARMHOLES: BO _____ sts at the beginning of the next two rows. BO _____ sts at the beginning of the following 2 rows. Decrease 1 st at each end of every RS row _____ times: _____ sts remain.

Work even until piece measures _____ from CO edge, ending with a WS row.

SHAPE NECK:

NEXT ROW (RS): Work _____ sts, attach a new ball of yarn and BO center _____ sts, work to end.

Working both sides of the neckline at the same time, decrease 1 st at neck edge of every RS row twice. _____ shoulder sts remain. Work even until piece measures _____ from CO edge, ending at the armhole edge for each side.

NEXT ROW: BO _____ sts, work to end. BO rem sts.

FRONT

Using long-tail cast-on method (or a different one, if you prefer), CO _____ sts. Work even in _____

until piece measures _____ from CO edge, ending with a WS row.

Switch to _____ and work even until piece measures _____ from CO edge, ending with a WS row.

On your last row, place markers on each side of center _____ sts.

DECREASE ROW (RS): Work to 2 sts before marker, ssk, sm, work to next marker, sm, k2tog, work to end.

Work decrease row every _____ rows _____ times total: _____ sts remain. Work even until piece measures _____ from CO edge, ending with a WS row.

INCREASE ROW (RS): Work to marker, M1-r, sm, work to next marker, sm, M1-l, work to end.

Work increase row every _____ rows _____ times total: _____ sts total. Work even until piece measures _____ from CO edge, ending with a WS row.

SHAPE ARMHOLES: BO _____ sts at the beginning of the next 2 rows. BO _____ sts at the beginning of the following 2 rows. Decrease 1 st at each end of every RS row _____ times: _____ sts remain.

SHAPE NECK: When armhole measures 1" (2.5 cm), ending with a WS row, shape neckline:

Mark center _____ sts.

NEXT ROW (RS): Work to marker. Attach a new ball of yarn and BO center _____ sts, work to end.

Decrease 1 st at neck edge every RS row _____ times, then every other RS row _____ times.

When all neck and armhole shaping is complete, _____ shoulder sts remain. Work even until piece measures _____ from CO edge, ending at the armhole edge for each side.

NEXT ROW: BO _____ sts, work to end. BO rem sts.

SLEEVE

Using long-tail cast-on method (or a different one, if you prefer), CO _____ sts.

Work even in _____ until piece measures _____ from CO edge, ending with a WS row.

Switch to _____ and work even until piece measures _____ from CO edge, ending with a WS row.

BOHEMIAN STYLE: DECREASE ROW (RS): K1, ssk, work to last 3 sts, K2tog, k1.

OTHER STYLES: INCREASE ROW (RS): K1, M1-r, work to last st, M1-l, k1.

Work increase or decrease row every _____ rows _____ times total: _____ sts total. Work even until sleeve measures _____ from CO edge, ending with a WS row.

SHAPE SLEEVE CAP: BO _____ sts at the beginning of the next 2 rows. BO _____ sts at the beginning of the following 2 rows. Decrease 1 st at each end of every 3rd RS row _____ times, then every other RS row _____ times, then every RS row _____ times.

BO _____ sts at the beginning of the next 4 rows.

BO final _____ sts.

FINISHING

Follow instructions on page 106.

BOHEMIAN   CASUAL   SPORTY

THE TUNIC

Tunics require a lot of knitting, it's true. But they're such a versatile wardrobe piece that they're more than worth the investment. Wear them with leggings, pants, or a skirt! Cold winter days call for layering with thick tights, while summer's heat allows for a linen tunic to be worn over a skirt.

By adjusting sleeve lengths, necklines, and of course the yarn involved, I've created three really different looks: a bohemian style with a deep V neckline, three-quarter sleeves, and intricate-looking (but simple!) colorwork; a casual style with an unexpected bit of lace on the back; and a sporty style with a henley neckline and super-long, ribbed sleeves with built-in thumbholes.

Of course, all of these options work well in any of the gauges I've provided. So have fun playing around with them, and knit a tunic that works perfectly for you.

Change it up!

Gauges offered
Fingering, DK, Aran

Necklines
Deep V, scoop, henley

Sleeves
Three-quarter-length, elbow, super-long with thumbholes

Make this
sweater suit
your
own style!

META-PATTERN #5

BOHEMIAN
The Tunic

V-neck trimmed with color.

Plain sleeves keep focus on hem's colorwork.

Intricate colorwork hem draws the eye down and layers well.

» Deedee is wearing size 40" (101.5 cm) in fingering gauge.

FINISHED BUST	**FINGERING:** 30¼ (32, 33¾, 35¾, 38¼, 40, 41¾, 43¾, 46¼, 48, 49¾, 54¼)" [76.5 (81.5, 86, 90.5, 97, 101.5, 106.5, 111, 117, 122, 126.5, 137.5) cm]	

DK: 30½ (32¾, 35, 36¼, 38½, 40¾, 43, 44¼, 46½, 48¾, 51, 54½): [77.5 (83, 88.5, 92.5, 98, 103.5, 109, 112.5, 118, 124, 129.5, 138.5) cm]

ARAN: 31 (33, 34¾, 36½, 39, 41, 42¾, 44½, 47, 49, 50¾, 55)" [79 (83.5, 88, 92.5, 99.5, 104, 108.5, 113, 119.5, 124, 128.5, 140) cm]

(Note: For ease in reading, the precise finished bust measurements have been rounded in the instructions below to 30 (32, 34, 36, 38, 40, 42, 44, 46, 48, 50, 54)" [76 (81.5, 86.5, 91.5, 96.5, 101.5, 106.5, 112, 117, 122, 127, 137) cm]. Your finished measurements will be as given above.

MATERIALS

See page 190 for fiber content.

FINGERING: Shibui Staccato in #2024 Lime (MC), #0016 Suit (CC1), #2027 Pool (CC2), and #0101 Ivory (CC3); 7 (8, 8, 9, 10, 10, 11, 11, 12, 13, 14, 15) hanks MC, 1 (1, 1, 1, 1, 1, 1, 1, 2, 2, 2) hanks CC1, and 1 hank each CC2 and CC3 all sizes

DK: Green Mountain Spinnery Alpaca Elegance in Cocoa, 6 (6, 7, 7, 8, 9, 9, 10, 11, 11, 12, 13) hanks

ARAN: Lorna's Laces Masham in Echo (MC) and Washington (CC), 6 (6, 6, 7, 7, 8, 8, 9, 9, 10, 10, 11) hanks MC and 1 hank CC all sizes

GAUGE

FINGERING: 26 sts and 40 rows = 4" (10 cm) in Stockinette st
DK: 22 sts and 32 rows = 4" (10 cm) in Stockinette st
ARAN: 18 sts and 22 rows = 4" (10 cm) in Stockinette st

NEEDLES

Change needle size if necessary to obtain the correct gauge.
FINGERING: US 2 / 2.75 mm
DK: US 5 / 3.75 mm
ARAN: US 8 / 5 mm

For Bohemian Style, needles in main needle size and one size smaller than main needle size.

NOTIONS

SPORTY STYLE: Two ¾ (20 mm) buttons

BACK

Using long-tail cast-on method (or a different one, if you prefer), CO

	30"	**32**	**34**	**36**	**38**	**40**	**42**	**44**	**46**	**48**	**50**	**54**
FINGERING	112	118	124	130	138	144	150	156	164	170	176	190
DK	94	100	106	110	116	122	128	132	138	144	150	160
ARAN	78	82	86	90	96	100	104	108	114	118	122	132

sts. Work even in trim of your choice, as follows:

BOHEMIAN STYLE: CO using MC and needles one size down from main needle size. Work even in Stockinette st for 1½" (4 cm), ending with a RS row. Switch to larger needles and knit 1 WS row to create turning ridge. *Note: All length measurements that follow are taken from turning ridge, not CO edge.*

Work 2 rows even in Stockinette st with main needle size and MC. Switch to Bohemian Body color pattern (page 127) and work 44-row chart pattern once. Switch to MC.

CASUAL STYLE: Work even in Garter st until piece measures 3½" (9 cm) from CO edge. Switch to Stockinette st.

SPORTY STYLE: CO using CC. Work even in 2x1 rib until piece measures ½" (1.5 cm). Switch to MC and work even in 2x1 rib until piece measures 3½" (9 cm) from CO edge. Switch to Stockinette st.

Work even until piece measures 7¾ (7¾, 7¾, 7¾, 8¾, 8¾, 8¾, 8¾, 8¾, 8¾, 8¾, 8¾)" [19.5 (19.5, 19.5, 19.5, 22, 22, 22, 22, 22, 22, 22, 22) cm] from CO edge, ending with a WS row.

On your last row, place two waist shaping markers, one on either side of the center section so that there are:

	30"	32	34	36	38	40	42	44	46	48	50	54
FINGERING	38	40	42	44	46	48	50	52	54	56	58	64
DK	32	34	36	36	38	40	42	44	46	48	50	54
ARAN	26	28	28	30	32	34	34	36	38	40	40	44

sts between waist shaping markers.

DECREASE ROW (RS): Work to 2 sts before first marker, ssk, sm, work to next marker, sm, k2tog, work to end. 2 sts decreased.

Work a decrease row every 4 rows

FINGERING: 12 / **DK:** 10 / **ARAN:** 8 times total.

When all decreases are complete,

	30"	32	34	36	38	40	42	44	46	48	50	54
FINGERING	88	94	100	106	114	120	126	132	140	146	152	166
DK	74	80	86	90	96	102	108	112	118	124	130	140
ARAN	62	66	70	74	80	84	88	92	98	102	106	116

sts remain. Work even until piece measures 14 (14, 14, 14, 15, 15, 15, 15, 15, 15, 15, 15)" [35.5 (35.5, 35.5, 35.5, 38, 38, 38, 38, 38, 38, 38, 38) cm] from CO edge, ending with a WS row.

ADDING THE CASUAL LACE DETAIL: Form the back lace detail by placing additional markers in the center of your sts and working those center sts in Dewdrop Lace (page 126) to back neck bind-off. Place markers around center

	30"	32	34	36	38	40	42	44	46	48	50	54
FINGERING	36	36	36	42	42	42	48	48	48	54	54	60
DK	30	30	30	30	36	36	36	42	42	42	48	48
ARAN	24	24	24	24	30	30	30	30	36	36	36	42

sts. Work sts between lace markers in Dewdrop Lace (page 126), beginning with Row 1, until back neck BO.

INCREASE ROW (RS): Work to first marker, M1-r, sm, work to next marker, sm, M1-l, work to end. 2 sts increased.

Work an increase row every

FINGERING: 12 / **DK:** 10 / **ARAN:** 8 rows

FINGERING: 5 / **DK:** 5 / **ARAN:** 4 times total.

When all increases are complete,

META-PATTERN #5

SPORTY

The Tunic

Henley neckline.

Softly shaded neutral with a pop of yellow.

Extra-long sleeves with thumbholes.

Long sleeves match the tunic length and keep you warm.

» Jackie is wearing size 38" (96.5 cm) in Aran gauge.

	30"	32	34	36	38	40	42	44	46	48	50	54
FINGERING	98	104	110	116	124	130	136	142	150	156	162	176
DK	84	90	96	100	106	112	118	122	128	134	140	150
ARAN	70	74	78	82	88	92	96	100	106	110	114	124

sts total. Work even until piece measures 20½ (20¾, 21, 21¼, 22½, 22¾, 23, 23, 23½, 23½, 23½, 23½)" [52 (52.5, 53.5, 54, 57, 58, 58.5, 58.5, 59.5, 59.5, 59.5, 59.5) cm] from CO edge, ending with a WS row.

SHAPE ARMHOLES

BO

	30"	32	34	36	38	40	42	44	46	48	50	54
FINGERING	8	8	8	8	8	8	8	8	8	10	12	12
DK	6	6	6	6	6	6	6	8	8	10	10	12
ARAN	6	6	6	6	6	6	6	8	8	10	10	12

sts at the beginning of the next 2 rows. BO

	30"	32	34	36	38	40	42	44	46	48	50	54
FINGERING	0	2	2	2	2	2	2	4	6	6	8	10
DK	2	2	2	2	2	4	4	4	6	6	8	10
ARAN	0	0	2	2	2	4	4	4	6	6	6	8

sts at the beginning of the following 2 rows. Decrease 1 st at each end of every RS row

	30"	32	34	36	38	40	42	44	46	48	50	54
FINGERING	3	3	4	5	6	7	9	9	10	10	9	10
DK	2	4	5	6	6	6	7	7	7	7	7	6
ARAN	3	3	2	3	4	3	4	3	4	3	4	3

times:

	30"	32	34	36	38	40	42	44	46	48	50	54
FINGERING	76	78	82	86	92	96	98	100	102	104	104	112
DK	64	66	70	72	78	80	84	84	86	88	90	94
ARAN	52	56	58	60	64	66	68	70	70	72	74	78

sts remain.
Work even until armhole measures 5½ (6, 6¼, 6½, 7, 7¼, 7½, 8, 8¼, 8¾, 9, 9½)" [14 (15, 16, 16.5, 18, 18.5, 19, 20.5, 21, 22, 23, 24) cm] and piece measures 26 (26¾, 27¼, 27¾, 29½, 30, 30½, 31, 31¾, 32¼, 32½, 33)" [66 (68, 69, 70.5, 75, 76, 77.5, 78.5, 80.5, 82, 82.5, 84) cm], ending with a WS row.

SHAPE NECK

NEXT ROW (RS): Work

	30"	32	34	36	38	40	42	44	46	48	50	54
FINGERING	22	22	23	24	25	26	27	27	28	28	28	30
DK	18	19	20	20	22	22	23	23	24	24	25	26
ARAN	16	16	17	17	18	19	19	20	20	20	21	22

sts, attach a new ball of yarn and BO center

	30"	32	34	36	38	40	42	44	46	48	50	54
FINGERING	32	34	36	38	42	44	44	46	46	48	48	52
DK	28	28	30	32	34	36	38	38	38	40	40	42
ARAN	20	24	24	26	28	28	30	30	30	32	32	34

sts, work to end. *You will now work both sides of the neckline at the same time.*

Decrease 1 st at neck edge of every RS row twice:

	30"	32	34	36	38	40	42	44	46	48	50	54
FINGERING	20	20	21	22	23	24	25	25	26	26	26	28
DK	16	17	18	18	20	20	21	21	22	22	23	24
ARAN	14	14	15	15	16	17	17	18	18	18	19	20

sts remain for each shoulder. Work even until armhole measures 6½ (7, 7¼, 7½, 8, 8¼, 8½, 9, 9¼, 9¾, 10, 10½)" [16.5 (18, 18.5, 19, 20.5, 21, 21.5, 23, 23.5, 25, 25.5, 26.5) cm] and piece measures 27 (27¾, 28¼, 28¾, 30½, 31, 31½, 32, 32¾, 33¼, 33½, 34)" [68.5 (70.5, 72, 73, 77.5, 78.5, 80, 81.5, 83, 84.5, 85, 86.5) cm] from CO edge, ending at the armhole edge for each side.

NEXT ROW: BO

	30"	32	34	36	38	40	42	44	46	48	50	54
FINGERING	10	10	11	11	12	12	13	13	13	13	13	14
DK	8	9	9	9	10	10	11	11	11	11	12	12
ARAN	7	7	8	8	8	9	9	9	9	9	10	10

sts, work to end. BO remaining sts.

FRONTS

Work as for back, aside from neck shaping, *except* place waist shaping markers around the center section so that there are:

	30"	32	34	36	38	40	42	44	46	48	50	54
FINGERING	56	58	62	64	68	72	74	78	82	84	88	94
DK	46	50	52	54	58	60	64	66	68	72	74	80
ARAN	38	40	42	44	48	50	52	54	56	58	60	66

sts between waist shaping markers.

Note: For Bohemian Style, neck shaping begins before armhole shaping starts. For Casual and Sporty Styles, neck shaping begins before armhole shaping is complete. Please read ahead.

SHAPE NECK

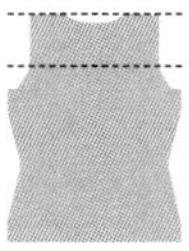

When piece measures

BOHEMIAN STYLE: 18½ (18¾, 19, 19¼, 20½, 20¾, 21, 21, 21½, 21½, 21½, 21½)" [47 (47.5, 48.5, 49, 52, 52.5, 53.5, 53.5, 54.5, 54.5, 54.5, 54.5) cm]

CASUAL STYLE: 21 (21¼, 21½, 21¾, 23, 23¼, 23½, 23½, 24, 24, 24, 24)" [53.5 (54, 54.5, 55, 58.5, 59, 59.5, 59.5, 61, 61, 61, 61) cm]

SPORTY STYLE: 21½ (21¾, 22, 22¼, 23½, 23¾, 24, 24, 24½, 24½, 24½, 24½)" [54.5 (55, 56, 56.5, 59.5, 60.5, 61, 61, 62, 62, 62, 62) cm]

from CO edge, *shape neckline* according to instructions for your style.

BOHEMIAN STYLE: Mark center

FINGERING: 12 / **DK:** 10 / **ARAN:** 8 sts

NEXT ROW (RS): Work to marker, attach a second ball of yarn and BO sts to next marker, work to end.

You will now work both sides of your neckline at the same time. *Note: Armhole shaping will begin before neck shaping is complete.*

Decrease 1 st at neck edge every

	30"	32	34	36	38	40	42	44	46	48	50	54
FINGERING	6	6	5	5	5	5	5	5	5	5	5	5
DK	5	5	5	5	5	4	4	5	5	5	5	5
ARAN	5	4	4	4	4	4	4	4	4	4	4	4

rows

	30"	32	34	36	38	40	42	44	46	48	50	54
FINGERING	12	13	14	15	17	18	18	19	19	20	20	22
DK	11	11	12	13	14	15	16	16	16	17	17	18
ARAN	8	10	10	11	12	12	13	13	13	14	14	15

times.

CASUAL STYLE: Mark center

	30"	32	34	36	38	40	42	44	46	48	50	54
FINGERING	16	16	16	18	20	20	20	20	20	22	22	24
DK	14	14	14	16	16	16	18	18	18	18	18	20
ARAN	10	12	12	12	14	14	14	14	14	16	16	16

sts.

NEXT ROW (RS): Work to marker, attach a new ball of yarn and BO sts to next marker, work to end. Working both sides of the neckline at the same time, decrease 1 st at neck edge every RS row

	30"	32	34	36	38	40	42	44	46	48	50	54
FINGERING	5	5	6	6	6	7	7	7	7	7	7	8
DK	4	4	5	5	5	6	6	6	6	6	6	6
ARAN	3	4	4	4	4	4	5	5	5	5	5	5

times, then every other RS row

	30"	32	34	36	38	40	42	44	46	48	50	54
FINGERING	5	6	6	6	7	7	7	8	8	8	8	8
DK	5	5	5	5	6	6	6	6	6	7	7	7
ARAN	4	4	4	5	5	5	5	5	5	5	5	6

times.

SPORTY STYLE: Mark center

FINGERING: 10 / **DK:** 8 / **ARAN:** 6 sts.

NEXT ROW (RS): Work to marker, attach a new ball of yarn and BO sts to next marker, work to end. You will now work both sides of the neckline at the same time. Work even for 3" (7.5 cm).
BO

	30"	32	34	36	38	40	42	44	46	48	50	54
FINGERING	3	3	3	4	5	5	5	5	5	6	6	7
DK	3	3	3	4	4	4	5	5	5	5	5	6
ARAN	2	3	3	3	4	4	4	4	4	5	5	5

sts at the beginning of the next neck-edge row, then decrease 1 st at neck edge every row

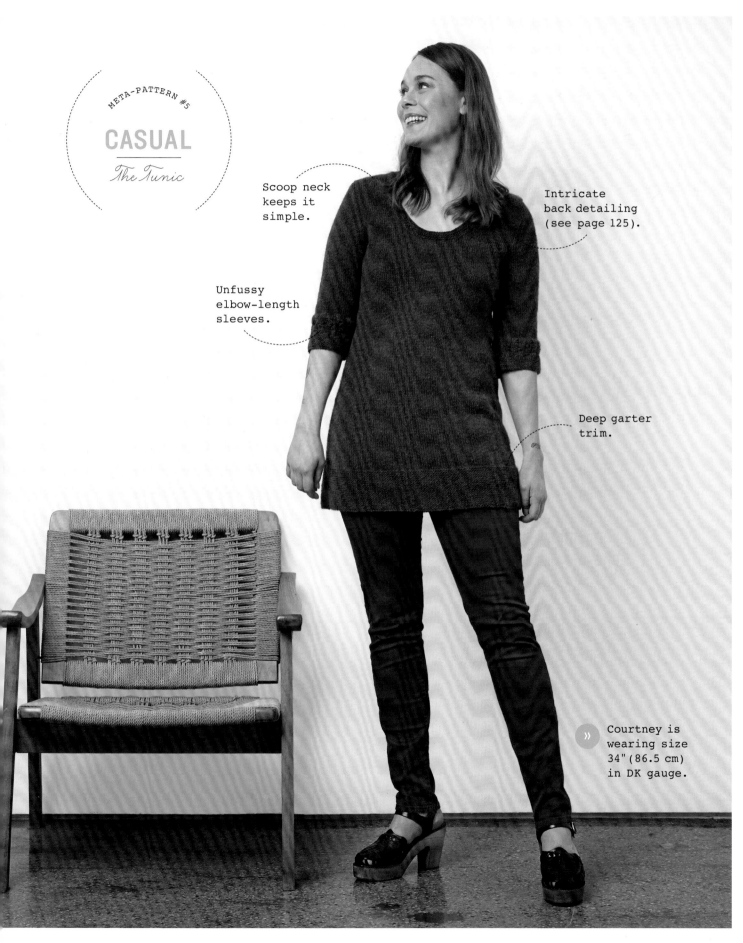

META-PATTERN #5

CASUAL

The Tunic

Scoop neck keeps it simple.

Intricate back detailing (see page 125).

Unfussy elbow-length sleeves.

Deep garter trim.

» Courtney is wearing size 34" (86.5 cm) in DK gauge.

	30"	32	34	36	38	40	42	44	46	48	50	54
FINGERING	5	5	6	6	6	7	7	7	7	7	7	8
DK	4	4	5	5	5	6	6	6	6	6	6	6
ARAN	3	4	4	4	4	4	5	5	5	5	5	5

times, then every RS row

	30"	32	34	36	38	40	42	44	46	48	50	54
FINGERING	5	6	6	6	7	7	7	8	8	8	8	8
DK	5	5	5	5	6	6	6	6	6	7	7	7
ARAN	4	4	4	5	5	5	5	5	5	5	5	6

times.

SHAPE ARMHOLES

When piece measures 20½ (20¾, 21, 21¼, 22½, 22¾, 23, 23, 23½, 23½, 23½, 23½)" [52 (52.5, 53.5, 54, 57, 58, 58.5, 58.5, 59.5, 59.5, 59.5, 59.5) cm] from CO edge, *shape armholes as directed for back.*

ALL STYLES, ALL SIZES: When all neck and armhole shaping is complete

	30"	32	34	36	38	40	42	44	46	48	50	54
FINGERING	20	20	21	22	23	24	25	25	26	26	26	28
DK	16	17	18	18	20	20	21	21	22	22	23	24
ARAN	14	14	15	15	16	17	17	18	18	18	19	20

sts remain. Work even and complete shoulder shaping as for back.

SLEEVES

BOHEMIAN STYLE: Using long-tail cast-on method (or a different one, if you prefer), MC, and needles one size down from main needle size, CO

	30"	32	34	36	38	40	42	44	46	48	50	54
FINGERING	72	76	78	82	84	88	92	98	104	110	118	124
DK	60	62	66	68	70	74	76	82	88	92	98	104
ARAN	50	52	54	56	58	62	64	68	72	76	82	86

sts.
Work even in Stockinette st until sleeve measures 1" (2.5 cm) from CO edge, ending with a RS row. Switch to main needle size and knit 1 WS row to create turning ridge.

Work even in MC and Stockinette st until sleeve measures 12 (12, 12, 13, 13, 13, 13½, 13½, 13½, 14, 14, 14)" [30.5 (30.5, 30.5, 33, 33, 33, 34.5, 34.5, 34.5, 35.5, 35.5, 35.5) cm] from turning ridge, ending with a WS row.

CASUAL STYLE: Using long-tail cast-on method (or a different one, if you prefer), CO

	30"	32	34	36	38	40	42	44	46	48	50	54
FINGERING	66	70	72	76	78	82	86	92	98	104	112	118
DK	56	58	62	64	66	70	72	78	84	88	94	100
ARAN	46	48	50	52	54	58	60	64	68	72	78	82

sts.
Work even in Garter st until sleeve measures 1" (2.5 cm) from CO edge, ending with a WS row. Switch to Dewdrop Lace (page 126) over center

	30"	32	34	36	38	40	42	44	46	48	50	54
FINGERING	66	66	72	72	78	78	84	90	96	102	108	114
DK	54	54	60	60	66	66	72	78	84	84	92	98
ARAN	42	48	48	48	54	54	60	60	66	72	78	78

sts, keeping remaining sts at sides (if any) in Stockinette st, and work until lace measures approximately 2" (5 cm), ending with a WS row.

Switch to Stockinette st and work 2 rows even.

INCREASE ROW (RS): K 1, M1-r, knit to last st, M1-l, k1.

Repeat increase row every

FINGERING: 12 / **DK:** 8 / **ARAN:** 6 rows until a total of

FINGERING: 3 / **DK:** 2 / **ARAN:** 2 increase rows have been worked:

	30"	32	34	36	38	40	42	44	46	48	50	54
FINGERING	72	76	78	82	84	88	92	98	104	110	118	124
DK	60	62	66	68	70	74	76	82	88	92	98	104
ARAN	50	52	54	56	58	62	64	68	72	76	82	86

sts total.

Work even until sleeve measures 8 (8½, 9, 9½, 10, 10, 10½, 10½, 11, 11, 11½, 11½)" [20.5 (21.5, 23, 24, 25.5, 25.5, 26.5, 26.5, 28, 28, 29, 29) cm] from CO edge, ending with a WS row.

SPORTY STYLE: Using CC and long-tail cast-on method (or a different one, if you prefer), CO

	30"	32	34	36	38	40	42	44	46	48	50	54
FINGERING	56	56	60	60	60	62	62	66	66	66	72	72
DK	48	48	50	50	50	54	54	56	56	56	62	62
ARAN	40	40	42	42	42	44	44	46	46	46	50	50

sts.

Work even in 2x1 rib and CC until piece measures ½" (1.5 cm) from CO edge. Switch to MC and continue until piece measures 1" (2.5 cm) from CO edge.

CREATE THUMBHOLE: *Work on RS row for right sleeve, WS row for left sleeve:*
Work

	30"	32	34	36	38	40	42	44	46	48	50	54
FINGERING	14	14	15	15	15	15	15	16	16	16	18	18
DK	12	12	12	12	12	13	13	14	14	14	15	15
ARAN	10	10	10	10	10	11	11	11	11	11	12	12

sts, attach a new ball of yarn and BO

FINGERING: 4 / **DK:** 3 / **ARAN:** 2 sts, work to end.

Working both sides at the same time, work even until thumbhole measures 1¾" (4.5 cm).

On your next row, work to thumbhole, CO

FINGERING: 4 / **DK:** 3 / **ARAN:** 2 sts to close the hole,

work to end with same ball of yarn. Cut second ball of yarn.

Continue in MC and rib until sleeve measures 7" (18 cm) from CO edge. Switch to Stockinette st.

INCREASE ROW (RS): K 1, M1-r, knit to last st, M1-l, k1.

INCREASE ROW (WS): P 1, M1-p, purl to last st, M1-p, p1.

Work increase row every

	30"	32	34	36	38	40	42	44	46	48	50	54
FINGERING	15	12	13	11	10	10	9	8	7	6	6	5
DK	16	14	12	11	10	10	9	8	6	6	6	5
ARAN	13	11	11	10	8	7	7	6	5	4	4	4

rows until a total of

	30"	32	34	36	38	40	42	44	46	48	50	54
FINGERING	8	10	9	11	12	13	15	16	19	22	23	26
DK	6	7	8	9	10	10	11	13	16	18	18	21
ARAN	5	6	6	7	8	9	10	11	13	15	16	18

increase rows have been worked:

	30"	32	34	36	38	40	42	44	46	48	50	54
FINGERING	72	76	78	82	84	88	92	98	104	110	118	124
DK	60	62	66	68	70	74	76	82	88	92	98	104
ARAN	50	52	54	56	58	62	64	68	72	76	82	86

sts total.

Work even until sleeve measures 21½ (21½, 21½, 22, 22, 22, 22½, 22½, 22½, 22½, 23, 23)" [54.5 (54.5, 54.5, 56, 56, 56, 57, 57, 57, 57, 58.5, 58.5) cm] from CO edge, ending with a WS row.

SHAPE SLEEVE CAP

ALL STYLES: BO

	30"	32	34	36	38	40	42	44	46	48	50	54
FINGERING	8	8	8	8	8	8	8	8	8	10	12	12
DK	6	6	6	6	6	6	6	8	8	10	10	12
ARAN	6	6	6	6	6	6	6	8	8	10	10	12

sts at the beginning of the next 2 rows. BO

	30"	32	34	36	38	40	42	44	46	48	50	54
FINGERING	0	2	2	2	2	2	2	4	6	6	8	9
DK	2	2	2	2	2	4	4	4	6	6	8	8
ARAN	0	0	2	2	2	4	4	4	6	6	6	6

sts at the beginning of the following 2 rows.

Decrease 1 st at each end of every 3rd RS row

	30"	32	34	36	38	40	42	44	46	48	50	54
FINGERING	2	3	3	3	4	3	4	5	5	6	6	8
DK	1	2	2	2	2	3	4	5	5	6	6	8
ARAN	0	0	1	1	1	1	2	3	3	4	2	5

time(s), then every other RS row

	30"	32	34	36	38	40	42	44	46	48	50	54
FINGERING	0	1	1	0	0	1	1	0	0	0	1	1
DK	1	1	0	0	0	0	1	0	0	0	0	0
ARAN	0	0	0	0	0	1	1	0	1	0	1	1

time(s), then every RS row

	30"	32	34	36	38	40	42	44	46	48	50	54
FINGERING	11	9	10	13	13	15	11	12	13	13	12	5
DK	9	9	12	13	14	13	5	6	7	6	7	1
ARAN	9	10	8	9	10	9	5	5	4	4	8	0

time(s). BO

	30"	32	34	36	38	40	42	44	46	48	50	54
FINGERING	3	3	3	3	3	3	4	4	4	4	4	6
DK	2	2	2	2	2	2	4	4	4	4	4	5
ARAN	2	2	2	2	2	2	3	3	3	3	3	4

sts at the beginning of the next 4 rows. BO final

	30"	32	34	36	38	40	42	44	46	48	50	54
FINGERING	18	18	18	18	18	18	24	24	24	24	24	30
DK	14	14	14	14	14	14	20	20	20	20	20	26
ARAN	12	12	12	12	12	12	16	16	16	16	16	22

sts.

FINISHING Wet-block all pieces to finished measurements. Sew shoulder seams using mattress stitch. Set in sleeves and sew side and sleeve seams using mattress stitch.

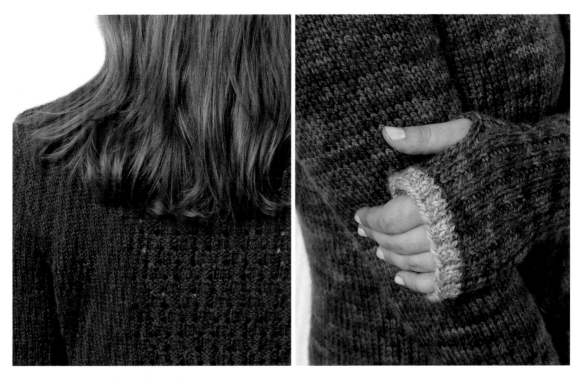

INTERESTING DETAILS: Casual lace on sweater back, sporty thumbholes for warmth.

BOHEMIAN STYLE: Fold body and sleeve hems to WS along turning ridge and sew in place.

NECKLINE: With RS facing and MC, starting at right front neck corner, pick up and knit sts around neck edge at the rate of 4 sts for every 5 rows along diagonal and vertical edges, and 1 st for every bound-off st, ending at left front neck corner. Count sts and adjust if necessary to make total a multiple of 8 sts. Switch to CC1 and purl 1 row.

Work 10 rows of Neck Colorwork Chart.

With CC1, work 5 rows in Garter st. BO all sts.

Sew sides of neck trim to bound-off edge of center front neck.

CASUAL STYLE: With RS facing, pick up and knit sts around neckline at the rate of 1 st for every bound-off st, 3 sts for every 4 rows along vertical edges, and 4 sts for every 5 rows along diagonal edges. Join for working in the round.

Work even in Garter st for 1" (2.5 cm). BO all sts.

SPORTY STYLE: With RS facing and CC, and starting at lower right front neck corner, pick up and knit sts along right front edge to neck edge at the rate of 3 sts for every 4 rows. Count sts and adjust if necessary to make total a multiple of 3 sts plus 2. Mark placement for 2 buttonholes with removable stitch markers.

Work

FINGERING: 7 / **DK:** 5 / **ARAN:** 3 rows even in 2x1 rib

BUTTONHOLE ROW (RS): *Work to marked buttonhole position, yo, k2tog; repeat from * once more, work to end.

Work

FINGERING: 7 / **DK:** 5 / **ARAN:** 3 more rows even in 2x1 rib,
BO all sts.

Repeat along left front neck edge, omitting buttonholes.

With RS facing and CC, starting at top of right front trim, pick up and knit sts around neckline at the rate of 1 st for every bound-off st, 3 sts for every 4 rows along vertical edges, and 4 sts for every 5 rows along diagonal edges. Work even in 2x1 rib until trim measures ½" (1.5 cm). BO all sts.

With RS facing and MC, pick up and knit sts around thumbhole at the rate of 1 st for every bound-off or cast-on st, and 3 sts for every 4 rows.

Knit 1 row. BO all sts.

SPECIAL STITCHES

DEWDROP LACE (multiple of 6 sts)

ROW 1 (RS): * P3, k3; repeat from * to end.

ROW 2: Repeat row 1.

ROW 3: *K3, yo, sl 1, k2tog, psso, yo; repeat from * to end.

ROWS 4, 5 AND 6: *K3, p3; repeat from * to end.

ROW 7: *Yo, sl 1, k2tog, psso, yo, k3; repeat from * to end.

ROW 8: Repeat row 1.

Repeat rows 1–8 for Dewdrop Lace.

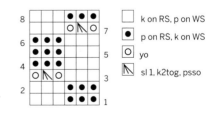

- □ k on RS, p on WS
- ● p on RS, k on WS
- ○ yo
- ◩ sl 1, k2tog, psso

BOHEMIAN BODY

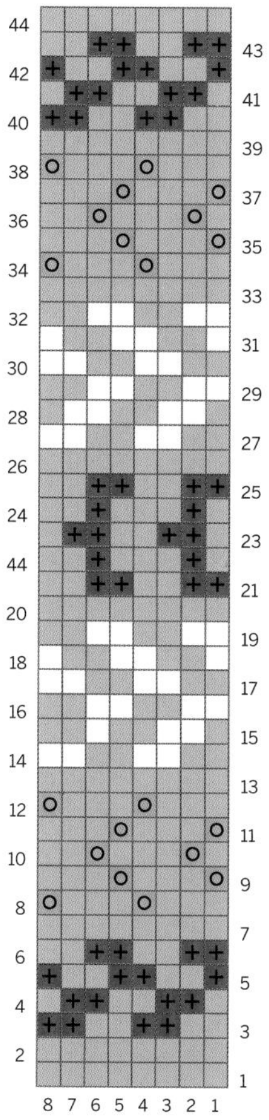

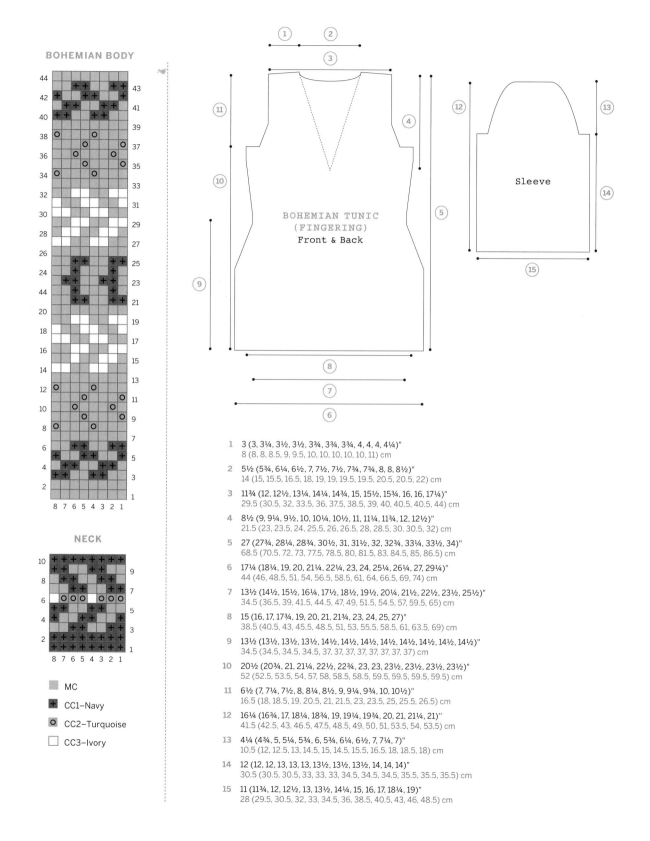

NECK

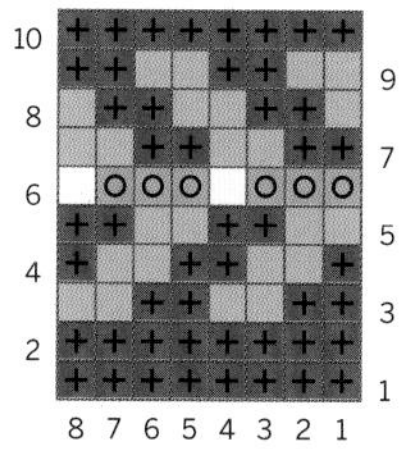

- MC
- CC1–Navy
- CC2–Turquoise
- CC3–Ivory

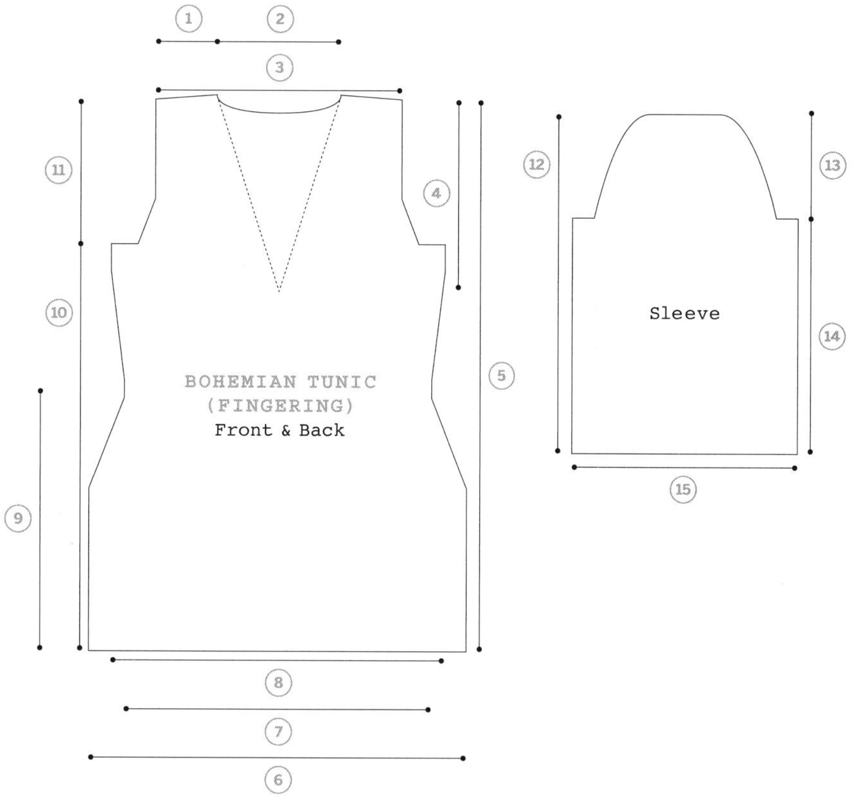
1
2
3
11
4
10
5
9
BOHEMIAN TUNIC
(FINGERING)
Front & Back
8
7
6
12
13
Sleeve
14
15

1 3 (3, 3¼, 3½, 3½, 3¾, 3¾, 3¾, 4, 4, 4, 4¼)"
8 (8, 8, 8.5, 9, 9.5, 10, 10, 10, 10, 10, 11) cm

2 5½ (5¾, 6¼, 6½, 7, 7½, 7½, 7¾, 7¾, 8, 8, 8½)"
14 (15, 15.5, 16.5, 18, 19, 19, 19.5, 19.5, 20.5, 20.5, 22) cm

3 11¾ (12, 12½, 13¼, 14¼, 14¾, 15, 15½, 15¾, 16, 16, 17¼)"
29.5 (30.5, 32, 33.5, 36, 37.5, 38.5, 39, 40, 40.5, 40.5, 44) cm

4 8½ (9, 9¼, 9½, 10, 10¼, 10½, 11, 11¼, 11¾, 12, 12½)"
21.5 (23, 23.5, 24, 25.5, 26, 26.5, 28, 28.5, 30, 30.5, 32) cm

5 27 (27¾, 28¼, 28¾, 30½, 31, 31½, 32, 32¾, 33¼, 33½, 34)"
68.5 (70.5, 72, 73, 77.5, 78.5, 80, 81.5, 83, 84.5, 85, 86.5) cm

6 17¼ (18¼, 19, 20, 21¼, 22¼, 23, 24, 25¼, 26¼, 27, 29¼)"
44 (46, 48.5, 51, 54, 56.5, 58.5, 61, 64, 66.5, 69, 74) cm

7 13½ (14½, 15½, 16¼, 17½, 18½, 19½, 20¼, 21½, 22½, 23½, 25½)"
34.5 (36.5, 39, 41.5, 44.5, 47, 49, 51.5, 54.5, 57, 59.5, 65) cm

8 15 (16, 17, 17¾, 19, 20, 21, 21¾, 23, 24, 25, 27)"
38.5 (40.5, 43, 45.5, 48.5, 51, 53, 55.5, 58.5, 61, 63.5, 69) cm

9 13½ (13½, 13½, 13½, 14½, 14½, 14½, 14½, 14½, 14½, 14½, 14½)"
34.5 (34.5, 34.5, 34.5, 37, 37, 37, 37, 37, 37, 37, 37) cm

10 20½ (20¾, 21, 21¼, 22½, 22¾, 23, 23, 23½, 23½, 23½, 23½)"
52 (52.5, 53.5, 54, 57, 58, 58.5, 58.5, 59.5, 59.5, 59.5, 59.5) cm

11 6½ (7, 7¼, 7½, 8, 8¼, 8½, 9, 9¼, 9¾, 10, 10½)"
16.5 (18, 18.5, 19, 20.5, 21, 21.5, 23, 23.5, 25, 25.5, 26.5) cm

12 16¼ (16¾, 17, 18¼, 18¾, 19, 19¼, 19¾, 20, 21, 21¼, 21)"
41.5 (42.5, 43, 46.5, 47.5, 48.5, 49, 50, 51, 53.5, 54, 53.5) cm

13 4¼ (4¾, 5, 5¼, 5¾, 6, 5¾, 6¼, 6½, 7, 7¼, 7)"
10.5 (12, 12.5, 13, 14.5, 15, 14.5, 15.5, 16.5, 18, 18.5, 18) cm

14 12 (12, 12, 13, 13, 13, 13½, 13½, 13½, 14, 14, 14)"
30.5 (30.5, 30.5, 33, 33, 33, 34.5, 34.5, 34.5, 35.5, 35.5, 35.5) cm

15 11 (11¾, 12, 12½, 13, 13½, 14¼, 15, 16, 17, 18¼, 19)"
28 (29.5, 30.5, 32, 33, 34.5, 36, 38.5, 40.5, 43, 46, 48.5) cm

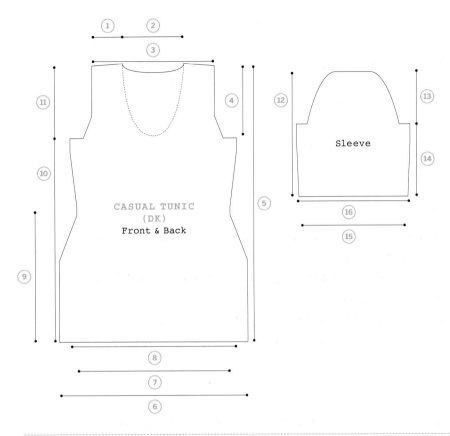

1 3 (3, 3¼, 3¼, 3¾, 3¾, 3¾, 3¾, 4, 4, 4¼, 4¼)"
   7.5 (8, 8.5, 8.5, 9, 9, 9.5, 9.5, 10, 10, 10.5, 11) cm

2 5¾ (5¾, 6¼, 6½, 7, 7¼, 7¾, 7¾, 7¾, 8, 8, 8¼)"
   15 (15, 15.5, 16.5, 17.5, 18.5, 19.5, 19.5, 19.5, 20.5, 20.5, 21) cm

3 11¾ (12, 12¾, 13, 14¼, 14½, 15¼, 15¼, 15¾, 16, 16¼, 17)"
   29.5 (30.5, 32.5, 33.5, 36, 37, 39, 39, 39.5, 40.5, 41.5, 43.5) cm

4 6 (6½, 6¾, 7, 7½, 7¾, 8, 8½, 8¾, 9¼, 9½, 10)"
   15 (16.5, 17, 18, 19, 19.5, 20.5, 21.5, 22, 23.5, 24, 25.5) cm

5 27 (27¾, 28¼, 28¾, 30½, 31, 31½, 32, 32¾, 33¼, 33½, 34)"
   68.5 (70.5, 72, 73, 77.5, 78.5, 80, 81.5, 83, 84.5, 85, 86.5) cm

6 17 (18¼, 19¼, 20, 21, 22¼, 23¼, 24, 25, 26¼, 27¼, 29)"
   43.5 (46, 49, 51, 53.5, 56.5, 59, 61, 63.5, 66.5, 69.5, 74) cm

7 13½ (14½, 15¾, 16¼, 17½, 18½, 19¾, 20¼, 21½, 22½, 23¾, 25½)"
   34 (37, 39.5, 41.5, 44.5, 47, 50, 51.5, 54.5, 57.5, 60, 64.5) cm

8 15¼ (16¼, 17½, 18¼, 19¼, 20¼, 21½, 22¼, 23¼, 24¼, 25½, 27¼)"
   39 (41.5, 44.5, 46, 49, 51.5, 54.5, 56.5, 59, 62, 64.5, 69.5) cm

9 13½ (13½, 13½, 13½, 14½, 14½, 14½, 14½, 14½, 14½, 14½, 14½)"
   34.5 (34.5, 34.5, 34.5, 37, 37, 37, 37, 37, 37, 37, 37) cm

10 20½ (20¾, 21, 21¼, 22½, 22¾, 23, 23, 23½, 23½, 23½, 23½)"
   52 (52.5, 53.5, 54, 57, 58, 58.5, 58.5, 59.5, 59.5, 59.5, 59.5) cm

11 6½ (7, 7¼, 7½, 8, 8¼, 8½, 9, 9¼, 9¾, 10, 10½)"
   16.5 (18, 18.5, 19, 20.5, 21, 21.5, 23, 23.5, 25, 25.5, 26.5) cm

12 12½ (13¾, 14½, 15¼, 16, 16½, 16¼, 16¾, 17½, 18, 18¾, 18¾)"
   32 (35, 37, 38.5, 40.5, 42, 41.5, 42.5, 44.5, 45.5, 47.5, 47.5) cm

13 4½ (5¼, 5½, 5¾, 6, 6½, 5¾, 6¼, 6½, 7, 7¼, 7¼)"
   11.5 (13.5, 14, 14.5, 15, 16.5, 14.5, 16, 16.5, 18, 18.5, 18.5) cm

14 8 (8½, 9, 9½, 10, 10, 10½, 10½, 11, 11, 11½, 11½)"
   20.5 (21.5, 23, 24, 25.5, 25.5, 26.5, 26.5, 28, 28, 29, 29) cm

15 10¼ (10½, 11¼, 11¾, 12, 12¾, 13, 14¼, 15¼, 16, 17, 18¼)"
   26 (27, 28.5, 29.5, 30.5, 32.5, 33.5, 36, 39, 40.5, 43.5, 46) cm

16 11 (11¼, 12, 12¼, 12¾, 13½, 13¾, 15, 16, 16¾, 17¾, 19)"
   27.5 (28.5, 30.5, 31.5, 32.5, 34, 35, 38, 40.5, 42.5, 45.5, 48) cm

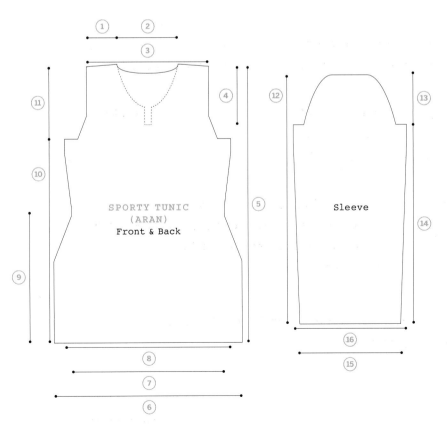

1 3 (3, 3¼, 3¼, 3½, 3¾, 3¾, 4, 4, 4, 4¼, 4½)"
   8 (8, 8.5, 8.5, 9, 9.5, 9.5, 10, 10, 10, 10.5, 11.5) cm

2 5¼ (6¼, 6¼, 6¾, 7, 7, 7½, 7½, 7½, 8, 8, 8½)"
   13.5 (16, 16, 17, 18, 18, 19, 19, 19, 20.5, 20.5, 21.5) cm

3 11½ (12½, 13, 13¼, 14¼, 14¾, 15, 15½, 15½, 16, 16½, 17¼)"
   29.5 (31.5, 32.5, 34, 36, 37.5, 38.5, 39.5, 39.5, 40.5, 42, 44) cm

4 5½ (6, 6¼, 6½, 7, 7¼, 7½, 8, 8¼, 8¾, 9, 9½)"
   14 (15, 16, 16.5, 18, 18.5, 19, 20.5, 21, 22, 23, 24) cm

5 27 (27¾, 28¼, 28¾, 30½, 31, 31½, 32, 32¾, 33¼, 33½, 34)"
   68.5 (70.5, 72, 73, 77.5, 78.5, 80, 81.5, 83, 84.5, 85, 86.5) cm

6 17¼ (18¼, 19, 20, 21¼, 22¼, 23, 24, 25¼, 26¼, 27, 29¼)"
   44 (46.5, 48.5, 51, 54, 56.5, 58.5, 61, 64.5, 66.5, 69, 74.5) cm

7 13¾ (14¾, 15½, 16½, 17¾, 18¾, 19½, 20½, 21¾, 22¾, 23½, 25¾)"
   35 (37.5, 39.5, 42, 45, 47.5, 49.5, 52, 55.5, 57.5, 60, 65.5) cm

8 15½ (16½, 17¼, 18¼, 19½, 20½, 21¼, 22¼, 23½, 24½, 25¼, 27½)"
   39.5 (42, 44, 46.5, 49.5, 52, 54, 56.5, 60, 62, 64.5, 70) cm

9 13½ (13½, 13½, 13½, 14½, 14½, 14½, 14½, 14½, 14½, 14½, 14½)"
   34.5 (34.5, 34.5, 34.5, 37, 37, 37, 37, 37, 37, 37, 37) cm

10 20½ (20¾, 21, 21¼, 22½, 22¾, 23, 23, 23½, 23½, 23½, 23½)"
   52 (52.5, 53.5, 54, 57, 58, 58.5, 58.5, 59.5, 59.5, 59.5, 59.5) cm

11 6½ (7, 7¼, 7½, 8, 8¼, 8½, 9, 9¼, 9¾, 10, 10½)"
   16.5 (18, 18.5, 19, 20.5, 21, 21.5, 23, 23.5, 25, 25.5, 26.5) cm

12 26¼ (26½, 27, 27¾, 28¼, 28½, 28¾, 29, 29½, 29¾, 30¼, 30¾)"
   66.5 (67.5, 68.5, 70.5, 72, 72.5, 73, 73.5, 75, 75.5, 77, 78) cm

13 4¾ (5, 5½, 5¾, 6¼, 6½, 6¼, 6½, 7, 7¼, 7¼, 7¾)"
   12 (13, 14, 15, 15.5, 16.5, 15.5, 16.5, 17.5, 18.5, 18.5, 19.5) cm

14 21½ (21½, 21½, 22, 22, 22, 22½, 22½, 22½, 22½, 23, 23)"
   54.5 (54.5, 54.5, 56, 56, 56, 57, 57, 57, 57, 58.5, 58.5) cm

15 9 (9, 9¼, 9¼, 9¼, 9¾, 9¾, 10¼, 10¼, 10¼, 11, 11)"
   23 (23, 23.5, 23.5, 23.5, 25, 25, 26, 26, 26, 28, 28) cm

16 11 (11½, 12, 12½, 13, 13¾, 14¼, 15, 16, 17, 18¼, 19)"
   28 (29.5, 30.5, 31.5, 32.5, 35, 36, 38.5, 40.5, 43, 46.5, 48.5) cm

META-PATTERN #5

THE TUNIC

Use this worksheet as a handy way to get all of the numbers for each individual tunic you knit in one simple place. You can photocopy these pages or download a fresh copy any time you like at www.amyherzogdesigns.com/knitwearlove.

BACK

Using long-tail cast-on method (or a different one, if you prefer), CO _____ sts. Work even in _____

until piece measures _____ from CO edge, ending with a WS row.

Switch to _____ and work even until piece measures _____ from CO edge, ending with a WS row.

On your last row, place markers on each side of center _____ sts.

DECREASE ROW (RS): Work to 2 sts before marker, ssk, sm, work to next marker, sm, k2tog, work to end.

Work decrease row every _____ rows _____ times total: _____ sts remain. Work even until piece measures _____ from CO edge, ending with a WS row.

CASUAL LACE PANEL–OPTIONAL INSERT

Mark center _____ sts with a fresh set of markers. Work these sts in Dewdrop Lace (page 126), starting with Row 1, until back neck bind-offs.

INCREASE ROW (RS): Work to marker, M1-r, sm, work to next marker, sm, M1-l, work to end.

Work increase row every _____ rows _____ times total: _____ sts total. Work even until piece measures _____ from CO edge, ending with a WS row.

SHAPE ARMHOLES: BO _____ sts at the beginning of the next 2 rows. BO _____ sts at the beginning of the following 2 rows. Decrease 1 st at each end of every RS row _____ times: _____ sts remain.

Work even until piece measures _____ from CO edge, ending with a WS row.

SHAPE NECK:

NEXT ROW (RS): Work _____ sts, attach a new ball of yarn and BO center _____ sts. Work to end.

Working both shoulders simultaneously, decrease 1 st at neck edge of every RS row twice. _____ shoulder sts remain.

Work even until piece measures _____ from CO edge, ending at the armhole edge for each side.

NEXT ROW: BO _____ sts, work to end. Work 1 row even. BO rem sts.

FRONT

Using long-tail cast-on method (or a different one, if you prefer), CO _____ sts. Work even in _____

until piece measures _____ from CO edge, ending with a WS row.

Switch to _____ and work even until piece measures _____ from CO edge, ending with a WS row. On your last row, place markers on each side of center _____ sts.

DECREASE ROW (RS): Work to 2 sts before marker, ssk, sm, work to next marker, sm, k2tog, work to end.

Work decrease row every _____ rows _____ times: _____ sts remain. Work even until piece measures _____ from CO edge, ending with a WS row.

INCREASE ROW (RS): Work to marker, M1-r, sm, work to next marker, sm, M1-l, work to end.

Work increase row every _____ rows _____ times: _____ sts total. Work even until piece measures _____ from CO edge, ending with a WS row.

Note: For Bohemian style, neck shaping begins before armhole shaping starts. For Casual and Sporty styles, neck shaping begins before armhole shaping is complete. Please read ahead.

SHAPE ARMHOLES: BO _____ sts at the beginning of the next 2 rows. BO _____ sts at the beginning of the following 2 rows. Decrease 1 st at each end of every RS row _____ times: _____ sts remain.

SHAPE NECK: When piece measures _____ from CO edge, ending with a WS row, shape neck:

BOHEMIAN STYLE—BOTH SIDES: Mark center _____ sts.

NEXT ROW (RS): Work to marker, attach new ball of yarn and BO center sts, work to end.

Working both sides of neckline at same time, decrease 1 st at neck edge every _____ rows _____ times.

CASUAL STYLE: Mark center _____ sts.

NEXT ROW (RS): Work to marked sts, attach a new ball of yarn and BO to the next marker, work to end.

Working both side of neckline at same time, decrease 1 st at neck edge every RS row _____ times, then every other RS row _____ times.

SPORTY STYLE: Mark center _____ sts.

NEXT ROW (RS): Work to marked sts, attach new ball of yarn and BO to next marker, work to end. Working both sides of neckline at same time, work straight for 3" (7.5 cm), then continue shaping neckline as follows.

BO _____ sts at the neck edge of the next row.

Decrease 1 st at neck edge every row _____ times, then every RS row _____ times.

ALL STYLES: When all neck and armhole shaping is complete, _____ shoulder sts remain. Work even until piece measures _____ from CO edge, ending at the armhole edge.

NEXT ROW: BO _____ sts, work to end. Work 1 row even. BO rem sts.

SLEEVES

BOHEMIAN STYLE: Using long-tail cast-on method (or a different one, if you prefer), MC, and needles one size smaller, CO _____ sts. Work even in Stockinette st until piece measures 1" (2.5 cm) from CO edge, ending with a RS row. Change to larger needles and knit 1 WS row to create turning ridge.

Work even in MC and Stockinette st until sleeve measures _____ from turning ridge, ending with a WS row.

CASUAL STYLE: Using long-tail cast-on method (or a different one, if you prefer), CO _____ sts. Work even in Garter st until sleeve measures 1" (2.5 cm) from CO edge.

Switch to Dewdrop Lace (page 126) over center _____ sts, keeping remaining sts at sides (if any) in Stockinette st, and work until lace measures approximately 2" (5 cm), ending with a WS row.

Switch to Stockinette st and work 2 rows even.

INCREASE ROW (RS): K1, M1-r, knit to last stitch, M1-l, k1.

Work increase row every _____ rows _____ times total. _____ sts total. Work even until sleeve measures _____ from CO edge, ending with a WS row.

SPORTY STYLE: Using CC and long-tail cast-on method (or a different one, if you prefer), CO _____ sts.

Work even in 2x1 rib and CC until piece measures ½" (1.5 cm) from CO edge. Switch to MC and continue until piece measures 1" (2.5 cm) from CO edge.

CREATE THUMBHOLE: *Work on RS row for right sleeve, WS row for left sleeve.*

Work _____ sts, attach a new ball of yarn and BO _____ sts, work to end. Working both sides at the same time, work even until thumbhole measures 1¾" (4.5 cm).

On your next row, work to thumbhole, CO _____ sts to close the hole, work to end with same ball of yarn. Cut second ball of yarn.

Continue in MC and rib until sleeve measures 7" (18 cm) from CO edge. Switch to Stockinette st.

INCREASE ROW (RS): K1, M1-r, knit to last st, M1-l, k1.

INCREASE ROW (WS): P1, M1-p, purl to last st, M1-p, p1.

Work increase row every _____ rows _____ times total. _____ sts total. Work even until sleeve measures _____ from CO edge, ending with a WS row.

SHAPE SLEEVE CAP: BO _____ sts at the beginning of the next 2 rows. BO _____ sts at the beginning of the following two rows. Decrease 1 st at each end of every 3rd RS row _____ times, then every other RS row _____ times, then every RS row _____ times.

BO _____ sts at the beginning of the next 4 rows.

BO final _____ sts.

FINISHING

Follow instructions on page 125.

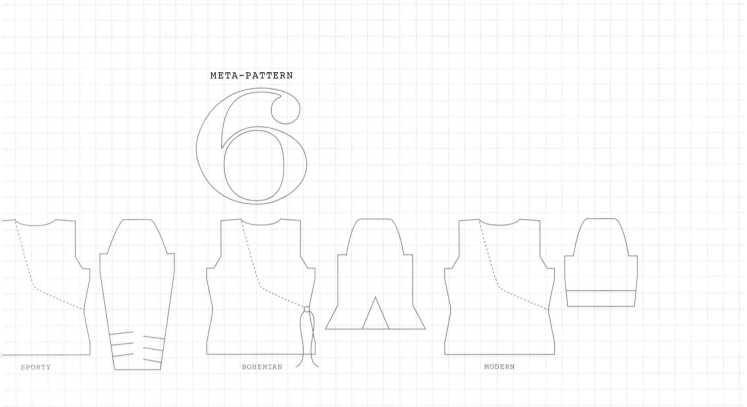

SPORTY   BOHEMIAN   MODERN

THE WRAP

Wrap sweaters are very figure-flattering. The diagonal lines create a curvy waist (when yours is straight) and highlight curves (when you've already got 'em). The fronts form an attractive V neckline, and there are tons of closure options.

The three very different styles are achieved by altering the sleeves and closures. A sporty look has ruching on cozy long sleeves and a bold zipper. A bohemian vibe comes from slightly flared sleeves, lace detailing, and fringed ties. Finally, a super-clean modern style pairs hidden snap closures with sleek elbow sleeves.

Of course, all of the gauges and customization options can be mixed and matched (though if you choose an Aran-weight yarn for the sporty sleeves, make sure it's more compressible than firm). So however you'd like to wear this wrap, grab your needles and get started!

Change it up!

Gauges offered
Sport, worsted, Aran

Sleeves
Long and ruched, Three-quarter-length and flared, elbow and straight

Closures
Sporty zipper, traditional ties, hidden snaps

Make this
sweater suit
your
own style!

SPORTY

The Wrap

Smooth yarn with climate control.

Comfortably scrunchy sleeves.

Sleek zipper closure.

Simple, functional garter stitch.

» Francesca is wearing size 38" (96.5 cm) in sport gauge.

FINISHED BUST	**SPORT:** 30 (32, 34, 36, 38, 40, 42, 44, 46, 48, 50, 54)" [76 (81.5, 86.5, 91.5, 96.5, 101.5, 106.5, 112, 117, 122, 127, 137) cm]

WORSTED: 30½ (32, 34¼, 36½, 38, 40½, 42¾, 44¼, 46½, 48, 50¼, 54)" [77.5 (81.5, 87, 93, 97, 102.5, 108.5, 112, 118, 122, 127.5, 137.5) cm]

ARAN: 30¼ (32, 34¾, 36½, 38¼, 40, 42¾, 44½, 46¼, 48, 50¾, 54¼)" [77 (81.5, 88, 92.5, 97, 101.5, 108.5, 113, 117.5, 122, 128.5, 137.5) cm]

(Note: For ease in reading, the precise finished bust measurements have been rounded in the instructions below to 30 (32, 34, 36, 38, 40, 42, 44, 46, 48, 50, 54)" [76 (81.5, 86.5, 91.5, 96.5, 101.5, 106.5, 112, 117, 122, 127, 137) cm]. Your finished measurements will be as given above.

MATERIALS

See page 190 for fiber content.

SPORT: Lorna's Laces Sportmate in Dobson, 5 (5, 5, 6, 6, 6, 7, 7, 8, 8, 9, 9) hanks

WORSTED: Classic Elite Classic Silk in #6927 Cool Cranberry, 8 (9, 9, 10, 11, 11, 12, 13, 14, 15, 16, 17) balls

ARAN: Brooklyn Tweed Shelter in #21 Hayloft, 6 (6, 7, 7, 8, 8, 9, 9, 10, 10, 11, 12) hanks

GAUGE

SPORT: 24 sts and 32 rows = 4" (10 cm) in Stockinette st
WORSTED: 21 sts and 30½ rows = 4" (10 cm) in Stockinette st
ARAN: 18 sts and 26 rows = 4" (10 cm) in Stockinette st

NEEDLES

Change needle size if necessary to obtain correct gauge:

SPORT: US 4 / 3.5 mm
WORSTED: US 6 / 4 mm
ARAN: US 8 / 5 mm
For Bohemian style, needles in main needle size and one size smaller than main needle size.

NOTIONS

SPORTY STYLE: One large snap, two small squares grosgrain ribbon, one 7" (18 cm) separating zipper
MODERN STYLE: 10 snaps, four 7" (18 cm) pieces grosgrain ribbon

BACK

Using long-tail cast-on method (or a different one, if you prefer), CO

	30"	32	34	36	38	40	42	44	46	48	50	54
SPORT	90	96	102	108	114	120	126	132	138	144	150	162
WORSTED	80	84	90	96	100	106	112	116	122	126	132	142
ARAN	68	72	78	82	86	90	96	100	104	108	114	122

stitches. Work even in trim of your choice, as follows:

SPORTY STYLE: Work even in Garter st until piece measures 1" (2.5 cm).
Switch to Stockinette st.

BOHEMIAN STYLE: Work a folded hem as follows:
CO sts using needles one size smaller. Work even in Stockinette st for 1½" (4 cm), then switch to larger needle and knit 1 WS row to create a turning ridge.

Note: All length measurements that follow are taken from turning ridge, not CO edge.
Switch to Stockinette st.

MODERN STYLE: Work even in 1x1 rib until piece measures 1¼" (3 cm).
Switch to Stockinette st.

Continue until piece measures 3" (7.5 cm) from CO edge, ending with a WS row.
On your last row, place two waist shaping markers, one on either side of the center section so that there are:

	30"	32	34	36	38	40	42	44	46	48	50	54
SPORT	30	32	34	36	38	40	42	44	46	48	50	54
WORSTED	26	28	30	32	34	36	38	38	40	42	44	48
ARAN	22	24	26	28	28	30	32	34	34	36	38	40

sts between waist shaping markers.
DECREASE ROW (RS): Work to 2 sts before first marker, ssk, sm, work to next marker, sm, k2tog, work to end. 2 sts decreased.
Work a decrease row every
SPORT: 8 / **WORSTED:** 10 / **ARAN:** 8 rows
SPORT: 5 / **WORSTED:** 4 / **ARAN:** 4 times total.
When all decreases are complete,

	30"	32	34	36	38	40	42	44	46	48	50	54
SPORT	80	86	92	98	104	110	116	122	128	134	140	152
WORSTED	72	76	82	88	92	98	104	108	114	118	124	134
ARAN	60	64	70	74	78	82	88	92	96	100	106	114

sts remain. Work even until piece measures 8" (20.5 cm) from CO edge, ending with a WS row.
INCREASE ROW (RS): Work to first marker, M1-r, sm, work to next marker, sm, M1-l, work to end. 2 sts increased.
Work an increase row every
SPORT: 8 / **WORSTED:** 10 / **ARAN:** 8 rows
SPORT: 5 / **WORSTED:** 4 / **ARAN:** 4 times total.
When all increases are complete,

	30"	32	34	36	38	40	42	44	46	48	50	54
SPORT	90	96	102	108	114	120	126	132	138	144	150	162
WORSTED	80	84	90	96	100	106	112	116	122	126	132	142
ARAN	68	72	78	82	86	90	96	100	104	108	114	122

sts total. Work even until piece measures 13½ (13¾, 14, 14¼, 14½, 14¾, 15, 15, 15½, 15½, 15½, 15½)" [34.5 (35, 35.5, 36, 37, 37.5, 38, 38, 39.5, 39.5, 39.5, 39.5) cm] from CO edge, ending with a WS row.

SHAPE ARMHOLES

BO

	30"	32	34	36	38	40	42	44	46	48	50	54
SPORT	6	6	6	6	6	6	8	8	10	10	12	14
WORSTED	6	6	6	6	6	6	6	6	8	8	10	12
ARAN	6	6	6	6	6	6	6	6	8	8	8	10

sts at the beginning of the next 2 rows. BO

META-PATTERN #6

MODERN
The Wrap

Warm, tweedy yarn.

Ribbing worked side-ways on sleeves, then folded up for the cuff.

Ultra-minimalist design.

Invisible snap closures.

» Kiki is wearing size 34" (86.5 cm) in Aran gauge.

	30"	32	34	36	38	40	42	44	46	48	50	54
SPORT	2	2	2	2	2	4	4	6	6	8	8	10
WORSTED	0	2	2	2	2	2	4	4	6	6	8	8
ARAN	0	0	2	2	2	2	2	4	4	4	6	6

sts at the beginning of the following 2 rows. Decrease 1 st at each end of every RS row

	30"	32	34	36	38	40	42	44	46	48	50	54
SPORT	2	4	5	7	7	6	6	6	6	6	7	6
WORSTED	3	2	4	5	5	6	6	7	6	7	6	6
ARAN	2	3	2	3	3	4	6	5	5	6	6	6

times:

	30"	32	34	36	38	40	42	44	46	48	50	54
SPORT	70	72	76	78	84	88	90	92	94	96	96	102
WORSTED	62	64	66	70	74	78	80	82	82	84	84	90
ARAN	52	54	58	60	64	66	68	70	70	72	74	78

sts remain. Work even until armhole measures 5½ (6, 6¼, 6½, 7, 7¼, 7½, 8, 8¼, 8¾, 9, 9½)" [14 (15, 16, 16.5, 18, 18.5, 19, 20.5, 21, 22, 23, 24) cm] and piece measures 19 (19¾, 20¼, 20¾, 21½, 22, 22½, 23, 23¾, 24¼, 24½, 25)" [48.5 (50, 51.5, 52.5, 54.5, 56, 57, 58.5, 60.5, 61.5, 62, 63.5) cm], ending with a WS row.

SHAPE
NECK

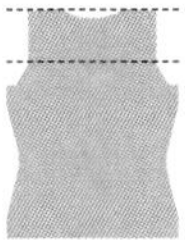

NEXT ROW (RS): Work

	30"	32	34	36	38	40	42	44	46	48	50	54
SPORT	20	20	22	22	23	25	25	25	26	26	26	28
WORSTED	18	18	19	20	21	22	23	23	23	23	23	25
ARAN	16	16	17	17	18	19	19	20	20	20	21	22

sts, attach a new ball of yarn and BO center

	30"	32	34	36	38	40	42	44	46	48	50	54
SPORT	30	32	32	34	38	38	40	42	42	44	44	46
WORSTED	26	28	28	30	32	34	34	36	36	38	38	40
ARAN	20	22	24	26	28	28	30	30	30	32	32	34

sts, work to end. *You will now work both sides of the neckline at the same time.*

Decrease 1 st at neck edge of every RS row twice:

	30"	32	34	36	38	40	42	44	46	48	50	54
SPORT	18	18	20	20	21	23	23	23	24	24	24	26
WORSTED	16	16	17	18	19	20	21	21	21	21	21	23
ARAN	14	14	15	15	16	17	17	18	18	18	19	20

sts remain for each shoulder. Work even until armhole measures 6½ (7, 7¼, 7½, 8, 8¼, 8½, 9, 9¼, 9¾, 10, 10½)" [16.5 (18, 18.5, 19, 20.5, 21, 21.5, 23, 23.5, 25, 25.5, 26.5) cm] and piece measures 20 (20¾, 21¼, 21¾, 22½, 23, 23½, 24, 24¾, 25¼, 25½, 26)" [51 (52.5, 54, 55, 57, 58.5, 59.5, 61, 63, 64, 65, 66) cm] from CO edge, ending at the armhole edge for each side.

NEXT ROW: BO

	30"	32	34	36	38	40	42	44	46	48	50	54
SPORT	9	9	10	10	11	12	12	12	12	12	12	13
WORSTED	8	8	9	9	10	10	11	11	11	11	11	12
ARAN	7	7	8	8	8	9	9	9	9	9	10	10

sts, work to end. Work 1 row even. BO remaining sts.

FRONTS

Using long-tail cast-on method (or a different one, if you prefer), CO

	30"	32	34	36	38	40	42	44	46	48	50	54
SPORT	90	96	102	108	114	120	126	132	138	144	150	162
WORSTED	80	84	90	96	100	106	112	116	122	126	132	142
ARAN	68	72	78	82	86	90	96	100	104	108	114	122

sts.

SPORTY STYLE: Work even in Garter stitch until piece measures 1" (2.5 cm). Switch all stitches to Stockinette st.

BOHEMIAN STYLE: Work a folded hem as follows:
CO sts using needles one size smaller. Work even in Stockinette st for 1½" (4 cm), then switch to larger needle and knit 1 WS row to create a turning ridge.
Note: All length measurements that follow are taken from turning ridge, not CO edge.
Switch to Stockinette st.

MODERN STYLE: Work even in 1x1 rib until piece measures 1¼" (3 cm), then switch to Stockinette st.

After edging is complete, continue shaping as for back to the waist, *except* place waist shaping markers around the center section so that there are:

	30"	32	34	36	38	40	42	44	46	48	50	54
SPORT	44	48	50	54	56	60	62	66	68	72	74	80
WORSTED	40	42	44	48	50	52	56	58	60	62	66	70
ARAN	34	36	38	40	42	44	48	50	52	54	56	60

sts between waist shaping markers.

SHAPE WRAP

When piece measures 7½" (19 cm) from CO edge, *shape wrap.*
Note: Armhole shaping and bust shaping begin before the wrap shaping is complete. Please read ahead.
WRAP SHAPING ROW–RIGHT FRONT (RS): K1, ssk, work to end.
WRAP SHAPING ROW–RIGHT FRONT (WS): Work to last 3 sts, ssp, p1.
WRAP SHAPING ROW–LEFT FRONT (RS): Work to last 3 sts, k2tog, k1.
WRAP SHAPING ROW–LEFT FRONT (WS): P1, p2tog, work to end.
Work wrap shaping row every row a total of

	30"	32	34	36	38	40	42	44	46	48	50	54
SPORT	50	53	56	59	62	65	68	71	74	77	80	86
WORSTED	44	46	49	52	54	57	60	62	65	67	70	75
ARAN	38	40	43	45	47	49	52	54	56	58	61	65

times, then every 3rd row

	30"	32	34	36	38	40	42	44	46	48	50	54
SPORT	7	8	8	9	11	11	12	13	13	14	14	15
WORSTED	7	8	8	9	10	11	11	12	12	13	13	14
ARAN	4	5	6	7	8	8	9	9	9	10	10	11

times.

Note: You will work bust increases as for back, but only in one place: At the first marker only for the left front, and the second marker only for the right front. Remove the unnecessary marker.
Work an increase row every
SPORT: 8 / **WORSTED:** 10 / **ARAN:** 8 rows
SPORT: 5 / **WORSTED:** 4 / **ARAN:** 4 times total

SHAPE ARMHOLES

When piece measures 13½ (13¾, 14, 14¼, 14½, 14¾, 15, 15, 15½, 15½, 15½, 15½)" [34.5 (35, 35.5, 36, 37, 37.5, 38, 38, 39.5, 39.5, 39.5, 39.5) cm] from CO edge, shape armholes as for back.

ALL STYLES: When all wrap and armhole shaping is complete

	30"	32	34	36	38	40	42	44	46	48	50	54
SPORT	18	18	20	20	21	23	23	23	24	24	24	26
WORSTED	16	16	17	18	19	20	21	21	21	21	21	23
ARAN	14	14	15	15	16	17	17	18	18	18	19	20

sts remain. Work even and complete shoulder shaping as for back.

SLEEVES

SPORTY STYLE: Using long-tail cast-on method (or a different one, if you prefer), CO

	30"	32	34	36	38	40	42	44	46	48	50	54
SPORT	42	42	46	46	48	48	52	52	54	54	58	58
WORSTED	38	38	40	40	42	42	46	46	48	48	50	50
ARAN	32	32	34	34	36	36	40	40	42	42	44	44

sts.

Work 5 rows in Garter st. Mark your center:

	30"	32	34	36	38	40	42	44	46	48	50	54
SPORT	40	40	44	44	46	46	50	50	52	52	56	56
WORSTED	36	36	38	38	40	40	44	44	46	46	48	48
ARAN	30	30	32	32	34	34	38	38	40	40	42	42

sts.

Switch to Stockinette st. *Note: You will be making the tucks and shaping the sleeve at the same time. Please read ahead.*
When sleeve measures 2" (5 cm) from CO edge, beginning with a WS row, make tucks:
MAKE TUCK (MT): With yarn in front, insert needle from top into the loop at the WS of the next st
SPORT: 10 / **WORSTED:** 8 / **ARAN:** 6 rows below,
pick up this loop, place on your left-hand needle and purl together with the next st on your current row.
MT ROW 1 (WS): Purl to first tuck marker, sm, MT over next

	30"	32	34	36	38	40	42	44	46	48	50	54
SPORT	20	20	22	22	23	23	25	25	26	26	28	28
WORSTED	18	18	19	19	20	20	22	22	23	23	24	24
ARAN	15	15	15	16	16	17	17	19	19	20	20	21

sts, purl to end.
MT ROW 2 (WS): Purl to first tuck marker, purl

	30"	32	34	36	38	40	42	44	46	48	50	54
SPORT	20	20	22	22	23	23	25	25	26	26	28	28
WORSTED	18	18	19	19	20	20	22	22	23	23	24	24
ARAN	15	15	15	16	16	17	17	19	19	20	20	21

sts, MT over remaining sts to next tuck marker, purl to end.

META-PATTERN #6

BOHEMIAN

The Wrap

Lace-trimmed neckline.

Rich, deep color and nubby texture.

Funky ties with fringe.

Lace repeated on belled sleeves.

Simple folded hem.

» Morgan is wearing size 38" (96.5 cm) in worsted gauge.

Alternate MT Rows 1 and 2 every

SPORT: 20 / **WORSTED:** 16 / **ARAN:** 12 rows

6 times total—3 tucks worked on each side of center.

At the same time, when sleeve measures 3" / 7.5 cm from beginning, work shaping:

INCREASE ROW (RS): K1, M1-r, knit to last st, M1-l, k1.

Work increase row every

	30"	32	34	36	38	40	42	44	46	48	50	54
SPORT	12	10	10	10	10	8	8	8	6	6	6	4
WORSTED	12	12	12	10	10	10	10	8	8	6	6	6
ARAN	12	10	10	10	10	10	10	8	8	8	6	6

rows until a total of

	30"	32	34	36	38	40	42	44	46	48	50	54
SPORT	12	14	13	15	15	17	16	19	21	24	27	31
WORSTED	10	11	11	13	13	14	14	16	18	20	23	27
ARAN	9	10	10	11	11	13	12	14	15	17	20	23

increase rows have been worked:

	30"	32	34	36	38	40	42	44	46	48	50	54
SPORT	66	70	72	76	78	82	84	90	96	102	112	120
WORSTED	58	60	62	66	68	70	74	78	84	88	96	104
ARAN	50	52	54	56	58	62	64	68	72	76	84	90

sts total.

Work even until sleeve measures 19 (19, 19, 19½, 19½, 19½, 19½, 19½, 20, 20, 20, 20)" [48 (48, 48, 49.5, 49.5, 49.5, 49.5, 49.5, 51, 51, 51, 51) cm] from CO edge, ending with a WS row.

- -

BOHEMIAN STYLE: Using long-tail cast-on method (or a different one, if you prefer), CO

	30"	32	34	36	38	40	42	44	46	48	50	54
SPORT	91	95	97	101	103	107	109	115	121	127	137	145
WORSTED	81	83	85	89	91	93	97	101	107	111	119	127
ARAN	69	71	73	75	77	81	83	87	91	95	103	109

sts. Beginning with a WS row, work 3 rows even in Garter st. On your last row, mark sts as follows:

LAST ROW (WS): Work

	30"	32	34	36	38	40	42	44	46	48	50	54
SPORT	25	27	28	30	31	33	34	37	40	43	48	52
WORSTED	25	26	27	29	30	31	33	35	38	40	44	48
ARAN	21	22	23	24	25	27	28	30	32	34	38	41

sts, place marker, work

SPORT: 41 / **WORSTED:** 31 / **ARAN:** 27 sts,

place marker, work to end. You will now change to Stockinette st outside of the markers, and a decreasing Arrow Lace Sleeve (page 146) and Garter panel between the markers.

NEXT ROW (RS): Knit to first marker, sm, knit

SPORT: 12 / **WORSTED:** 11 / **ARAN:** 9 sts,

place marker, work Row 1 of Arrow Lace Sleeve (page 146) over center

SPORT: 17 / **WORSTED:** 9 / **ARAN:** 9 sts,

place marker, knit to next marker, sm, knit to end.

NEXT ROW (WS): Purl to first marker, sm, knit to next marker, sm, work Row 2 of Arrow Lace to next marker, sm, knit to next marker, sm, purl to end.

Stockinette, Garter, and Arrow Lace pattern established.

Work

SPORT: 6 / **WORSTED:** 8 / **ARAN:** 12 rows even as established.

DECREASE ROW (RS): Knit to first marker, sm, ssk, work as established to 2 sts before last marker, k2tog, sm, knit to end. 2 sts decreased from Garter portion of center panel.

Repeat decrease row every RS row until a total of

SPORT: 12 / **WORSTED:** 11 / **ARAN:** 9 decrease rows have been worked.

Second full repeat of 16-row Arrow Lace pattern completes at the same time.

NEXT ROW (WS): Purl to center st, p2tog, purl to end.

	30"	32	34	36	38	40	42	44	46	48	50	54
SPORT	66	70	72	76	78	82	84	90	96	102	112	120
WORSTED	58	60	62	66	68	70	74	78	84	88	96	104
ARAN	50	52	54	58	58	62	64	68	72	76	84	90

sts remain. Switch to Stockinette st.

Work even until sleeve measures 12 (12, 12, 12, 12½, 12½, 12½, 12½, 13, 13, 13, 13)" [30.5 (30.5, 30.5, 30.5, 32, 32, 32, 32, 33, 33, 33, 33) cm] from CO edge, ending with a WS row.

MODERN STYLE: Using long-tail cast-on method (or a different one, if you prefer), CO

SPORT: 19 / **WORSTED:** 15 / **ARAN:** 13 sts.

Work even in 1x1 rib, slipping the first st of every RS row purlwise, until ribbed band measures 10¼ (10¾, 11, 11½, 12, 13, 13¼, 14¼, 15, 16, 17¾, 19)" [26 (27, 28, 29.5, 30.5, 32.5, 34, 36, 38.5, 40.5, 45, 48.5) cm]. BO all sts.

Rotate ribbed piece 90 degrees. Pick up and knit:

	30"	32	34	36	38	40	42	44	46	48	50	54
SPORT	60	64	66	70	72	76	78	84	90	96	106	114
WORSTED	54	56	58	62	64	66	70	74	80	84	92	100
ARAN	46	48	50	52	54	58	60	64	68	72	80	86

sts along top edge. Work even in Stockinette st for 10 rows.

INCREASE ROW (RS): K1, M1-r, knit to last st, M1-l, k1.

Work increase row every

SPORT: 12 / **WORSTED:** 10 / **ARAN:** 8 rows until a total of

SPORT: 3 / **WORSTED:** 2 / **ARAN:** 2 increase rows have been worked:

	30"	32	34	36	38	40	42	44	46	48	50	54
SPORT	66	70	72	76	78	82	84	90	96	102	112	120
WORSTED	58	60	62	66	68	70	74	78	84	88	96	104
ARAN	50	52	54	56	58	62	64	68	72	76	84	90

sts total.

Work even until sleeve measures 8 (8, 8, 8, 8½, 8½, 8½, 8½, 9, 9, 9, 9)" [20.5 (20.5, 20.5, 20.5, 21.5, 21.5, 21.5, 21.5, 23, 23, 23, 23) cm] from edge where sts were picked up, ending with a WS row.

SHAPE SLEEVE CAP

ALL STYLES : BO

	30"	32	34	36	38	40	42	44	46	48	50	54
SPORT	6	6	6	6	6	6	8	8	10	10	12	14
WORSTED	6	6	6	6	6	6	6	6	8	8	10	12
ARAN	6	6	6	6	6	6	6	6	8	8	8	10

sts at the beginning of the next 2 rows. BO

	30"	32	34	36	38	40	42	44	46	48	50	54
SPORT	2	2	2	2	2	4	4	6	6	8	8	9
WORSTED	0	2	2	2	2	2	4	4	6	6	7	7
ARAN	0	0	2	2	2	2	2	4	4	4	6	6

sts at the beginning of the following 2 rows. Decrease 1 st at each end of every 3rd RS row

	30"	32	34	36	38	40	42	44	46	48	50	54
SPORT	1	1	1	0	1	1	2	3	4	5	3	4
WORSTED	0	2	2	1	2	2	2	2	5	4	5	4
ARAN	1	1	2	2	2	1	1	2	4	3	2	3

time(s), then every other RS row

	30"	32	34	36	38	40	42	44	46	48	50	54
SPORT	0	0	0	1	0	1	1	0	1	0	1	1
WORSTED	1	0	1	1	0	0	1	1	0	1	0	1
ARAN	0	0	0	0	1	1	1	1	0	1	1	0

time(s), then every RS row

	30"	32	34	36	38	40	42	44	46	48	50	54
SPORT	10	12	13	15	16	15	13	14	8	9	13	13
WORSTED	11	9	9	12	13	14	13	15	7	9	10	12
ARAN	8	9	7	8	8	11	12	11	6	8	11	12

times. BO

	30"	32	34	36	38	40	42	44	46	48	50	54
SPORT	3	3	3	3	3	3	3	3	4	4	4	4
WORSTED	2	2	2	2	2	2	2	2	3	3	3	3
ARAN	2	2	2	2	2	2	2	2	3	3	3	3

sts at the beginning of the next 4 rows. BO final

	30"	32	34	36	38	40	42	44	46	48	50	54
SPORT	16	16	16	16	16	16	16	16	22	22	22	22
WORSTED	14	14	14	14	14	14	14	14	20	20	20	20
ARAN	12	12	12	12	12	12	12	12	16	16	16	16

sts.

FINISHING

Wet-block all pieces to finished measurements. Sew shoulder seams using mattress stitch. Set in sleeves and sew side and sleeve seams using mattress stitch.
Note: For Bohemian Style, leave approximately a 1" (2.5 cm) gap in the left side seam at the waist to allow for wrap tie to slip through the side seam.

SPORTY STYLE: With RS facing, beginning at start of right front wrap shaping and ending at beginning of left front wrap shaping, pick up and knit sts around neckline at the rate of 4 sts for every

THREE CLOSURES (clockwise from top left): Bohemian tie with fringe, sporty zipper, invisible modern snaps.

5 rows along diagonal edges of neck, 3 sts for every 4 rows along vertical edges of neck, and one st for every bound-off st.

Work 1" (2.5 cm) even in Garter st. BO all sts.

TRIM SIDE EDGES OF WRAP WITH GARTER STITCH: With RS facing, pick up and knit sts along side edges of wrap at the rate of 3 sts for every 4 rows. Work 3 rows even in Garter st. BO all sts. Hand-sew a small square of grosgrain ribbon on RS of left front just inside trim. Sew another piece of ribbon to WS of right front where it meets the left front edge. Sew one half of snap on each piece of ribbon.

Hand-sew zipper to WS of right front wrap edge, and to RS of left front at side seam (see photo on page 145).

Knit facing for zipper on left front side seam edge by picking up sts at the rate of 3 sts for every 4 rows along size of zipper. Work ½" (1.5 cm) in Garter st, then BO all sts. Tack zipper to facing.

BOHEMIAN STYLE: Using long-tail cast-on method (or a different one if you prefer), CO
SPORT: 78 / **WORSTED:** 68 / **ARAN:** 58 sts,
then with RS facing, beginning at right front wrap shaping and ending at left front wrap shaping, pick up and knit stitches around neckline at the rate of 4 sts for every 5 rows along diagonal edges of neck, 3 sts for every 4 rows along vertical edges of neck, and 1 st for every bound-off st. At end of left front wrap shaping, CO an additional

	30"	32	34	36	38	40	42	44	46	48	50	54
SPORT	168	174	180	186	192	198	204	210	216	222	228	240
WORSTED	148	152	158	164	168	174	180	184	190	194	200	210
ARAN	126	130	136	140	144	148	154	158	162	166	172	180

sts. Count sts and adjust if necessary to make total a multiple of 8 sts + 1.
Work 12 rows even in Arrow Lace Neck pattern. Work 3 rows of Garter st and then BO all sts.

Fringe ties by cutting 4 groups of 5 strands of yarn at desired length (fringe shown measures 6" [15 cm] total). Weave through ends of ties and knot.

MODERN STYLE: Using long-tail cast-on method (or a different one if you prefer), CO
SPORT: 14 / **WORSTED:** 12 / **ARAN:** 10 sts.
Work even in 1x1 rib, slipping the first st of every RS row, until ribbed piece, slightly stretched, matches length of wrap edge from CO edge of front to center of back neck.

Make another strip of ribbing the same, *except* slipping the first st of every WS row.

Sew non-slipped edges of pieces to front and neck edges using mattress stitch, easing around corner.

SNAP CLOSURES: Hand-sew 7" (18 cm) pieces of grosgrain ribbon to wrap to anchor snaps as follows: On WS of the right front, sew one piece of ribbon along front edge and another where edge of left front meets WS of right front. On RS of the left front, sew one piece of ribbon along front edge and another where left of right front meets RS of left front.

Hand-sew 5 snaps evenly spaced along each pair of ribbons.

SPECIAL STITCHES

ARROW LACE SLEEVE
(multiple of 8 sts + 1)
ROW 1 (RS): K1, *yo, ssk, k3, k2tog, yo, k1;
repeat from * to end.
ROW 2 AND ALL WS ROWS: Purl.

ROW 3: K1, *k1, yo, ssk, k1, k2tog, yo, k2; repeat from * to end.
ROW 5: P1, *k2, yo, sl 1, k2tog, psso, yo, k2, p1; repeat from * to end.
ROWS 7, 9, 11, 13 AND 15: P1, *ssk, [k1, yo] twice, k1, k2tog, p1; repeat from * to end.
ROW 16: Purl.
Repeat Rows 1–16 for Arrow Lace Sleeve.

ARROW LACE NECK

ROWS 1, 3, AND 5 (RS): P1, *ssk, [k1, yo] twice, k1, k2tog, p1; repeat from * to end.
ROW 2 AND ALL WS ROWS: Purl.
ROW 7: P1, *yo, ssk, k3, k2tog, yo, p1; repeat from * to end.
ROW 9: P1, *p1, yo, ssk, k1, k2tog, yo, p2; repeat from * to end.
ROW 11: P1; *p2, yo, sl 1, k2tog, psso, yo, p3; repeat from * to end.
ROW 12: Purl.
Repeat Rows 1–12 for Arrow Lace Neck.

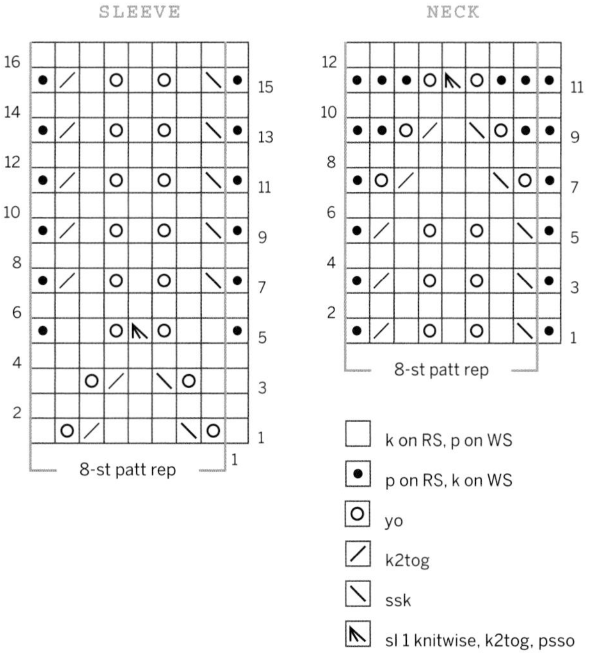

SLEEVE
NECK
8-st patt rep
8-st patt rep
k on RS, p on WS
p on RS, k on WS
yo
k2tog
ssk
sl 1 knitwise, k2tog, psso

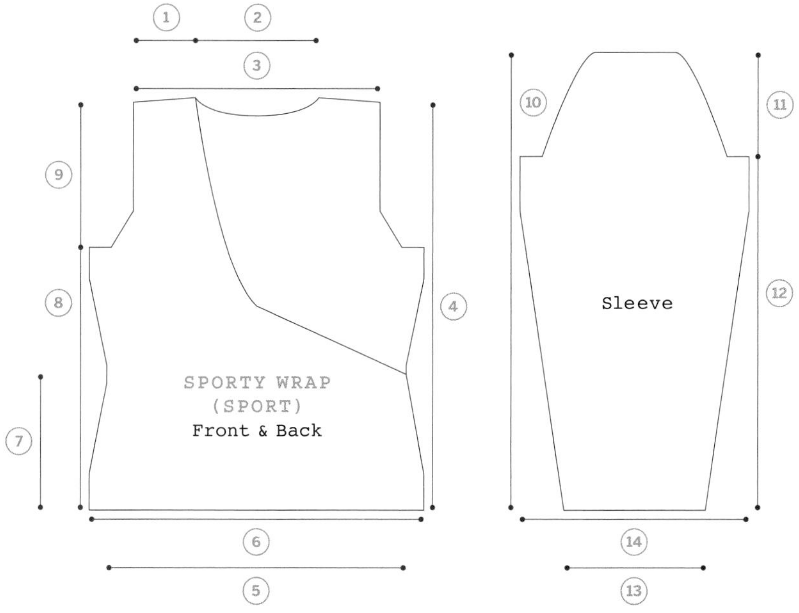

SPORTY WRAP (SPORT) Front & Back
Sleeve

1. 3 (3, 3¼, 3¼, 3½, 3¾, 3¾, 3¾, 4, 4, 4, 4¼)"
7.5 (7.5, 8.5, 8.5, 9, 9.5, 9.5, 9.5, 10, 10, 10, 11) cm
2. 5¾ (6, 6, 6¼, 7, 7, 7¼, 7¾, 7¾, 8, 8, 8¼)"
14.5 (15, 15, 16, 18, 18, 18.5, 19.5, 19.5, 20.5, 20.5, 21) cm
3. 11¾ (12, 12¾, 13, 14, 14¾, 15, 15¼, 15¾, 16, 16, 17)"
29.5 (30.5, 32, 33, 35.5, 37.5, 38, 39, 40, 40.5, 40.5, 43) cm
4. 20 (20¾, 21¼, 21¾, 22½, 23, 23½, 24, 24¾, 25¼, 25½, 26)"
51 (52.5, 54, 55, 57, 58.5, 59.5, 61, 63, 64, 65, 66) cm
5. 13¼ (14¼, 15¼, 16¼, 17¼, 18¼, 19¼, 20¼, 21¼, 22¼, 23¼, 25¼)"
34 (36.5, 39, 41.5, 44, 46.5, 49, 51.5, 54, 56.5, 59.5, 64.5) cm
6. 15 (16, 17, 18, 19, 20, 21, 22, 23, 24, 25, 27)"
38 (40.5, 43, 45.5, 48.5, 51, 53.5, 56, 58.5, 61, 63.5, 68.5) cm
7. 7½"/19 cm
8. 13½ (13¾, 14, 14¼, 14½, 14¾, 15, 15, 15½, 15½, 15½, 15½)"
34.5 (35, 35.5, 36, 37, 37.5, 38, 38, 39.5, 39.5, 39.5, 39.5) cm
9. 6½ (7, 7¼, 7½, 8, 8¼, 8½, 9, 9¼, 9¾, 10, 10½)"
16.5 (18, 18.5, 19, 20.5, 21, 21.5, 23, 23.5, 25, 25.5, 26.5) cm
10. 23¼ (24, 24, 24¾, 25¼, 25½, 26¼, 26¾, 26½, 27½, 27½, 28¼)"
59 (61, 61, 63, 64, 65, 67, 68, 67.5, 70, 70, 72) cm
11. 4¼ (5, 5, 5¼, 5¾, 6, 6¼, 6¾, 6½, 7, 7, 7¾)"
11 (12.5, 12.5, 13.5, 14.5, 15, 16, 17, 16.5, 18, 18, 19.5) cm
12. 19 (19, 19, 19½, 19½, 19½, 19½, 19½, 20, 20, 20, 20)"
48 (48, 48, 49.5, 49.5, 49.5, 49.5, 49.5, 51, 51, 51, 51) cm
13. 7 (7, 7¾, 7¾, 8, 8, 8¾, 8¾, 9, 9, 9¾, 9¾)"
18 (18, 19.5, 19.5, 20.5, 20.5, 22, 22, 23, 23, 24.5, 24.5) cm
14. 11 (11¼, 12, 12¾, 13, 13¼, 14, 15, 16, 17, 18¾, 20)"
28 (29, 30.5, 32, 33, 34, 35.5, 38, 40.5, 43, 47.5, 51) cm

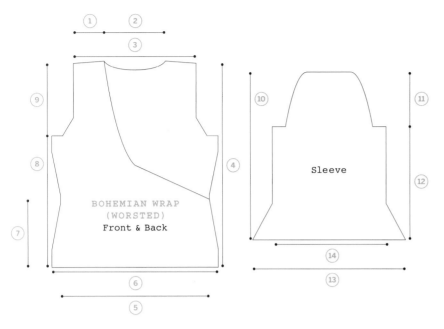

1 3 (3, 3¼, 3½, 3½, 3¾, 4, 4, 4, 4, 4½)"
   7.5 (7.5, 8, 8.5, 9, 9.5, 10, 10, 10, 10, 11) cm

2 5¾ (6, 6, 6½, 6¾, 7¼, 7¼, 7½, 7½, 8, 8, 8½)"
   14.5 (15, 15.5, 16.5, 17.5, 18.5, 18.5, 19.5, 19.5, 20.5, 20.5, 21.5) cm

3 11¾ (12¼, 12½, 13¼, 14, 14¾, 15¼, 15½, 15½, 16, 16, 17¼)"
   30 (31, 32, 34, 36, 37.5, 38.5, 39.5, 39.5, 40.5, 40.5, 43.5) cm

4 20 (20¾, 21¼, 21¾, 22½, 23, 23½, 24, 24¾, 25¼, 25½, 26)"
   51 (52.5, 54, 55, 57, 58.5, 59.5, 61, 63, 64, 65, 66) cm

5 13¾ (14½, 15½, 16¾, 17½, 18¾, 19¾, 20½, 21¾, 22½, 23½, 25½)"
   35 (37, 39.5, 42.5, 44.5, 47.5, 50.5, 52.5, 55, 57, 60, 65) cm

6 15¼ (16, 17¼, 18¼, 19, 20¼, 21¼, 22, 23¼, 24, 25¼, 27)"
   38.5 (40.5, 43.5, 46.5, 48.5, 51.5, 54, 56, 59, 61, 64, 68.5) cm

7 7½"/19 cm

8 13½ (13¾, 14, 14¼, 14½, 14¾, 15, 15, 15½, 15½, 15½, 15½)"
   34.5 (35, 35.5, 36, 37, 37.5, 38, 38, 39.5, 39.5, 39.5, 39.5) cm

9 6½ (7, 7¼, 7½, 8, 8¼, 8½, 9, 9¼, 9¾, 10, 10½)"
   16.5 (18, 18.5, 19, 20.5, 21, 21.5, 23, 23.5, 25, 25.5, 26.5) cm

10 16½ (17, 17¼, 17½, 18½, 18½, 19, 19¼, 19¾, 20, 20¼, 20¾)"
   41.5 (43, 43.5, 44.5, 47, 47, 48.5, 49, 50, 51, 51.5, 53) cm

11 4½ (5, 5¼, 5½, 6, 6, 6½, 6¾, 6¾, 7, 7¼, 7¾)"
   11.5 (12.5, 13.5, 14, 15, 15, 16.5, 17, 17, 18, 18.5, 20) cm

12 12 (12, 12, 12, 12½, 12½, 12½, 12½, 13, 13, 13, 13)"
   30.5 (30.5, 30.5, 30.5, 32, 32, 32, 32, 33, 33, 33, 33) cm

13 15½ (16¼, 16½, 17, 17¾, 18, 18½, 19½, 20½, 21½, 23, 24½)"
   39.5 (41.5, 42, 43, 45, 45.5, 47, 49.5, 52, 54.5, 58.5, 62) cm

14 11 (11¾, 12¼, 12½, 13¼, 13¾, 14, 15¼, 16, 17¼, 18¾, 20¼)"
   28 (30, 31, 32, 34, 35, 36, 38.5, 40.5, 43.5, 47.5, 51.5) cm

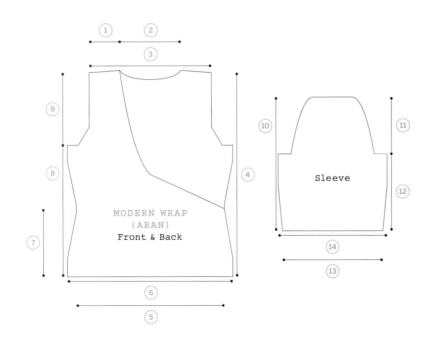

1 3 (3, 3¼, 3¼, 3½, 3¾, 3¾, 4, 4, 4, 4¼, 4½)"
   8 (8, 8.5, 8.5, 9, 9.5, 9.5, 10, 10, 10, 10.5, 11.5) cm

2 5¼ (5¾, 6¼, 6¾, 7, 7, 7½, 7½, 7½, 8, 8, 8½)"
   13.5 (14.5, 16, 17, 18, 18, 19, 19, 19, 20.5, 20.5, 21.5) cm

3 11½ (12, 13, 13¼, 14¼, 14¾, 15, 15½, 15½, 16, 16½, 17¼)"
   29.5 (30.5, 32.5, 34, 36, 37.5, 38.5, 39.5, 39.5, 40.5, 42, 44) cm

4 20 (20¾, 21¼, 21¾, 22½, 23, 23½, 24, 24¾, 25¼, 25½, 26)"
   51 (52.5, 54, 55, 57, 58.5, 59.5, 61, 63, 64, 65, 66) cm

5 13¼ (14¼, 15½, 16½, 17¼, 18¼, 19½, 20½, 21¼, 22¼, 23½, 25¼)"
   34 (36, 39.5, 42, 44, 46.5, 49.5, 52, 54, 56.5, 60, 64.5) cm

6 15 (16, 17¼, 18¼, 19, 20, 21¼, 22¼, 23, 24, 25¼, 27)"
   38.5 (40.5, 44, 46.5, 48.5, 51, 54, 56.5, 58.5, 61, 64.5, 69) cm

7 7½"/19 cm

8 13½ (13¾, 14, 14¼, 14½, 14¾, 15, 15, 15½, 15½, 15½, 15½)"
   34.5 (35, 35.5, 36, 37, 37.5, 38, 38, 39.5, 39.5, 39.5, 39.5) cm

9 6½ (7, 7¼, 7½, 8, 8¼, 8½, 9, 9¼, 9¾, 10, 10½)"
   16.5 (18, 18.5, 19, 20.5, 21, 21.5, 23, 23.5, 25, 25.5, 26.5) cm

10 12½ (13, 13¼, 13½, 14¾, 14¾, 15, 15½, 15¾, 16, 16, 16¾)"
   32 (33, 33.5, 34.5, 37, 37, 38, 39.5, 40, 41, 41, 42.5) cm

11 4½ (5, 5¼, 5½, 6¼, 6¼, 6½, 7, 6¾, 7, 7, 7¾)"
   11.5 (12.5, 13.5, 14, 15.5, 15.5, 16.5, 18, 17, 18, 18, 19.5) cm

12 8 (8, 8, 8, 8½, 8½, 8½, 8½, 9, 9, 9, 9)"
   20.5 (20.5, 20.5, 20.5, 21.5, 21.5, 21.5, 21.5, 23, 23, 23, 23) cm

13 10¼ (10¾, 11, 11½, 12, 13, 13¼, 14¼, 15, 16, 17¾, 19)"
   26 (27, 28, 29.5, 30.5, 32.5, 34, 36, 38.5, 40.5, 45, 48.5) cm

14 11 (11½, 12, 12½, 13, 13¾, 14¼, 15, 16, 17, 18¾, 20)"
   28 (29.5, 30.5, 31.5, 32.5, 35, 36, 38.5, 40.5, 43, 47.5, 51) cm

META-PATTERN #6
THE WRAP

Use this worksheet as a handy way to get all of the numbers for each individual
wrap you knit in one simple place. You can photocopy these pages or download a
fresh copy any time you like at www.amyherzogdesigns.com/knitwearlove.

BACK

Using long-tail cast-on method (or a different one, if you prefer), CO _____ sts.

EDGING: Work even in _____ until piece measures _____ from CO edge, ending with a WS row.

Switch to _____ and work even until piece measures _____ from CO edge, ending with a WS row.

On your last row, place markers on each side of center _____ sts.

DECREASE ROW (RS): Work to 2 sts before marker, ssk, sm, work to next marker, sm, k2tog, work to end.

Work decrease row every _____ rows _____ times total: _____ sts remain. Work even until piece measures _____ from CO edge, ending with a WS row.

INCREASE ROW (RS): Work to marker, M1-r, sm, work to next marker, sm, M1-l, work to end.

Work increase row every _____ rows _____ times total: _____ sts total. Work even until piece measures _____ from CO edge, ending with a WS row.

SHAPE ARMHOLES: BO _____ sts at the beginning of the next 2 rows. BO _____ sts at the beginning of the following 2 rows. Decrease 1 st at each end of every RS row _____ times: _____ sts remain.

Work even until piece measures _____ from CO edge, ending with a WS row.

SHAPE NECK:

NEXT ROW (RS): Work _____ sts, attach a new ball of yarn and BO center _____ sts, work to end.

Working both sides of the neckline at the same time, decrease 1 st at neck edge of every RS row twice. _____ shoulder sts remain. Work even until piece measures _____ from CO edge, ending at the armhole edge for each side.

NEXT ROW: BO _____ sts, work to end. Work 1 row even. BO rem sts.

FRONTS

Using long-tail cast-on method (or a different one, if you prefer), CO _____ sts.

Work even in _____ until piece measures _____ from CO edge, ending with a WS row.

Switch to _____ and work even until piece measures _____ from CO edge, ending with a WS row.

On your last row, place markers on each side of center _____ sts.

DECREASE ROW (RS): Work to 2 sts before marker, ssk, sm, work to next marker, sm, k2tog, work to end.

Work decrease row every _____ rows _____ times total: _____ sts remain. Work even until piece measures _____ from CO edge, ending with a WS row.

Note: Wrap shaping, increases, and armhole shaping will all occur at the same time—please read ahead.

SHAPE WRAP: When piece measures _____ from CO edge, ending with a WS row, shape wrap:

WRAP SHAPING ROW–RIGHT FRONT (RS): K1, ssk, work to end.

WRAP SHAPING ROW–RIGHT FRONT (WS): Work to last 3 sts, p2tog tbl, p1.

WRAP SHAPING ROW–LEFT FRONT (RS): Work to last 3 sts, k2tog, k1.

WRAP SHAPING ROW–LEFT FRONT (WS): P1, p2tog, work to end.

Work wrap shaping every row _____ times, then every 3rd row _____ times.

BUST INCREASES: When piece measures _____ from CO edge, shape bust:

Remove first marker for right front, or second marker for left front.

INCREASE ROW–RIGHT FRONT (RS): Work to marker, sm, M1-l, work to end.

INCREASE ROW–LEFT FRONT (RS): Work to marker, M1-r, sm, work to end.

Work increase row every _____ rows _____ times total.

SHAPE ARMHOLES: When piece measures _____ from CO edge, shape armholes:

BO _____ sts at the beginning of the next armhole edge.

BO _____ sts at the beginning of the following armhole edge.

Decrease 1 st at armhole end of every RS row _____ times: _____ sts remain.

ALL: When all wrap and armhole shaping is complete, _____ shoulder sts remain. Work even until piece measures _____ from CO edge, ending at the armhole edge.

NEXT ROW: BO _____ sts, work to end. Work 1 row even. BO rem sts.

SLEEVES

Using long-tail cast-on method (or a different one, if you prefer), CO _____ sts.

- -

SPORTY STYLE: Work 5 row in Garter st. Mark center _____ sts and switch to Stockinette st. Make the tucks and shape the sleeve at the same time. Please read ahead.

When sleeve measures 2" (5 cm) from CO edge, beginning with a WS row, make tucks:

MAKE TUCK (MT): With yarn in front, insert needle from top into the loop at the WS of the next st _____ rows below, pick up this loop, place on your left-hand needle and purl together with the next st on your current row.

MT ROW 1 (WS): Purl to first tuck marker, sm, MT over next _____ sts, purl to end.

MT ROW 2 (WS): Purl to first tuck marker, purl _____ sts, MT over remaining sts to next tuck marker, purl to end.

Alternate MT Rows 1 and 2 every _____ rows 6 times total—3 tucks on each side of center. *At the same time,* shape sleeve when sleeve measures 3" (7.5 cm) from beginning:

INCREASE ROW (RS): Work 1, M1-r, work to last st, M1-l, work 1.

Work increase row every _____ rows _____ times total: _____ sts total. Work even until sleeve measures _____ from CO edge, ending with a WS row.

BOHEMIAN STYLE: Work 2 rows even in Garter st, then mark stitches as follows: Work _____ sts, place marker, work _____ sts, place marker, work to end. Change to Stockinette st outside of the markers and decreasing Arrow Lace Sleeve (page 146) between the markers.

NEXT ROW (RS): Knit to first marker, sm, knit _____ sts, place marker, work row 1 of Arrow Lace over center _____ sts, place marker, knit to next marker, sm, knit to end.

NEXT ROW (WS): Purl to first marker, sm, knit to next marker, sm, work row 2 of Arrow Lace to next marker, sm, knit to next marker, sm, purl to end. Stockinette, Garter, and Arrow Lace pattern established. Work _____ rows even as established.

DECREASE ROW (RS): Knit to first marker, sm, ssk, work as established to 2 sts before last marker, k2tog, sm, knit to end. 2 sts decreased from Garter portion of center panel.

Repeat decrease row every RS row until a total of _____ decrease rows have been worked. Second full repeat of 16-row Arrow Lace pattern completes at the same time.

NEXT ROW (WS): Purl to center st, p2tog, purl to end: _____ sts remain. Switch to Stockinette st and work even until sleeve measures _____ from CO edge, ending with a WS row.

MODERN STYLE: Using long-tail cast-on method (or a different one, if you prefer), CO _____ sts. Work even in 1x1 rib, slipping the first st of every RS row purlwise, until ribbed band measures _____. BO all sts.

Rotate ribbed piece 90 degrees. Pick up and knit _____ sts along top edge. Work even in Stockinette st for 10 rows.

INCREASE ROW (RS): K1, M1-r, work to last st, M1-l, k1.

Work increase row every _____ rows _____ times: _____ sts total. Work even until sleeve measures _____ from edge where sts were picked up, ending with a WS row.

ALL STYLES:

SHAPE SLEEVE CAP: BO _____ sts at the beginning of the next 2 rows. BO _____ sts at the beginning of the following 2 rows. Decrease 1 st at each end of every 3rd RS row _____ times, then every other RS row _____ times, then every RS row _____ times.

BO _____ sts at the beginning of the next 4 rows.

BO final _____ sts.

FINISHING

Follow instructions on page 144.

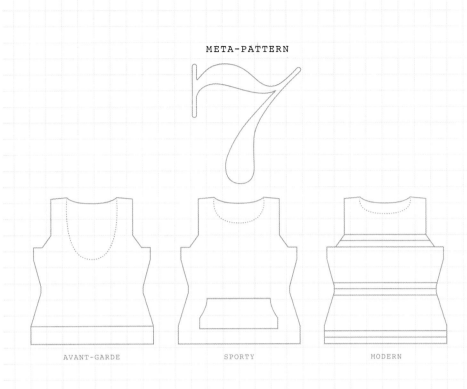

META-PATTERN

AVANT-GARDE   SPORTY   MODERN

THE TANK

We often think of sweaters as fundamentally cozy, cold-weather attire. But, really, sweaters are just knit tops—and tanks are another top style to knit! They represent a smaller commitment (both in time and in yarn), they offer a great range of styling options, and they're comfortable to boot.

These tanks work either as layering pieces or on their own, and the three versions I provide give you a range of fashion choices. Make it edgy and avant-garde with an industrial look achieved with a futuristic chained linen yarn and plenty of dropped stitches; take the basic shell in a sporty direction with a hood and kangaroo pocket; go sleek and modern with intentionally mismatched stripes and a smooth folded hem.

Again, all of these options mix and match well—so make a sample just like these in any gauge you like, or change things up to create a tank that's uniquely you.

Change it up!

Gauges offered
Fingering, DK, worsted

Necklines
Scoop, crew, boat

Textures and finishing
Dropped stitches, pocket & hood, stripes

Make this sweater suit your own style!

Hood leaves
front neck open.

Hard-wearing
cormo blend.

Simple
ribbed trim.

Super-snuggly
kangaroo
pocket.

» Jackie is wearing
size 38" (96.5 cm)
in DK gauge.

The Tank

| FINISHED BUST | **FINGERING:** 30¼ (32½, 34¼, 36½, 38¼, 40½, 42¼, 44½, 46¼, 48½, 50¼, 54¼)" [77 (82.5, 87, 93, 97, 103, 107.5, 113, 117.5, 123.5, 127.5, 138) cm] |

DK: 30 (32, 34, 36¼, 38¼, 40¼, 42½, 44½, 46, 48, 50, 54¼)" [76 (81.5, 86.5, 92, 97, 102.5, 108, 113, 116.5, 122, 127, 138) cm]

WORSTED: 30¼ (32¾, 34½, 37, 38¾, 40½, 43, 44¾, 46¼, 48¾, 50½, 54¾)" [77 (83.5, 87.5, 94, 98.5, 102.5, 109, 113.5, 117.5, 124, 128.5, 139) cm]

(Note: For ease in reading, the precise finished bust measurements have been rounded in the instructions below to 30 (32, 34, 36, 38, 40, 42, 44, 46, 48, 50, 54)" [76 (81.5, 86.5, 91.5, 96.5, 101.5, 106.5, 112, 117, 122, 127, 137) cm]. Your finished measurements will be as given above.

MATERIALS

See page 190 for fiber content.

FINGERING: Shibui Linen in Cypress, 3 (3, 4, 4, 4, 4, 5, 5, 5, 6, 6, 6) hanks

DK: Foxfire Farms Cormo Silk Alpaca, in Poppy, 5 (5, 5, 6, 6, 6, 7, 7, 7, 8, 8, 9) hanks

WORSTED: Swans Island Worsted in Oatmeal (MC), 2 (2, 2, 2, 2, 2, 2, 3, 3, 3, 3, 3) hanks and Garnet (CC), 1 hank all sizes (actual CC required will vary between 1/3 and 2/3 of a hank)

GAUGE

FINGERING: 28 sts and 36 rows = 4" (10 cm) in Stockinette st
DK: 23 sts and 34 rows = 4" (10 cm) in Stockinette st
WORSTED: 19 sts and 30 rows = 4" (10 cm) in Stockinette st

NEEDLES

Change needle size if necessary to obtain correct gauge:
FINGERING: US 3 / 3.25 mm
DK: US 6 / 4 mm
WORSTED: US 7 / 4.5 mm

For Modern Style, needles in size to obtain gauge and needles one size smaller.

BACK

Using long-tail cast-on method (or a different one, if you prefer), CO:

	30"	32	34	36	38	40	42	44	46	48	50	54
FINGERING	112	120	126	134	140	148	154	162	168	176	182	196
DK	92	98	104	110	116	122	128	134	138	144	150	162
WORSTED	76	82	86	92	96	100	106	110	114	120	124	134

sts.

SPORTY STYLE: Work even in 1x1 rib for 1" (2.5 cm), then switch to Stockinette st. Continue with All Styles instruction page 156.

MODERN STYLE: Work a folded hem as follows:
CO using MC and needles one size smaller than main needle size. Work 1½" (4 cm) even in Stockinette st, ending with a RS row. Switch to main needle size and knit 1 WS row to create turning ridge.
Note: All length measurements that follow are taken from turning ridge, not CO edge.
Switch to Stockinette st and stripe pattern (page 156).

Work 16 rows with MC in Stockinette st. Then, establish stripe pattern on back as follows:

STRIPE PATTERN:

Work 4 rows in CC.

Work 2 rows in MC.

Work 4 rows in CC.

Work 36 rows in MC.

Repeat these 46 rows.

AVANT GARDE STYLE: Work even in 2x2 rib for 2" (6.5 cm), ending with a RS row. Knit 1 WS row. The dropped sts for this style should be placed in a fairly free-form fashion, wherever the whim strikes you. If you wish to make dropped sts like the ones shown, create and place the dropped sts as follows. *Note: The sts to be dropped are not included in st counts in shaping instructions.* On first RS row after rib, knit to last

	30"	32	34	36	38	40	42	44	46	48	50	54
FINGERING	16	18	18	20	21	22	23	24	25	26	27	29
DK	13	14	15	16	17	18	19	20	20	21	22	24
WORSTED	11	12	12	13	14	15	15	16	17	18	18	20

sts, pm, make 3 (insert left needle, from back to front, under strand of yarn which runs between next st on left needle and last st on right needle, k1, p1, k1 into this st), pm, knit to end.

Work in Stockinette st for 2½" (5 cm), ending with a WS row.

NEXT ROW: Knit to the new sts and drop them from needle, remove markers. Encourage the sts to unravel all the way down.

When you reach the narrowest part of waist, just before your first increase row, knit to marker, sm, k2, place dropped st marker, make 2 sts, place dropped st marker, knit to end. Work the new sts in Stockinette st until neck shaping, then drop them.

ALL STYLES: Work until piece measures 4" (10 cm) from CO edge. On your last row, place two waist shaping markers, one on either side of the center section so that there are:

	30"	32	34	36	38	40	42	44	46	48	50	54
FINGERING	38	40	42	44	46	50	52	54	56	58	60	66
DK	30	32	34	36	38	40	42	44	46	48	50	54
WORSTED	26	28	28	30	32	34	36	36	38	40	42	44

sts between waist shaping markers.

DECREASE ROW (RS): Work to 2 sts before first marker, ssk, sm, work to next marker, sm, k2tog, work to end. 2 sts decreased.

Work a decrease row every

FINGERING: 6 / **DK:** 6 / **WORSTED:** 8 rows

FINGERING: 9 / **DK:** 8 / **WORSTED:** 6 times total.

When all decreases are complete,

	30"	32	34	36	38	40	42	44	46	48	50	54
FINGERING	94	102	108	116	122	130	136	144	150	158	164	178
DK	76	82	88	94	100	106	112	118	122	128	134	146
WORSTED	64	70	74	80	84	88	94	98	102	108	112	122

sts remain. Work even until piece measures 9½" (24 cm) from CO edge, ending with a WS row.

META-PATTERN #7

AVANT-GARDE

The Tank

Deep, ribbed
neckline.

Crunchy
linen yarn.

Eye-catching
dropped
stitches.

» Morgan is wearing
size 40" (101.5 cm)
in fingering gauge.

INCREASE ROW (RS): Work to first marker, M1-r, sm, work to next marker, sm, M1-l, work to end. 2 sts increased.

Work an increase row every

FINGERING: 8 / **DK:** 8 / **WORSTED:** 10 rows

FINGERING: 6 / **DK:** 5 / **WORSTED:** 4 times total.

When all increases are complete,

	30"	32	34	36	38	40	42	44	46	48	50	54
FINGERING	106	114	120	128	134	142	148	156	162	170	176	190
DK	86	92	98	104	110	116	122	128	132	138	144	156
WORSTED	72	78	82	88	92	96	102	106	110	116	120	130

sts total. Work even until piece measures 15 (15¼, 15½, 15¾, 16, 16¼, 16½, 16½, 17, 17, 17, 17)" [38 (38.5, 39.5, 40, 40.5, 41.5, 42, 42, 43, 43, 43, 43) cm] from CO edge, ending with a WS row.

SHAPE ARMHOLES

BO

	30"	32	34	36	38	40	42	44	46	48	50	54
FINGERING	8	8	8	8	8	8	8	10	10	12	14	14
DK	6	6	6	6	6	6	6	8	8	10	10	12
WORSTED	6	6	6	6	6	6	6	6	8	8	10	10

sts at the beginning of the next 2 rows. BO

	30"	32	34	36	38	40	42	44	46	48	50	54
FINGERING	2	2	2	2	2	4	4	6	8	8	10	12
DK	0	2	2	2	2	2	4	4	6	6	8	10
WORSTED	0	2	2	2	2	2	2	4	4	6	6	8

sts at the beginning of the following 2 rows. Decrease 1 st at each end of every RS row

	30"	32	34	36	38	40	42	44	46	48	50	54
FINGERING	2	4	6	8	8	8	9	8	8	9	8	9
DK	3	3	5	6	6	8	7	8	7	7	8	7
WORSTED	2	2	3	5	4	5	7	6	6	6	6	6

times:

	30"	32	34	36	38	40	42	44	46	48	50	54
FINGERING	82	86	88	92	98	102	106	108	110	112	112	120
DK	68	70	72	76	82	84	88	88	90	92	92	98
WORSTED	56	58	60	62	68	70	72	74	74	76	76	82

sts remain. Work even until armhole measures 5½ (6, 6¼, 6½, 7, 7¼, 7½, 8, 8¼, 8¾, 9, 9½)" [14 (15, 16, 16.5, 18, 18.5, 19, 20.5, 21, 22, 23, 24) cm] and piece measures 20½ (21¼, 21¾, 22¼, 23, 23½, 24, 24½, 25¼, 25¾, 26, 26½)" [52 (54, 55, 56.5, 58.5, 59.5, 61, 62, 64, 65.5, 66, 67.5) cm], ending with a WS row.

SHAPE NECK

NEXT ROW (RS): Work

	30"	32	34	36	38	40	42	44	46	48	50	54
FINGERING	19	20	20	21	22	23	24	24	25	25	25	26
DK	16	16	17	18	19	19	20	20	20	21	21	22
WORSTED	14	14	14	15	16	16	17	17	17	18	18	19

sts, attach a new ball of yarn and BO center

	30"	32	34	36	38	40	42	44	46	48	50	54
FINGERING	44	46	48	50	54	56	58	60	60	62	66	68
DK	36	38	38	40	44	46	48	48	50	50	50	54
WORSTED	28	30	32	32	36	38	38	40	40	40	40	44

sts, work to end. *You will now work both sides of the neckline at the same time.*

Decrease 1 st at neck edge of every RS row twice:

	30"	32	34	36	38	40	42	44	46	48	50	54
FINGERING	17	18	18	19	20	21	22	22	23	23	23	24
DK	14	14	15	16	17	17	18	18	18	19	19	20
WORSTED	12	12	12	13	14	14	15	15	15	16	16	17

sts remain for each shoulder. Work even until armhole measures 6½ (7, 7¼, 7½, 8, 8¼, 8½, 9, 9¼, 9¾, 10, 10½)" [16.5 (18, 18.5, 19, 20.5, 21, 21.5, 23, 23.5, 25, 25.5, 26.5) cm], ending at the armhole edge for each side.

NEXT ROW: BO

	30"	32	34	36	38	40	42	44	46	48	50	54
FINGERING	9	9	9	10	10	11	11	11	12	12	12	12
DK	7	7	8	8	9	9	9	9	9	10	10	10
WORSTED	6	6	6	7	7	7	8	8	8	8	8	9

sts, work to end. Work 1 row even. BO remaining sts.

FRONT

MODERN STYLE: The stripe sequence on front is intentionally different than on back, to form the positive/negative line at the side seams.

After folded hem, work 12 rows with MC in Stockinette st. Then, establish stripe pattern on Front as follows:

Work 4 rows in CC.
Work 4 rows in MC.
Work 2 rows in CC.
Work 4 rows in MC.
Work 4 rows in CC.
Work 28 rows in MC.
Repeat these 46 rows.

AVANTE GARDE STYLE: The dropped sts for this style should be placed in a fairly free-form fashion, wherever the whim strikes you. If you wish to make dropped sts like the ones shown, create and place the dropped sts as follows. *Note: The sts to be dropped are not included in st counts in shaping instructions.*

On first RS row after rib, knit

	30"	32	34	36	38	40	42	44	46	48	50	54
FINGERING	39	42	44	47	49	51	53	56	58	61	63	67
DK	33	35	37	39	41	43	45	47	48	50	52	56
WORSTED	27	29	31	33	34	35	37	39	40	42	43	47

sts, pm, make 1, pm, knit to last

	30"	32	34	36	38	40	42	44	46	48	50	54
FINGERING	16	18	18	20	21	22	23	24	25	26	27	29
DK	13	14	15	16	17	18	19	20	20	21	22	24
WORSTED	11	12	12	13	14	15	15	16	17	18	18	20

sts, pm, make 3, pm, knit to end. Work first marked st in Stockinette st to neck shaping, then drop all the way down. Work 3 marked sts in Stockinette st for 2½" (6.5 cm), then drop and remove markers.

When you reach 2" (5 cm) below neck shaping, create another dropped st:
Knit

	30"	32	34	36	38	40	42	44	46	48	50	54
FINGERING	73	78	82	87	91	97	101	106	110	115	119	129
DK	59	63	67	71	75	79	83	87	90	94	98	106
WORSTED	49	53	55	59	62	65	69	71	74	78	81	87

sts, pm, make 2, pm, work to end. Work these sts in Stockinette st to neck shaping, then drop.

Work front as for back aside from neck shaping, *except* place waist shaping markers around the center sts so that there are:

	30"	32	34	36	38	40	42	44	46	48	50	54
FINGERING	56	60	62	66	70	74	76	80	84	88	90	98
DK	46	48	52	54	58	60	64	66	68	72	74	80
WORSTED	38	40	42	46	48	50	52	54	56	60	62	66

sts between waist shaping markers.
When piece measures:

AVANT-GARDE STYLE: 13 (13¼, 13½, 13¾, 14, 14¼, 14½, 14½, 15, 15, 15, 15)" [33 (33.5, 34.5, 35, 35.5, 36, 37, 37, 38, 38, 38, 38) cm]

SPORTY STYLE: 17½ (18¼, 18¾, 19¼, 20, 20½, 21, 21½, 22¼, 22¾, 23, 23½)" [44.5 (46.5, 47.5, 49, 51, 52, 53.5, 54.5, 56.5, 58, 58.5, 59.5) cm]

MODERN STYLE: 19 (19¾, 20¼, 20¾, 21½, 22, 22½, 23, 23¾, 24¼, 24½, 25)" [48.5 (50, 51.5, 52.5, 54.5, 56, 57, 58.5, 60.5, 61.5, 62, 63.5) cm]

from CO edge, *shape neckline according to style. Note: Avant-Garde neckline begins before waist increases are complete, please read ahead. Waist, armholes and shoulders will be shaped same as back.*

SHAPE NECK

AVANT-GARDE STYLE: Mark the center

	30"	32	34	36	38	40	42	44	46	48	50	54
FINGERING	22	24	24	26	28	28	28	30	30	30	30	34
DK	18	20	20	20	22	24	24	24	26	26	26	28
WORSTED	16	16	18	18	18	20	20	20	20	20	20	22

sts.

NEXT ROW (RS): Work to marker, attach a new ball of yarn and BO marked sts, work to end. You'll now work both sides of neckline (including armhole shaping) at the same time.
Decrease 1 st at neck edge every RS row

META-PATTERN #7

MODERN

The Tank

Simple edge trims.

Stripe sequence different on front and back.

Clean, bold colors.

Plain folded hem.

» Kiki is wearing size 34" (86.5 cm) in worsted gauge.

	30"	32	34	36	38	40	42	44	46	48	50	54
FINGERING	7	7	7	7	8	8	9	9	9	9	9	10
DK	6	6	6	6	7	7	7	7	7	7	7	8
WORSTED	4	5	5	5	6	6	6	6	6	6	6	7

times, then every other RS row

	30"	32	34	36	38	40	42	44	46	48	50	54
FINGERING	6	6	7	7	7	8	8	8	8	9	9	9
DK	5	5	5	6	6	6	7	7	7	7	7	7
WORSTED	4	4	4	4	5	5	5	6	6	6	6	6

times.

SPORTY STYLE: Mark the center

	30"	32	34	36	38	40	42	44	46	48	50	54
FINGERING	22	24	24	26	28	28	28	30	30	30	30	34
DK	18	20	20	20	22	24	24	24	26	26	26	28
WORSTED	16	16	18	18	18	20	20	20	20	20	20	22

sts.

NEXT ROW (RS): Work to marker, attach a new ball of yarn and BO marked sts, work to end. You'll now work both sides of neckline at the same time.

Decrease 1 st at neck edge every row

	30"	32	34	36	38	40	42	44	46	48	50	54
FINGERING	7	7	7	7	8	8	9	9	9	9	9	10
DK	6	6	6	6	7	7	7	7	7	7	7	8
WORSTED	4	5	5	5	6	6	6	6	6	6	6	7

times, then every RS row

	30"	32	34	36	38	40	42	44	46	48	50	54
FINGERING	6	6	7	7	7	8	8	8	8	9	9	9
DK	5	5	5	6	6	6	7	7	7	7	7	7
WORSTED	4	4	4	4	5	5	5	6	6	6	6	6

times.

MODERN STYLE: Mark the center

	30"	32	34	36	38	40	42	44	46	48	50	54
FINGERING	42	44	46	48	52	54	56	58	58	60	60	66
DK	34	36	36	38	42	44	46	46	48	48	48	52
WORSTED	26	28	30	30	34	36	36	38	38	38	38	42

sts.

NEXT ROW (RS): Work to marker, attach a new ball of yarn and BO marked sts, work to end. You'll now work both sides of neckline at the same time. Decrease 1 st at neck edge every RS row 3 times.

ALL STYLES: When all neck and armhole shaping is complete,

	30"	32	34	36	38	40	42	44	46	48	50	54
FINGERING	17	18	18	19	20	21	22	22	23	23	23	24
DK	14	14	15	16	17	17	18	18	18	19	19	20
WORSTED	12	12	12	13	14	14	15	15	15	16	16	17

sts remain for each shoulder. Work even and complete shoulder shaping as for back.

FINISHING

Wet-block all pieces to finished measurements. Sew shoulder seams using mattress stitch.

TRIM ARMHOLE EDGES WITH APPLIED I-CORD: With RS facing and circular needle, beginning at under-arm, pick up and knit sts around armhole edge at the rate of 1 st for every bound off st and 1 st for each row.

Using double-pointed needles, CO 3 sts. K2 on dpns, sl 1 knitwise, knit first st from circular needle onto dpn, psso. Slide sts to the other end of the dpn.

Using the other dpn and drawing yarn across the WS of the sts, k2, sl 1 knitwise, knit next st from circular needle onto dpn, psso. Slide sts to the other end of the dpn. Continue in this manner until all armhole sts have been worked. BO 3 i-cord sts. Cut yarn.

Repeat for other armhole.
Weave in ends.

AVANT-GARDE STYLE: Sew side seams using mattress stitch with WS facing to create an exposed seam.

With RS facing, beginning at right shoulder seam, pick up and knit sts along neck edge at the rate of 3 sts for every 4 rows along vertical edges, 4 sts for every 5 rows along diagonal edges, and 1 st for every bound-off st along horizontal edges. Count sts and adjust if necessary to make total a multiple of 4 sts.

Join for working in the round. Purl 1 round, then work even in 2x2 rib until neck trim measures 2" (5 cm). BO all sts firmly in rib.

SPORTY STYLE:
POCKET: CO

	30"	32	34	36	38	40	42	44	46	48	50	54
FINGERING	84	90	96	102	106	112	116	122	126	132	138	148
DK	70	74	78	84	88	92	96	102	104	108	114	122
WORSTED	58	62	66	70	72	76	80	84	86	90	94	102

sts. Work 2" (5 cm) even in Stockinette st.
Decrease 1 st at each end of every row

	30"	32	34	36	38	40	42	44	46	48	50	54
FINGERING	7	7	8	8	9	9	9	10	10	11	11	12
DK	6	6	6	7	7	7	8	8	8	9	9	10
WORSTED	5	5	5	6	6	6	6	7	7	7	8	8

times, then every RS row

	30"	32	34	36	38	40	42	44	46	48	50	54
FINGERING	7	8	8	9	9	10	10	10	11	11	12	13
DK	6	6	7	7	8	8	8	9	9	9	10	10
WORSTED	5	5	6	6	6	7	7	7	7	8	8	9

times:

	30"	32	34	36	38	40	42	44	46	48	50	54
FINGERING	56	60	64	68	70	74	78	82	84	88	92	98
DK	46	50	52	56	58	62	64	68	70	72	76	82
WORSTED	38	42	44	46	48	50	54	56	58	60	62	68

sts remain.

Work even until pocket measures 6½" (16.5) cm from CO edge. BO all sts.

Trim curved edges of pocket with applied i-cord as for armholes.

Using mattress stitch, sew straight edges of pocket to front of tank, centering pocket on front and placing lower edge of pocket at top of rib.

Sew side seams using mattress stitch.

HOOD: With RS facing and beginning at right edge of neck BOs, pick up and knit sts around neckline to left edge of front neck BOs at the rate of 3 sts for every 4 rows along vertical edges, 4 sts for every 5 rows along diagonal edges, and 1 st for every bound-off st along horizontal edges. Count sts and adjust if necessary to make total an even number of sts. *Note: Bound-off edge at center front neck is finished edge.*

Work even in Stockinette st until hood measures 13" (33 cm). Place marker on either side of center 2 sts.

SHAPE HOOD: DECREASE ROW (RS): Decrease 2 sts this row, then every other row 6 times, as follows: Work to 2 sts before first marker, ssk, sm, k2, sm, k2tog, work to end.

Divide sts evenly onto 2 needles, fold hood in half with RSs together, and using Three-Needle BO, join halves together.

TRIM HOOD: Pick up sts around hood at the rate of 3 sts for every 4 rows. Work 3 rows even in Garter st and then BO all sts.

MODERN STYLE: Sew folded hems into place. Sew side seams using mattress stitch.

TRIM NECKLINE: With RS facing and beginning at right shoulder seam, pick up and knit sts around neckline at the rate of 4 sts for every 5 rows along diagonal edges, and 1 st for every bound-off st. Join for working in the round. Work 5 rounds in Stockinette st. BO all sts, encouraging edge to roll.

PLAYING WITH DETAIL (left to right): avant-garde dropped stitches, modern stripe sequences.

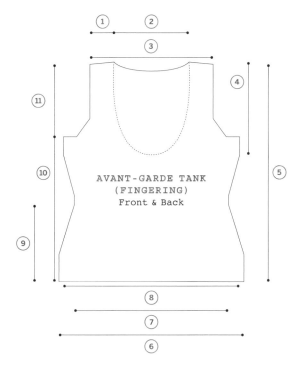

AVANT-GARDE TANK
(FINGERING)
Front & Back

1   2½ (2½, 2½, 2¾, 2¾, 3, 3¼, 3¼, 3¼, 3¼, 3¼, 3½)"
    6 (6.5, 6.5, 7, 7.5, 7.5, 8, 8, 8.5, 8.5, 8.5, 8.5) cm

2   6¾ (7¼, 7½, 7¾, 8¼, 8½, 8¾, 9¼, 9¼, 9½, 9½, 10¼)"
    17.5 (18, 19, 19.5, 21, 22, 22.5, 23, 23, 24, 24, 26) cm

3   11¾ (12¼, 12½, 13¼, 14, 14½, 15¼, 15½, 15¾, 16, 16, 17¼)"
    30 (31, 32, 33.5, 35.5, 37, 38.5, 39, 40, 40.5, 40.5, 43.5) cm

4   8½ (9, 9¼, 9½, 10, 10¼, 10½, 11, 11¼, 11¾, 12, 12½)"
    21.5 (23, 23.5, 24, 25.5, 26, 26.5, 28, 28.5, 30, 30.5, 32) cm

5   21½ (22¼, 22¾, 23¼, 24, 24½, 25, 25½, 26¼, 26¾, 27, 27½)"
    54.5 (56.5, 58, 59, 61, 62, 63.5, 65, 66.5, 68, 68.5, 70) cm

6   16 (17¼, 18, 19¼, 20, 21¼, 22, 23¼, 24, 25¼, 26, 28)"
    40.5 (43.5, 45.5, 48.5, 51, 53.5, 56, 59, 61, 64, 66, 71) cm

7   13½ (14½, 15½, 16½, 17½, 18½, 19½, 20½, 21½, 22½, 23½, 25½)"
    34 (37, 39, 42, 44.5, 47, 49.5, 52.5, 54.5, 57.5, 59.5, 64.5) cm

8   15¼ (16¼, 17¼, 18¼, 19¼, 20¼, 21¼, 22¼, 23¼, 24¼, 25¼, 27¼)"
    38.5 (41.5, 43.5, 46.5, 48.5, 51.5, 53.5, 56.5, 59, 61.5, 64, 69) cm

9   9"/23 cm

10 15 (15¼, 15½, 15¾, 16, 16¼, 16½, 16½, 17, 17, 17, 17)"
    38 (38.5, 39.5, 40, 40.5, 41.5, 42, 42, 43, 43, 43, 43) cm

11 6½ (7, 7¼, 7½, 8, 8¼, 8½, 9, 9¼, 9¾, 10, 10½)"
    16.5 (18, 18.5, 19, 20.5, 21, 21.5, 23, 23.5, 25, 25.5, 26.5) cm

1 2½ (2½, 2½, 2¾, 3, 3, 3¼, 3¼, 3¼, 3¼, 3¼, 3½)"
6 (6, 6.5, 7, 7.5, 7.5, 8, 8, 8, 8.5, 8.5, 9) cm

2 7 (7¼, 7¼, 7¾, 8¼, 8¾, 9, 9, 9½, 9½, 9½, 10)"
17.5 (18.5, 18.5, 19.5, 21, 22, 23. 23, 24, 24, 24, 25.5) cm

3 11¾ (12¼, 12½, 13¼, 14¼, 14½, 15¼, 15¼, 15¾, 16, 16, 17)"
30 (31, 32, 33.5, 36, 37, 39, 39, 40, 40.5, 40.5, 43.5) cm

4 4"/10cm

5 21½ (22¼, 22¾, 23¼, 24, 24½, 25, 25½, 26¼, 26¾, 27, 27½)"
54.5 (56.5, 58, 59, 61, 62, 63.5, 65, 66.5, 68, 68.5, 70) cm

6 16 (17, 18, 19¼, 20¼, 21¼, 22¼, 23¼, 24, 25, 26, 28¼)"
40.5 (43.5, 46, 48.5, 51, 54, 56.5, 59, 61, 63.5, 66.5, 71.5) cm

7 13¼ (14¼, 15¼, 16¼, 17½, 18½, 19½, 20½, 21¼, 22¼, 23¼, 25½)"
33.5 (36, 39, 41.5, 44, 47, 49.5, 52, 54, 56.5, 59, 64.5) cm

8 15 (16, 17, 18, 19¼, 20¼, 21¼, 22¼, 23, 24, 25, 27¼)"
38 (40.5, 43.5, 46, 48.5, 51, 54, 56.5, 58.5, 61, 63.5, 69) cm

9 9"/23 cm

10 15 (15¼, 15½, 15¾, 16, 16¼, 16½, 16½, 17, 17, 17, 17)"
38 (38.5, 39.5, 40, 40.5, 41.5, 42, 42, 43, 43, 43, 43) cm

11 6½ (7, 7¼, 7½, 8, 8¼, 8½, 9, 9¼, 9¾, 10, 10½)"
16.5 (18, 18.5, 19, 20.5, 21, 21.5, 23, 23.5, 25, 25.5, 26.5) cm

1 2½ (2½, 2½, 2¾, 3, 3, 3¼, 3¼, 3¼, 3¼, 3¼, 3½)"
6.5 (6.5, 6.5, 7, 7.5, 7.5, 8, 8, 8, 8.5, 8.5, 9) cm

2 6¾ (7¼, 7½, 7½, 8½, 8¾, 8¾, 9¼, 9¼, 9¼, 9¼, 10)"
17 (18, 19.5, 19.5, 21.5, 22.5, 22.5, 23.5, 23.5, 23.5, 23.5, 25.5) cm

3 11¾ (12¼, 12¾, 13, 14¼, 14¾, 15¼, 15½, 15½, 16, 16, 17¼)"
30 (31, 32, 33, 36.5, 37.5, 38.5, 39.5, 39.5, 40.5, 40.5, 44) cm

4 2½"/6.5 cm

5 21½ (22¼, 22¾, 23¼, 24, 24½, 25, 25½, 26¼, 26¾, 27, 27½)"
54.5 (56.5, 58, 59, 61, 62, 63.5, 65, 66.5, 68, 68.5, 70) cm

6 16 (17¼, 18, 19¼, 20¼, 21, 22¼, 23¼, 24, 25¼, 26, 28¼)"
40.5 (44, 46, 49, 51.5, 53.5, 56.5, 59, 61, 64, 66.5, 71.5) cm

7 13½ (14¾, 15½, 16¾, 17¾, 18½, 19¾, 20¾, 21½, 22¾, 23½, 25¾)"
34 (37.5, 39.5, 43, 45, 47, 50.5, 52.5, 54.5, 58, 60, 65) cm

8 15¼ (16½, 17¼, 18½, 19¼, 20¼, 21½, 22¼, 23¼, 24½, 25¼, 27¼)"
38.5 (41.5, 44, 47, 49, 51.5, 54.5, 56.5, 59, 62, 64, 69.5) cm

9 9"/23 cm

10 15 (15¼, 15½, 15¾, 16, 16¼, 16½, 16½, 17, 17, 17, 17)"
38 (38.5, 39.5, 40, 40.5, 41.5, 42, 42, 43, 43, 43, 43) cm

11 6½ (7, 7¼, 7½, 8, 8¼, 8½, 9, 9¼, 9¾, 10, 10½)"
16.5 (18, 18.5, 19, 20.5, 21, 21.5, 23, 23.5, 25, 25.5, 26.5) cm

META-PATTERN #7
THE TANK

Use this worksheet as a handy way to get all of the numbers for each individual tank you knit in one simple place. You can photocopy these pages or download a fresh copy any time you like at www.amyherzogdesigns.com/knitwearlove.

BACK

Using long-tail cast-on method (or a different one, if you prefer), CO _____ sts.

Work even in _____ until piece measures _____ from CO edge, ending with a WS row.

AVANT-GARDE STYLE: Work dropped stitches like the ones shown as follows:

On first RS row after rib, knit to final _____ sts, pm, make 3 (pick up bar before next stitch, k1, p1, k1 into bar), pm, work to end. Knit these stitches in Stockinette st for 2½" (5 cm), then drop and remove markers.

When you reach the narrowest part of waist, just before your first increase row, knit to marker, sm, knit 2, place dropped stitch marker, make 2, place dropped stitch marker, knit to end. Work these stitches in Stockinette st until neck shaping, then drop them.

Switch to Stockinette st and work even until piece measures _____ from CO edge, ending with a WS row.

MODERN STYLE: Establish stripe pattern after folded hem as follows:

Work 16 rows after folded hem in MC in Stockinette st. Then, establish stripe pattern on back as follows:

Work 4 rows in CC.

Work 2 rows in MC.

Work 4 rows in CC.

Work 36 rows in MC.

Repeat these 46 rows.

On your last row, place markers as follows: Work _____ sts, pm, work _____ sts, pm, work to end.

DECREASE ROW (RS): Work to 2 sts before marker, ssk, sm, work to next marker, sm, k2tog, work to end.

Work decrease row every _____ rows _____ times total: _____ sts remain. Work even until piece measures _____ from CO edge, ending with a WS row.

INCREASE ROW (RS): Work to marker, M1-r, sm, work to next marker, sm, M1-l, work to end.

Work increase row every _____ rows _____ times total: _____ sts total. Work even until piece measures _____ from CO edge, ending with a WS row.

SHAPE ARMHOLES: BO _____ sts at the beginning of the next 2 rows. BO _____ sts at the beginning of the following 2 rows. Decrease 1 st at each end of every RS row _____ times: _____ sts remain.

Work even until piece measures _____ from CO edge, ending with a WS row.

NEXT ROW (RS): Work _____ sts, attach a new ball of yarn and BO center _____ sts, work to end.

Working both sides of neckline at the same time, decrease 1 st at neck edge of every RS row twice. _____ shoulder sts remain. Work even until piece measures _____ from CO edge, ending at the armhole edge.

NEXT ROW: BO _____ sts, work to end. Work 1 row even. BO rem sts.

FRONT

Using long-tail cast-on method (or a different one, if you prefer), CO _____ sts. Work even in _____ until piece measures _____ from CO edge, ending with a WS row.

Switch to _____ and work even until piece measures _____ from CO edge, ending with a WS row.

MODERN STYLE: Stripe sequence on front is intentionally different than on back, to form the positive/negative stripe sequence when seamed.

Establish stripe pattern after folded hem as follows:

Work 12 rows after folded hem in MC in Stockinette st. Then, establish stripe pattern on front as follows:

Work 4 rows in CC.

Work 4 rows in MC.

Work 2 rows in CC.

Work 4 rows in MC.

Work 4 rows in CC.

Work 28 rows in MC.

Repeat these 46 rows.

AVANT-GARDE STYLE: Work dropped sts like the ones shown as follows:

On first RS row after rib, knit _____ sts, pm, make 1, pm, knit to final _____ sts, pm, make 3, pm, knit to end. Knit first marked st in Stockinette st to neck shaping, then drop all the way down to rib. Knit 3 marked sts in Stockinette st for 2½" (6.5 cm), then drop and remove markers.

When you reach 2" (6 cm) below neck shaping, create another dropped stitch: Knit _____ sts, pm, make 2, pm, knit to end. Work these sts in Stockinette st until neck shaping, then drop.

On your last row, place markers on each side of center _____ sts.

DECREASE ROW (RS): Work to 2 sts before marker, ssk, sm, work to next marker, sm, k2tog, work to end.

Work decrease row every _____ rows _____ times total: _____ sts remain. Work even until piece measures _____ from CO edge, ending with a WS row.

Note: For Avant-Garde style, neck shaping begins before armhole shaping. Please read ahead!

INCREASE ROW (RS): Work to marker, M1-r, sm, work to next marker, sm, M1-l, work to end.

Work increase row every _____ rows _____ times total: _____ sts total. Work even until piece measures _____ from CO edge, ending with a WS row.

AVANT-GARDE STYLE:

SHAPE NECK: When piece measures _____ from CO edge, ending with a WS row, shape neck: Mark center _____ sts.

NEXT ROW (RS): Work to marker, attach a new ball of yarn and BO center _____ sts, work to end.

Decrease 1 st at neck edge every RS row _____ times, then every other RS row _____ times.

ALL STYLES: Work until piece measures _____ from CO edge, ending with a WS row.

SHAPE ARMHOLES: BO _____ sts at the beginning of the next 2 rows. BO _____ sts at the beginning of the following 2 rows. Decrease 1 st at each end of every RS row _____ times: _____ sts remain.

SPORTY STYLE:

SHAPE NECK: When piece measures _____ from CO edge, ending with a WS row, shape neckline:

Mark center _____ sts.

NEXT ROW (RS): Work to marker, attach a new ball of yarn and BO to next marker, work to end.

Decrease 1 st at neck edge every row _____ times, then every RS row _____ times.

MODERN STYLE:

SHAPE NECK: When piece measures _____ from CO edge, ending with a WS row, shape neckline:

Mark center _____ sts.

NEXT ROW (RS): Work to marker, attach a new ball of yarn and BO center sts, work to end.

Decrease 1 st at neck edge every RS row 3 times.

When all neck and armhole shaping is complete, _____ shoulder sts remain. Work even until piece measures _____ from CO edge, ending at the armhole edge.

NEXT ROW: BO _____ sts, work to end. Work 1 row even. BO rem sts.

FINISHING

Follow instructions on page 163.

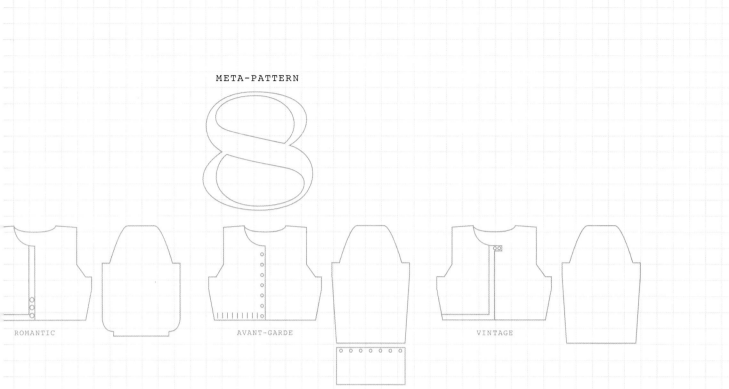

ROMANTIC

AVANT-GARDE

VINTAGE

THE BOLERO

Boleros aren't for everyone, but they definitely have some of the most passionate fashion fans around. (And if you've never tried one, consider doing so! They do an amazing job at calling attention to a curvy waist and can look especially divine with dresses and skirts.) They're pretty quick to knit, can be created in a variety of styles, and are just plain fun.

I've given you three versions: a soft, floaty romantic look achieved through slightly ballooned elbow sleeves and a plunging neckline; a super-funky avant-garde style with detachable sleeve cuffs and custom buttons; and a fun vintage look with an asymmetrical neck closure and trim three-quarter sleeves.

Change it up!

Gauges offered
Fingering,
Worsted, Bulky

Sleeves
Ballooned elbow,
detachable long,
tapered three-
quarter-length

Closures
Buttons at waist,
fully buttoned,
buttoned only
at top

Make this
sweater suit
your
own style!

META-PATTERN #8

VINTAGE
The Bolero

Thick yarn
pairs with
simple Stock-
inette and
ribbing.

Asymmetrical
buttons
highlight
neckline.

Trim fit and
three-quarter
sleeves.

» Kiki is wearing
size 34" (86.5 cm)
in bulky gauge.

FINISHED BUST

FINGERING: 30½ (32, 34¼, 36¼, 38½, 40, 42¼, 44¼, 46½, 48, 50¼, 54½)" [77 (81.5, 86.5, 92, 97.5, 101.5, 107, 112.5, 118, 122, 127.5, 138) cm]

WORSTED: 30½ (32, 34½, 36, 38½, 40, 42½, 44, 46½, 48, 50½, 54½)" [77 (81.5, 87.5, 91.5, 97.5, 101.5, 107.5, 112, 118, 122, 128, 138) cm]

BULKY: 30¾ (32, 34¾, 36, 38¾, 40, 42¾, 44, 46¾, 48, 50¾, 54¾)" [78 (81.5, 88, 91.5, 98, 101.5, 108.5, 112, 118.5, 122, 128.5, 139) cm]

(Note: For ease in reading, the precise finished bust measurements have been rounded in the instructions below to 30 (32, 34, 36, 38, 40, 42, 44, 46, 48, 50, 54)" [76 (81.5, 86.5, 91.5, 96.5, 101.5, 106.5, 112, 117, 122, 127, 137) cm]. Your finished measurements will be as given above.

MATERIALS

See page 190 for fiber content.

FINGERING: Rowan Yarns Fine Lace in #925 Quaint, 4 (4, 4, 5, 5, 6, 6, 6, 7, 7, 8, 9) hanks [worked with 2 strands held together throughout]

WORSTED: SweetGeorgia Yarns Trinity Worsted in Terra Firma, 4 (4, 4, 5, 5, 5, 6, 6, 7, 7, 7, 8) hanks

BULKY: Quince and Co. Puffin in Carrie's Yellow, 3 (4, 4, 4, 4, 5, 5, 5, 6, 6, 7, 7) hanks

GAUGE

FINGERING: 30 sts and 40 rows = 4" (10 cm) in Stockinette st, with yarn held double

WORSTED: 20 sts and 28 rows = 4" (10 cm) in Stockinette st

BULKY: 12 sts and 18 rows = 4" (10 cm) in Stockinette st

NEEDLES

Adjust needle size if necessary to obtain correct gauge:

FINGERING: US 2 / 2.75 mm

WORSTED: US 7 / 4.5 mm

BULKY: US 11 / 8 mm

NOTIONS

ROMANTIC: Three ¾" (20 mm) buttons

AVANT-GARDE: Sixteen ½" (13 mm) buttons and 6 (6, 7, 7, 7, 8, 8, 8, 9, 9, 9, 10) ⅞" (22 mm) buttons

VINTAGE: Two 1" (25 mm) buttons

BACK

Using long-tail cast-on method (or a different one, if you prefer), CO

	30"	32	34	36	38	40	42	44	46	48	50	54
FINGERING	102	108	116	124	132	138	146	154	162	168	176	192
WORSTED	68	72	78	82	88	92	98	102	108	112	118	128
BULKY	40	42	46	48	52	54	58	60	64	66	70	76

sts. Work even in trim of your choice, as follows:

ROMANTIC STYLE: Work even in Seed st for 1½" (4 cm), then switch to Stockinette st.

AVANT-GARDE STYLE: Work even in Corded Rib pattern (page 183) for 1½" (4 cm), then switch to Reverse Stockinette st.

VINTAGE STYLE: Work even in 1x1 rib for 1" (2.5 cm), then switch to Stockinette st.

Continue until piece measures 2" (5 cm) from CO edge, ending with a WS row.

On your last row, place two waist shaping markers, one on either side of the center section so that there are:

	30"	32	34	36	38	40	42	44	46	48	50	54
FINGERING	38	40	42	46	48	50	52	56	58	60	62	68
WORSTED	26	26	28	30	32	34	36	36	38	40	42	46
BULKY	16	16	18	18	20	20	22	22	24	24	26	28

sts between waist shaping markers.

INCREASE ROW (RS): Work to first marker, M1-r, sm, work to next marker, sm, M1-l, work to end. 2 sts increased.

Work an increase row every 6 rows

FINGERING: 6 / **WORSTED:** 4 / **BULKY:** 3 times total.

When all increases are complete,

	30"	32	34	36	38	40	42	44	46	48	50	54
FINGERING	114	120	128	136	144	150	158	166	174	180	188	204
WORSTED	76	80	86	90	96	100	106	110	116	120	126	136
BULKY	46	48	52	54	58	60	64	66	70	72	76	82

sts total. Work even until piece measures 6 (6¼, 6½, 6¾, 7, 7¼, 7½, 7½, 8, 8, 8, 8)" [15 (16, 16.5, 17, 18, 18.5, 19, 19, 20.5, 20.5, 20.5, 20.5) cm] from CO edge, ending with a WS row.

SHAPE ARMHOLES

BO

	30"	32	34	36	38	40	42	44	46	48	50	54
FINGERING	8	8	8	8	8	8	8	10	10	12	14	16
WORSTED	6	6	6	6	6	6	6	6	8	8	10	12
BULKY	3	4	4	4	4	4	4	6	6	6	6	8

sts at the beginning of the next 2 rows. BO

	30"	32	34	36	38	40	42	44	46	48	50	54
FINGERING	2	2	2	2	2	2	4	6	8	8	10	12
WORSTED	0	2	2	2	2	2	4	4	6	6	8	8
BULKY	0	0	0	0	0	2	2	2	2	4	4	4

sts at the beginning of the following 2 rows. Decrease 1 st at each end of every RS row

	30"	32	34	36	38	40	42	44	46	48	50	54
FINGERING	3	5	7	9	9	10	10	9	10	10	10	10
WORSTED	3	2	3	4	4	5	5	6	5	6	5	5
BULKY	2	2	3	3	3	2	3	2	3	2	3	3

times:

	30"	32	34	36	38	40	42	44	46	48	50	54
FINGERING	88	90	94	98	106	110	114	116	118	120	120	128
WORSTED	58	60	64	66	72	74	76	78	78	80	80	86
BULKY	36	36	38	40	44	44	46	46	48	48	50	52

sts remain. Work even until armhole measures 5½ (6, 6¼, 6½, 7, 7¼, 7½, 8, 8¼, 8¾, 9, 9½)" [14 (15, 16, 16.5, 18, 18.5, 19, 20.5, 21, 22, 23, 24) cm], ending with a WS row.

Laceweight held double gives an airy, light fabric.

ROMANTIC

The Bolero

Simple seed-stitch trim.

Slightly ballooned sleeves.

» DeeDee is wearing size 42" (106.5 cm) in fingering gauge.

SHAPE NECK

NEXT ROW (RS): Work

	30"	32	34	36	38	40	42	44	46	48	50	54
FINGERING	24	25	26	27	29	30	31	31	32	32	32	34
WORSTED	17	17	18	19	20	21	21	22	22	22	22	24
BULKY	11	11	12	12	14	14	14	14	14	14	15	15

sts, attach a new ball of yarn and BO center

	30"	32	34	36	38	40	42	44	46	48	50	54
FINGERING	40	40	42	44	48	50	52	54	54	56	56	60
WORSTED	24	26	28	28	32	32	34	34	34	36	36	38
BULKY	14	14	14	16	16	16	18	18	20	20	20	22

sts, work to end. *You will now work both sides of the neckline at the same time.*
Decrease 1 st at neck edge of every RS row twice:

	30"	32	34	36	38	40	42	44	46	48	50	54
FINGERING	22	23	24	25	27	28	29	29	30	30	30	32
WORSTED	15	15	16	17	18	19	19	20	20	20	20	22
BULKY	9	9	10	10	12	12	12	12	12	12	13	13

sts remain for each shoulder. Work even until armhole measures 6½ (7, 7¼, 7½, 8, 8¼, 8½, 9, 9¼, 9¾, 10, 10½)" [16.5 (18, 18.5, 19, 20.5, 21, 21.5, 23, 23.5, 25, 25.5, 26.5) cm] and piece measures 12½ (13¼, 13¾, 14¼, 15, 15½, 16, 16½, 17¼, 17¾, 18, 18½)" [32 (33.5, 35, 36, 38, 39.5, 40.5, 42, 44, 45, 46.5, 47) cm] from CO edge, ending at the armhole edge for each side.

NEXT ROW: BO

	30"	32	34	36	38	40	42	44	46	48	50	54
FINGERING	11	12	12	13	14	14	15	15	15	15	15	16
WORSTED	8	8	8	9	9	10	10	10	10	10	10	11
BULKY	5	5	5	5	6	6	6	6	6	6	7	7

sts, work to end. Work 1 row even. BO remaining sts.

FRONTS

Using long-tail cast-on method (or a different one, if you prefer), CO

	30"	32	34	36	38	40	42	44	46	48	50	54
FINGERING	52	54	58	62	66	70	74	78	82	84	88	96
WORSTED	34	36	40	42	44	46	50	52	54	56	60	64
BULKY	21	21	23	25	27	27	29	31	33	33	35	39

sts. Work even in trim of your choice, as follows:

ROMANTIC STYLE: Work even in Seed st for 1½" (4 cm), then switch to Stockinette st.

AVANTE-GARDE STYLE: Work even in Corded Rib pattern (page 183) for 1½" (4 cm), ending with a WS row.
Place a marker:
FINGERING: 17 / **WORSTED:** 9 / **BULKY:** 7 sts in from neck edge.
Note: Neck edge is at beginning of RS row for the right front, and at the end of the RS row for the left front.

Keeping marked sts in Corded Rib throughout fronts, switch remainder of the sts to Reverse Stockinette st.

Work Buttonhole Row on left front immediately, and then every 1½" (4 cm) thereafter as follows:

FINGERING BUTTONHOLE ROW 1 (RS): Work 6 sts, BO 5 sts, work to end.

FINGERING BUTTONHOLE ROW 2 (WS): Work to bound-off sts, CO 5 sts, work to end. Work sts on either side of buttonhole through back loop to tighten.

WORSTED BUTTONHOLE ROW 1 (RS): Work 3 sts, BO 3 sts, work to end.

WORSTED BUTTONHOLE ROW 2 (WS): Work to bound-off sts, CO 3 sts, work to end.

BULKY BUTTONHOLE ROW 1 (RS): Work 2 sts, BO 2 sts, work to end.

BULKY BUTTONHOLE ROW 2 (WS): Work to bound-off sts, CO 2 sts, work to end.

VINTAGE STYLE: Work even in 1x1 rib for 1" (2.5 cm), slipping the first st at beginning of RS rows for right front and at beginning of WS rows for left front.

Place marker:

FINGERING: 8 / **WORSTED:** 6 / **BULKY:** 4 sts in from neck edge.

Note: Neck edge is at beginning of RS row for the right front, and at the end of the RS row for the left front.

Keeping the marked edge sts in 1x1 rib throughout fronts, switch remainder of the sts to Stockinette st.

ALL STYLES: Continue until piece measures 2" (5 cm) from CO edge, ending with a WS row.

On your last row, place a waist shaping marker in the center of sts. If you have an odd number of sts, place marker to left of center st for left front, to right of center st for right front.

INCREASE ROW–RIGHT FRONT (RS): Work to marker, sm, M1-l, work to end. 1 st increased.

INCREASE ROW–LEFT FRONT (RS): Work to marker, M1-r, sm, work to end. 1 st increased.

Work an increase row every 6 rows

FINGERING: 6 / **WORSTED:** 4 / **BULKY:** 3 times total.

When all increases are complete,

	30"	32	34	36	38	40	42	44	46	48	50	54
FINGERING	58	60	64	68	72	76	80	84	88	90	94	102
WORSTED	38	40	44	46	48	50	54	56	58	60	64	68
BULKY	24	24	26	28	30	30	32	34	36	36	38	42

sts total. Work even until piece measures 6 (6¼, 6½, 6¾, 7, 7¼, 7½, 7½, 8, 8, 8, 8)'' [15 (16, 16.5, 17, 18, 18.5, 19, 19, 20.5, 20.5, 20.5, 20.5) cm] from CO edge, ending with a WS row for the left front and a RS row for the right front.

SHAPE ARMHOLES

BO

	30"	32	34	36	38	40	42	44	46	48	50	54
FINGERING	8	8	8	8	8	8	8	10	10	12	14	16
WORSTED	6	6	6	6	6	6	6	6	8	8	10	12
BULKY	3	4	4	4	4	4	4	6	6	6	6	8

sts at the beginning of the next row. Work 1 row even.

BO

	30"	32	34	36	38	40	42	44	46	48	50	54
FINGERING	2	2	2	2	2	2	4	6	8	8	10	12
WORSTED	0	2	2	2	2	2	4	4	6	6	8	8
BULKY	0	0	0	0	0	2	2	2	2	4	4	4

sts at the beginning of the following row. Work 1 row even.

Decrease 1 st at armhole edge of every RS row

	30"	32	34	36	38	40	42	44	46	48	50	54
FINGERING	3	5	7	9	9	10	10	9	10	10	10	10
WORSTED	3	2	3	4	4	5	5	6	5	6	5	5
BULKY	2	2	3	3	3	2	3	2	3	2	3	3

times:

	30"	32	34	36	38	40	42	44	46	48	50	54
FINGERING	45	45	47	49	53	56	58	59	60	60	60	64
WORSTED	29	30	33	34	36	37	39	40	39	40	41	43
BULKY	19	18	19	21	23	22	23	24	25	24	25	27

sts remain. Work even until armhole measures 3½ (4, 4¼, 4½, 5, 5¼, 5½, 6, 6¼, 6¾, 7, 7½)" [9 (10, 11, 11.5, 12.5, 13.5, 14, 15, 16, 17, 18, 19) cm], ending with a WS row for the right front and a RS row for the left front.

- -

SHAPE NECK

BO

	30"	32	34	36	38	40	42	44	46	48	50	54
FINGERING	12	11	12	12	13	14	15	15	15	15	15	16
WORSTED	7	8	9	9	9	9	10	10	10	10	11	11
BULKY	5	5	5	6	6	5	6	6	7	6	6	7

sts at the beginning of the next row.

Decrease 1 st at neck edge of every row

	30"	32	34	36	38	40	42	44	46	48	50	54
FINGERING	6	6	6	6	7	7	7	8	8	8	8	8
WORSTED	4	4	4	4	5	5	5	5	5	5	5	5
BULKY	3	2	2	3	3	3	3	3	3	3	3	4

times, then every RS row

	30"	32	34	36	38	40	42	44	46	48	50	54
FINGERING	5	5	5	6	6	7	7	7	7	7	7	8
WORSTED	3	3	4	4	4	4	5	5	4	5	5	5
BULKY	2	2	2	2	2	2	2	3	3	3	3	3

times:

	30"	32	34	36	38	40	42	44	46	48	50	54
FINGERING	22	23	24	25	27	28	29	29	30	30	30	32
WORSTED	15	15	16	17	18	19	19	20	20	20	20	22
BULKY	9	9	10	10	12	12	12	12	12	12	13	13

sts remain for each shoulder. Work even until armhole measures 6½ (7, 7¼, 7½, 8, 8¼, 8½, 9, 9¼, 9¾, 10, 10½)" [16.5 (18, 18.5, 19, 20.5, 21, 21.5, 23, 23.5, 25, 25.5, 26.5) cm] and piece measures 12 (13, 13½, 14, 15, 15½, 16, 17, 17½, 18½, 19, 20)" [30.5 (33, 34.5, 35.5, 38, 39.5, 40.5, 43, 44.5, 47, 48.5, 51) cm] from CO edge, ending at the armhole edge.

NEXT ROW: BO

	30"	32	34	36	38	40	42	44	46	48	50	54
FINGERING	11	12	12	13	14	14	15	15	15	15	15	16
WORSTED	8	8	8	9	9	10	10	10	10	10	10	11
BULKY	5	5	5	5	6	6	6	6	6	6	7	7

sts, work to end. BO remaining sts.

META-PATTERN #8

AVANT-GARDE
The Bolero

Bold
variegated
yarn.

Custom
buttons.

Reverse
Stockinette
stitch and
a corded rib
trim.

Detachable
sleeve
extensions.

» Francesca is wearing
size 38" (96.5 cm)
in worsted gauge.

SLEEVES

ROMANTIC STYLE: *Note: The puffed bottom of the Romantic sleeve works best in an extremely lightweight, floaty yarn. Instructions for bulkier gauges are provided, but please be sure to use an incredibly lightweight fabric at these gauges. For an example, please see the Romantic Cowl on page 99.*

Using long-tail cast-on method (or a different one, if you prefer), CO

	30"	32	34	36	38	40	42	44	46	48	50	54
FINGERING	76	80	84	88	92	96	98	106	114	122	134	144
WORSTED	50	52	56	58	60	62	66	72	76	80	88	96
BULKY	32	32	34	36	38	38	40	44	46	48	54	58

sts.

Work even in 1x1 rib until sleeve measures ½" (1.5 cm), ending with a WS row. Work 2 rows even in Stockinette st.

INCREASE ROW (RS): *K2, M1-r; rep from * around until a total of

	30"	32	34	36	38	40	42	44	46	48	50	54
FINGERING	38	40	42	44	46	48	48	52	56	60	66	72
WORSTED	24	26	28	28	30	30	32	36	38	40	44	48
BULKY	16	16	16	18	18	18	20	22	22	24	26	28

increase rows have been worked:

	30"	32	34	36	38	40	42	44	46	48	50	54
FINGERING	114	120	126	132	138	144	146	158	170	182	200	216
WORSTED	74	78	84	86	90	92	98	108	114	120	132	144
BULKY	48	48	50	54	56	56	60	66	68	72	80	86

sts total. Work even in Stockinette st until piece measures 2" (5 cm), ending with a WS row.

DECREASE ROW (RS): K1, k2tog, knit to last 3 sts, ssk, k1.

DECREASE ROW (WS): P1, ssp, purl to last 3 sts, p2tog, p1.

Work a decrease row every

	30"	32	34	36	38	40	42	44	46	48	50	54
FINGERING	4	4	4	4	4	3	3	3	3	3	2	2
WORSTED	4	4	4	4	4	4	3	3	3	3	3	2
BULKY	5	5	4	5	4	4	4	4	3	4	3	3

rows

	30"	32	34	36	38	40	42	44	46	48	50	54
FINGERING	16	17	18	19	20	22	21	23	25	27	30	33
WORSTED	10	11	12	12	13	13	14	16	17	18	20	22
BULKY	7	7	7	8	8	8	9	10	10	11	12	13

times. When all decreases have been worked,

	30"	32	34	36	38	40	42	44	46	48	50	54
FINGERING	82	86	90	94	98	100	104	112	120	128	140	150
WORSTED	54	56	60	62	64	66	70	76	80	84	92	100
BULKY	34	34	36	38	40	40	42	46	48	50	56	60

sts remain.

Work even until sleeve measures 10½ (10½, 10½, 11, 11, 11, 11½, 11½, 11½, 12, 12, 12)'' [26.5 (26.5, 26.5, 28, 28, 28, 29, 29, 29, 30.5, 30.5, 30.5) cm] from CO edge, ending with a WS row.

AVANT-GARDE STYLE:

MAKE DETACHABLE PIECES FIRST: Using long-tail cast-on method (or a different one, if you prefer), CO

	30"	32	34	36	38	40	42	44	46	48	50	54
FINGERING	74	78	82	86	90	94	98	102	110	110	122	138
WORSTED	50	54	58	58	62	62	66	70	74	74	82	94
BULKY	34	34	34	38	38	38	42	42	46	46	50	58

sts. Work even in Corded Rib pattern (page 183) until sleeve piece measures 5" (12.5 cm) from CO edge, ending with a WS row. Switch to Seed st and work ½" (1.5 cm) even.

Place markers for 8 buttonholes evenly spaced along the row, aligning markers with purl sections of Corded Rib pattern.

BUTTONHOLE ROW (RS): *Work in pattern to marker, remove marker, yo, p2tog; repeat from * 7 more times, work in pattern to end.

Work ½" (1.5 cm) even in Seed st. BO all sts.

MAKE SLEEVES: Using long-tail cast-on method (or a different one, if you prefer), CO

	30"	32	34	36	38	40	42	44	46	48	50	54
FINGERING	72	76	80	84	88	90	94	98	106	106	118	136
WORSTED	48	50	54	56	58	60	64	66	70	70	78	90
BULKY	30	30	32	34	36	36	38	40	42	42	48	54

sts. Work even in Corded Rib until sleeve measures 1" (2.5 cm) from CO edge. Switch to Reverse Stockinette st and work 2 rows even.

INCREASE ROW (RS): P1, M1-p, purl to last stitch, M1-p, p1.

Work increase row every

FINGERING: 10 / **WORSTED:** 12 / **BULKY:** 12 rows

	30"	32	34	36	38	40	42	44	46	48	50	54
FINGERING	5	5	5	5	5	5	5	7	7	11	11	7
WORSTED	3	3	3	3	3	3	3	5	5	7	7	5
BULKY	2	2	2	2	2	2	2	3	3	4	4	3

times:

	30"	32	34	36	38	40	42	44	46	48	50	54
FINGERING	82	86	90	94	98	100	104	112	120	128	140	150
WORSTED	54	56	60	62	64	66	70	76	80	84	92	100
BULKY	34	34	36	38	40	40	42	46	48	50	56	60

sts total. Work even until sleeve measures 13 (13, 13, 13½, 13½, 13½, 13½, 14, 14, 14, 14, 14)" [33 (33, 33, 34.5, 34.5, 34.5, 34.5, 35.5, 35.5, 35.5, 35.5, 35.5) cm] from CO edge, ending with a WS row.

VINTAGE STYLE: Using long-tail cast-on method (or a different one, if you prefer), CO

	30"	32	34	36	38	40	42	44	46	48	50	54
FINGERING	72	76	80	84	88	90	94	98	106	106	118	136
WORSTED	48	50	54	56	58	60	64	66	70	70	78	90
BULKY	30	30	32	34	36	36	38	40	42	42	48	54

sts. Work even in 1x1 rib until sleeve measures 1" (2.5 cm) from CO edge. Switch to Stockinette st and work 2 rows even.

INCREASE ROW (RS): K1, M1-r, knit to last stitch, M1-l, k1.

Work increase row every

FINGERING: 10 / **WORSTED:** 12 / **BULKY:** 12 rows

	30"	32	34	36	38	40	42	44	46	48	50	54
FINGERING	5	5	5	5	5	5	5	7	7	11	11	7
WORSTED	3	3	3	3	3	3	3	5	5	7	7	5
BULKY	2	2	2	2	2	2	2	3	3	4	4	3

times:

	30"	32	34	36	38	40	42	44	46	48	50	54
FINGERING	82	86	90	94	98	100	104	112	120	128	140	150
WORSTED	54	56	60	62	64	66	70	76	80	84	92	100
BULKY	34	34	36	38	40	40	42	46	48	50	56	60

sts total. Work even until sleeve measures 13 (13, 13, 13½, 13½, 13½, 13½, 14, 14, 14, 14, 14)" [33 (33, 33, 34.5, 34.5, 34.5, 34.5, 35.5, 35.5, 35.5, 35.5, 35.5) cm] from CO edge, ending with a WS row.

SHAPE SLEEVE CAP

ALL STYLES: BO

	30"	32	34	36	38	40	42	44	46	48	50	54
FINGERING	8	8	8	8	8	8	8	10	10	12	14	16
WORSTED	6	6	6	6	6	6	6	6	8	8	10	12
BULKY	3	4	4	4	4	4	4	6	6	6	6	8

sts at the beginning of the next 2 rows. BO

	30"	32	34	36	38	40	42	44	46	48	50	54
FINGERING	2	2	2	2	2	2	4	6	8	8	10	11
WORSTED	0	2	2	2	2	2	4	4	6	6	7	7
BULKY	0	0	0	0	0	2	2	2	2	4	4	4

sts at the beginning of the following 2 rows. Decrease 1 st at each end of every 3rd RS row

	30"	32	34	36	38	40	42	44	46	48	50	54
FINGERING	1	1	1	1	1	1	2	3	5	5	4	5
WORSTED	1	2	1	1	2	2	2	1	4	4	4	4
BULKY	0	0	0	0	0	0	0	1	2	3	2	3

time(s), then every other RS row

	30"	32	34	36	38	40	42	44	46	48	50	54
FINGERING	1	1	1	0	0	0	0	0	0	0	1	0
WORSTED	0	1	1	1	0	0	1	1	1	0	0	0
BULKY	1	1	1	1	1	2	2	1	2	1	1	0

time(s), then every RS row

	30"	32	34	36	38	40	42	44	46	48	50	54
FINGERING	13	15	17	20	22	23	22	21	13	15	17	19
WORSTED	9	6	9	10	11	12	11	15	6	9	10	12
BULKY	7	6	7	8	9	6	7	7	2	1	2	5

time(s). BO

	30"	32	34	36	38	40	42	44	46	48	50	54
FINGERING	3	3	3	3	3	3	3	3	5	5	5	5
WORSTED	2	2	2	2	2	2	2	2	3	3	3	3
BULKY	1	1	1	1	1	1	1	1	2	2	2	2

sts at the beginning of the next 4 rows. BO final

	30"	32	34	36	38	40	42	44	46	48	50	54
FINGERING	20	20	20	20	20	20	20	20	28	28	28	28
WORSTED	14	14	14	14	14	14	14	14	18	18	18	18
BULKY	8	8	8	8	8	8	8	8	12	12	12	12

sts.

FINISHING

Wet-block all pieces to finished measurements. Sew shoulder seams using mattress stitch. Set in sleeves and sew side and sleeve seams using mattress stitch.

ROMANTIC STYLE: With RS facing and beginning at lower edge of right front, pick up and knit sts along right front edge at the rate of 3 sts for every 4 rows. Place 3 markers along bottom 4" (10 cm) of button band edge for button holes.

Work even in Seed st for ½" (1.5 cm).

BUTTONHOLE ROW 1 (RS): Work to marker, BO

FINGERING: 6 / **WORSTED:** 3 / **BULKY:** 1 st(s); repeat from * to end.

BUTTONHOLE ROW 2 (WS): Work to bound-off sts, CO same number of sts using backward loop cast-on method; repeat from * to end.

Work even in Seed st until button band measures 1" (2.5 cm). BO all sts.

Repeat for left front, beginning at neck edge, omitting buttonholes.

With RS facing and beginning at right front neck edge, pick up and knit sts along neck edge at the rate of 1 st for each bound-off st, 3 sts for every 4 rows along vertical edges, and 4 sts for every 5 rows along diagonal edges. Work even in Seed st for ½" (1.5 cm). BO all sts.

AVANT-GARDE STYLE: Sew side edges of detachable sleeve cuffs together. Lining up the cuff seam with the sleeve seam, mark button positions at lower edge of sleeves. Sew smaller buttons in place. Sew buttons to left front edge opposite buttonholes.

With RS facing and beginning at right front neck edge, pick up and knit sts along neck edge at the rate of 1 st for every bound-off st, 3 sts for every 4 rows along vertical edges, and 4 sts for every 5 rows along diagonal edges. Work even in Corded Rib pattern (below) for 1" (2.5 cm). BO all sts.

VINTAGE STYLE: Using long-tail cast-on method (or a different one, if you prefer), CO

FINGERING: 20 / **WORSTED:** 12 / **BULKY:** 10 sts,

then beginning at right front neck edge, pick up and knit sts around neck edge at the rate of 1 st for every bound-off st, 4 sts for every 5 rows along diagonal edges, and 3 sts for every 4 rows along vertical edges.

Work even in 1x1 rib for ½" (1.5 cm), ending with a WS row.

BUTTONHOLE ROW (RS): Work

FINGERING: 8 / **WORSTED:** 4 / **BULKY:** 2 sts,

[yo, k2tog, k2] twice, work to end.

Work even in 1x1 rib for ½" (1.5 cm).

BO all sts. Sew buttons to left side of neckband.

SPECIAL STITCHES

CORDED RIB (multiple of 4 sts + 1)

ROW 1: Knit 1, *ssk, M1-r, p 2; repeat from * to end.

Repeat Row 1 for Corded Rib.

BUTTONS EVERYWHERE (left to right): vintage glass, custom ceramic created by Jennie the Potter.

ROMANTIC BOLERO
(FINGERING)
Front & Back

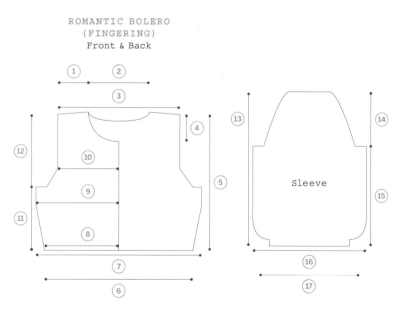

1   3 (3, 3¼, 3¼, 3½, 3¾, 3¾, 3¾, 4, 4, 4, 4¼)"
    7.5 (8, 8, 8.5, 9, 9.5, 10, 10, 10, 10, 10, 11) cm

2   5¾ (5¾, 6¼, 6½, 7, 7¼, 7½, 7¾, 7¾, 8, 8, 8½)"
    15 (15, 15.5, 16.5, 17.5, 18.5, 19, 19.5, 19.5, 20.5, 20.5, 21.5) cm

3   11¾ (12, 12½, 13, 14¼, 14¾, 15¼, 15½, 15¾, 16, 16, 17)"
    30 (30.5, 32, 33, 36, 37.5, 38.5, 39.5, 40, 40.5, 40.5, 43.5) cm

4   3"/7.5 cm

5   12.5 (13.25, 13.75, 14.25, 15, 15.5, 16, 16.5, 17.25, 17.75, 18, 18.5)"
    32 (33.5, 35, 36, 38, 39.5, 40.5, 42, 44, 45, 45.5, 47) cm

6   13½ (14½, 15½, 16½, 17½, 18½, 19½, 20½, 21½, 22½, 23½, 25½)"
    34.5 (36.5, 39.5, 42, 44.5, 46.5, 49.5, 52, 55, 57, 59.5, 65) cm

7   15¼ (16, 17, 18¼, 19¼, 20, 21, 22¼, 23¼, 24, 25, 27¼)"
    38.5 (40.5, 43.5, 46, 49, 51, 53.5, 56, 59, 61, 63.5, 69) cm

8   7 (7¼, 7¾, 8¼, 8¾, 9¼, 9¾, 10½, 11, 11¼, 11¾, 12¾)"
    17.5 (18.5, 19.5, 21, 22.5, 23.5, 25, 26.5, 28, 28.5, 30, 32.5) cm

9   7¾ (8, 8½, 9, 9½, 10¼, 10¾, 11¼, 11¾, 12, 12½, 13½)"
    19.5 (20.5, 21.5, 23, 24.5, 25.5, 27, 28.5, 30, 30.5, 32, 34.5) cm

10 6 (6, 6¼, 6½, 7, 7½, 7¾, 7¾, 8, 8, 8, 8½)"
    15 (15, 16, 16.5, 18, 19, 19.5, 20, 20.5, 20.5, 20.5, 21.5) cm

11 6 (6¼, 6½, 6¾, 7, 7¼, 7½, 7½, 8, 8, 8)"
    15 (16, 16.5, 17, 18, 18.5, 19, 19, 20.5, 20.5, 20.5, 20.5) cm

12 6½ (7, 7¼, 7½, 8, 8¼, 8½, 9, 9¼, 9¾, 10, 10½)"
    16.5 (18, 18.5, 19, 20.5, 21, 21.5, 23, 23.5, 25, 25.5, 26.5) cm

13 15 (15.25, 15.75, 16.5, 16.75, 17, 18, 18.25, 18, 18.75, 19, 19.5)"
    38 (38.5, 40, 42, 42.5, 43, 45.5, 46.5, 45.5, 47.5, 48.5, 49.5) cm

14 4½ (4¾, 5¼, 5½, 5¾, 6, 6½, 6¾, 6½, 6¾, 7, 7½)"
    11 (12, 13, 13.5, 14.5, 15, 16.5, 17.5, 16.5, 17.5, 18, 19.5) cm

15 10½ (10½, 10½, 11, 11, 11, 11½, 11½, 11½, 12, 12, 12)"
    26.5 (26.5, 26.5, 28, 28, 28, 29, 29, 29, 30.5, 30.5, 30.5) cm

16 9½ (10¼, 10¾, 11¼, 11¾, 12, 12½, 13, 14¼, 14¼, 15¾, 18¼)"
    24.5 (25.5, 27, 28.5, 30, 30.5, 32, 33, 36, 36, 40, 46) cm

17 11 (11½, 12, 12½, 13, 13¼, 13¾, 15, 16, 17, 18¾, 20)"
    28 (29, 30.5, 32, 33, 34, 35, 38, 40.5, 43.5, 47.5, 51) cm

AVANT-GARDE BOLERO
(WORSTED)
Front & Back

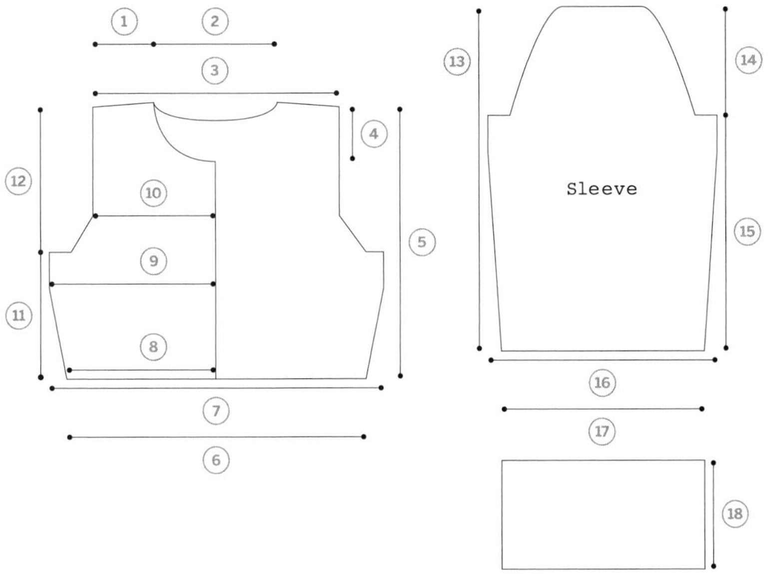

1 3 (3, 3¼, 3½, 3½, 3¾, 3¾, 4, 4, 4, 4, 4½)"
7.5 (7.5, 8, 8.5, 9, 9.5, 9.5, 10, 10, 10, 10, 11) cm

2 5½ (6, 6½, 6½, 7¼, 7¼, 7½, 7½, 7½, 8, 8, 8½)"
14 (15, 16.5, 16.5, 18.5, 18.5, 19.5, 19.5, 19.5, 20.5, 20.5, 21.5) cm

3 11½ (12, 12¾, 13¼, 14½, 14¾, 15¼, 15½, 15½, 16, 16, 17¼)"
29.5 (30.5, 32.5, 33.5, 36.5, 37.5, 38.5, 39.5, 39.5, 40.5, 40.5, 43.5) cm

4 3"/7.5 cm

5 12½ (13¼, 13¾, 14¼, 15, 15½, 16, 16½, 17¼, 17¾, 18, 18½)"
32 (33.5, 35, 36, 38, 39.5, 40.5, 42, 44, 45, 45.5, 47) cm

6 13½ (14½, 15½, 16½, 17½, 18½, 19½, 20½, 21½, 22½, 23½, 25½)"
34.5 (36.5, 39.5, 41.5, 44.5, 46.5, 50, 52, 55, 57, 60, 65) cm

7 15¼ (16, 17¼, 18, 19¼, 20, 21¼, 22, 23¼, 24, 25¼, 27¼)"
38.5 (40.5, 43.5, 45.5, 49, 51, 54, 56, 59, 61, 64, 69) cm

8 6¾ (7¼, 8, 8½, 8¾, 9¼, 10, 10½, 10¾, 11¼, 12, 12¾)"
17.5 (18.5, 20.5, 21.5, 22.5, 23.5, 25.5, 26.5, 27.5, 28.5, 30.5, 32.5) cm

9 7½ (8, 8¾, 9¼, 9½, 10, 10¾, 11¼, 11½, 12, 12¾, 13½)"
19.5 (20.5, 22.5, 23.5, 24.5, 25.5, 27.5, 28.5, 29.5, 30.5, 32.5, 34.5) cm

10 5¾ (6, 6½, 6¾, 7¼, 7½, 7¾, 8, 7¾, 8, 8¼, 8½)"
14.5 (15, 17, 17.5, 18.5, 19, 20, 20.5, 20, 20.5, 21, 22) cm

11 6 (6¼, 6½, 6¾, 7, 7¼, 7½, 7½, 8, 8, 8, 8)"
15 (16, 16.5, 17, 18, 18.5, 19, 19, 20.5, 20.5, 20.5, 20.5) cm

12 6½ (7, 7¼, 7½, 8, 8¼, 8½, 9, 9¼, 9¾, 10, 10½)"
16.5 (18, 18.5, 19, 20.5, 21, 21.5, 23, 23.5, 25, 25.5, 26.5) cm

13 17½ (18¼, 18¼, 19, 19½, 19¾, 20, 20¾, 20¾, 21¼, 21½, 22)"
44.5 (46, 46, 48, 49.5, 50.5, 51, 53, 53, 53.5, 54.5, 56) cm

14 4½ (5¼, 5¼, 5½, 6, 6¼, 6½, 6¾, 6¾, 7¼, 7½, 8)"
11.5 (13, 13, 14, 15, 16, 16.5, 17.5, 17.5, 18, 19, 20.5) cm

15 13 (13, 13, 13½, 13½, 13½, 13½, 14, 14, 14, 14, 14)"
33 (33, 33, 34.5, 34.5, 34.5, 34.5, 35.5, 35.5, 35.5, 35.5, 35.5) cm

16 9½ (10, 10¾, 11¼, 11½, 12, 12¾, 13¼, 14, 14, 15½, 18)"
24.5 (25.5, 27.5, 28.5, 29.5, 30.5, 32.5, 33.5, 35.5, 35.5, 39.5, 45.5) cm

17 10¾ (11¼, 12, 12½, 12¾, 13¼, 14, 15¼, 16, 16¾, 18½, 20)"
27.5 (28.5, 30.5, 31.5, 32.5, 33.5, 35.5, 38.5, 40.5, 42.5, 46.5, 51) cm

18 6"/15 cm

VINTAGE BOLERO
(BULKY)
Front & Back

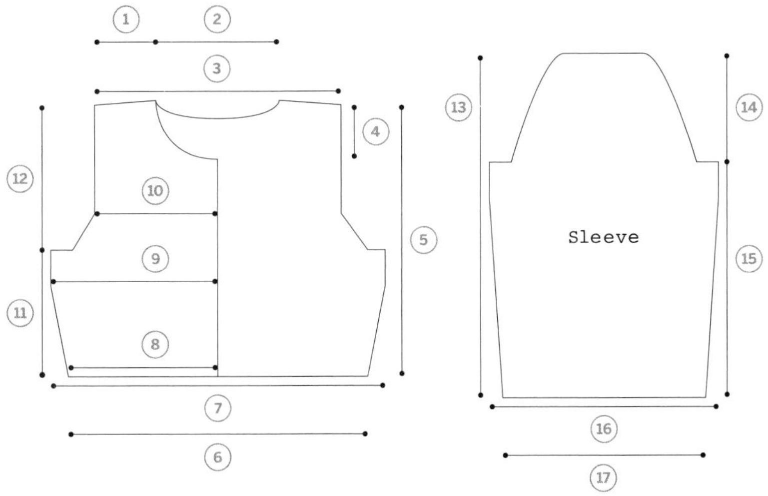

1 3 (3, 3¼, 3¼, 4, 4, 4, 4, 4, 4, 4¼, 4¼)"
7.5 (7.5, 8.5, 8.5, 10, 10, 10, 10, 10, 10, 11, 11) cm

2 6 (6, 6, 6¾, 6¾, 6¾, 7¼, 7¼, 8, 8, 8, 8¾)"
15 (15, 15, 17, 17, 17, 18.5, 18.5, 20.5, 20.5, 20.5, 22) cm

3 12 (12, 12¾, 13¼, 14¾, 14¾, 15¼, 15¼, 16, 16, 16¾, 17¼)"
30.5 (30.5, 32, 34, 37.5, 37.5, 39, 39, 40.5, 40.5, 42.5, 44) cm

4 3"/7.5 cm

5 12.5 (13.25, 13.75, 14.25, 15, 15.5, 16, 16.5, 17.25, 17.75, 18, 18.5)"
32 (33.5, 35, 36, 38, 39.5, 40.5, 42, 44, 45, 45.5, 47) cm

6 13¼ (14, 15¼, 16, 17¼, 18, 19¼, 20, 21¼, 22, 23¼, 25¼)"
34 (35.5, 39, 40.5, 44, 45.5, 49, 51, 54, 56, 59.5, 64.5) cm

7 15¼ (16, 17¼, 18, 19¼, 20, 21¼, 22, 23¼, 24, 25¼, 27¼)"
39 (40.5, 44, 45.5, 49, 51, 54, 56, 59.5, 61, 64.5, 69.5) cm

8 7 (7, 7¾, 8¼, 9, 9, 9¾, 10¼, 11, 11, 11¾, 13)"
18 (18, 19.5, 21, 23, 23, 24.5, 26, 28, 28, 29.5, 33) cm

9 8 (8, 8¾, 9¼, 10, 10, 10¾, 11¼, 12, 12, 12¾, 14)"
20.5 (20.5, 22, 23.5, 25.5, 25.5, 27, 29, 30.5, 30.5, 32, 35.5) cm

10 6¼ (6, 6¼, 7, 7¾, 7¼, 7¾, 8, 8¼, 8, 8¼, 9)"
16 (15, 16, 18, 19.5, 18.5, 19.5, 20.5, 21, 20.5, 21, 23) cm

11 6 (6¼, 6½, 6¾, 7, 7¼, 7½, 7½, 8, 8, 8, 8)"
15 (16, 16.5, 17, 18, 18.5, 19, 19, 20.5, 20.5, 20.5, 20.5) cm

12 6½ (7, 7¼, 7½, 8, 8¼, 8½, 9, 9¼, 9¾, 10, 10½)"
16.5 (18, 18.5, 19, 20.5, 21, 21.5, 23, 23.5, 25, 25.5, 26.5) cm

13 17½ (17¾, 18¼, 19¼, 19¾, 19¾, 20¼, 21, 21, 21, 21½, 22) "
44.5 (45.5, 46.5, 49, 50, 50, 51, 53.5, 53.5, 53.5, 54.5, 56) cm

14 4½ (5, 5¼, 5¾, 6¼, 6¼, 6¾, 7, 7, 7, 7½, 8)"
11.5. (12.5, 13.5, 14.5, 16, 16, 17, 18, 18, 18, 19, 20.5) cm

15 13 (13, 13, 13½, 13½, 13½, 13½, 14, 14, 14, 14, 14)"
33 (33, 33, 34.5, 34.5, 34.5, 34.5, 35.5, 35.5, 35.5, 35.5, 35.5) cm

16 10 (10, 10¾, 11¼, 12, 12, 12¾, 13¼, 14, 14, 16, 18)"
25.5 (25.5, 27, 29, 30.5, 30.5, 32, 34, 35.5, 35.5, 40.5, 45.5) cm

17 11¼ (11¼, 12, 12¾, 13¼, 13¼, 14, 15¼, 16, 16¾, 18¾, 20)"
29 (29, 30.5, 32, 34, 34, 35.5, 39, 40.5, 42.5, 47.5, 51) cm

META-PATTERN #8
THE BOLERO

Use this worksheet as a handy way to get all of the numbers for each individual bolero you knit in one simple place. You can photocopy these pages or download a fresh copy any time you like at www.amyherzogdesigns.com/knitwearlove.

BACK

Using long-tail cast-on method (or a different one, if you prefer), CO _____ sts.

EDGING: Work even in _____ until piece measures _____ from CO edge, ending with a WS row.

Switch to _____ and work even until piece measures _____ from CO edge, ending with a WS row.

On your last row, place markers on each side of center _____ sts.

INCREASE ROW (RS): Work to marker, M1-r, sm, work to next marker, sm, M1-l, work to end.

Work increase row every _____ rows _____ times total: _____ sts total. Work even until piece measures _____ from CO edge, ending with a WS row.

SHAPE ARMHOLES: BO _____ sts at the beginning of the next 2 rows. BO _____ sts at the beginning of the following 2 rows. Decrease 1 st at each end of every RS row _____ times: _____ sts remain.

Work even until armhole measures _____ from CO edge, ending with a WS row.

SHAPE NECK:

NEXT ROW (RS): Work _____ sts. Attach a new ball of yarn. BO center _____ sts and work to end.

Working both sides of neckline at the same time, decrease 1 st at neck edge of every RS row twice. _____ shoulder sts remain. Work even until piece measures _____ from CO edge, ending at the armhole edge.

NEXT ROW: BO _____ sts, work to end. Work 1 row even. BO rem sts.

FRONTS

Using long-tail cast-on method (or a different one, if you prefer), CO _____ sts.

EDGING: Work even in _____ until piece measures _____ from CO edge, ending with a WS row.

Switch to _____ and work even until piece measures _____ from CO edge, ending with a WS row.

Note: Avant-Garde style buttonhole rows should be worked on left front immediately, and then every 1½" (4 cm) thereafter as specified here:

BUTTONHOLE ROW 1 (RS): Work _____ sts, BO _____ sts, work to end.

BUTTONHOLE ROW 2 (WS): Work to bound-off sts, CO _____, work to end. For fingering buttonhole, work stitches on either side of buttonhole through the back loop to tighten.

On last row, mark center of sts.

INCREASE ROW–RIGHT FRONT (RS): Work to marker, sm, M1-l, work to end.

INCREASE ROW–LEFT FRONT(RS): Work to marker, M1-r, sm, M1-l, work to end.

Work increase row every _____ rows _____ times total: _____ sts total. Work even until piece measures _____ from CO edge, ending with a WS row for left front, RS row for right front.

Note: Armhole and neck shaping may occur at the same time—please read ahead.

SHAPE ARMHOLES: BO _____ sts at the beginning of the row. Work 1 row even.

BO _____ sts at the beginning of the following row.

Decrease 1 st at armhole end of every RS row _____ times. _____ sts remain.

SHAPE NECK: When armhole shaping measures _____, BO _____ sts at the beginning of the next neck edge row.

Decrease 1 st at neck edge every row _____ times, then every RS row _____ times.

ALL: When all neck and armhole shaping is complete, _____ shoulder sts remain. Work even until piece measures _____ from CO edge, ending at the armhole edge.

NEXT ROW: BO _____ sts, work to end. Work 1 row even. BO rem sts.

SLEEVES

ROMANTIC STYLE: Using long-tail cast-on method (or a different one, if you prefer), CO _____ sts.

Work even in 1x1 rib until sleeve measures ½" (1.5 cm), ending with a WS row. Work 2 rows even in Stockinette st.

INCREASE ROW (RS): *K2, M1-r, rep from * around until a total of _____ increases have been worked: _____ sts total.

Work even as established until piece measures 2" (5 cm), ending with a WS row.

DECREASE ROW (RS): K1, k2tog, work to last 3 sts, ssk, k1.

DECREASE ROW (WS): P1, ssp, work to last 3 sts, p2tog, p1.

Work a decrease row every _____ rows _____ times: _____ sts remain. Work even until sleeve measures _____ from CO edge, ending with a WS row.

AVANT-GARDE STYLE:

DETACHABLE SLEEVE CUFFS: Using long-tail cast-on method (or a different one, if you prefer), CO _____ sts. Work even in Corded Rib (page 183) until cuff measures 5" (12.5 cm) from CO edge, ending with a WS row. Switch to Seed st and work ½" (1.5 cm) even.

Place markers for 8 buttonholes evenly spaced along the row, aligning markers with purl sections of Corded Rib.

BUTTONHOLE ROW (RS): *Work in pattern to marker, remove marker, yo, p2tog; repeat from * 7 more times, work in pattern to end.

Work ½" (1.5 cm) even in Seed st. BO all sts.

MAIN SLEEVES: Using long-tail cast-on method (or a different one, if you prefer), CO _____ sts. Work even in Corded Rib until sleeve measures 1" (2.5 cm) from CO edge. Switch to Reverse Stockinette st and work even for 2 rows.

INCREASE ROW (RS): P1, M1-p, purl to last st, M1-p, p1.

Work increase row every _____ rows _____ times total: _____ sts total. Work even until sleeve measures _____ from CO edge, ending with a WS row.

VINTAGE STYLE: Using long-tail cast-on method (or a different one, if you prefer), CO _____ sts. Work even in 1x1 rib until sleeve measures 1" (2.5 cm) from CO edge. Switch to Stockinette st and work even for 2 rows.

INCREASE ROW (RS): K1, M1-r, knit to last st, M1-l, k1.

Work increase row every _____ rows _____ times total: _____ sts total. Work even until sleeve measures _____ from CO edge, ending with a WS row.

ALL STYLES:

SHAPE SLEEVE CAP: BO _____ sts at the beginning of the next 2 rows. BO _____ sts at the beginning of the following 2 rows. Decrease 1 st at each end of every 3rd RS row _____ times, then every other RS row _____ times, then every RS row _____ times.

BO _____ sts at the beginning of the next 4 rows.

BO final _____ sts.

FINISHING

Follow instructions on page 183.

CHECKLIST FOR SUCCESS

I hope these pages have given you a new outlook on sweaters—one that feels flexible, and adventurous, and is rooted in the kind of clothing you love to put on. I hope I've inspired you to use your knowledge to approach your next sweater with imagination and to truly create your next favorite piece of clothing.

While sweater knitting doesn't have to be technically challenging, it's often intimidating, and there's definitely a lot of information to mull over. So I want to leave you with a quick checklist of what I think is the best way to approach your next sweater.

CHOOSE A FABRIC YOU LOVE. First and foremost, you're going to be wearing your sweater as clothing, paired with your other clothes. So please take some time and swatch (more detail on this on page 27) until you've got a fabric that fits well with your other clothing that you can't wait to wear.

CHOOSE A SILHOUETTE YOU LOVE. The greatest fabric in the world should be matched with a sweater silhouette you love to wear. Are you a tunic girl? Check out page 112. More of a

classic, preppy pullover kind of person? See my version on page 40. Of course you can always branch out from there, but if the sweater's silhouette works for you, you're going to love the finished garment.

CHOOSE DETAILS YOU LOVE. How do you want your sweater described? What stitch patterns, edgings, necklines, and so forth best evoke those adjectives? Swatch a bit to ensure that all of the details are ones you love.

CHOOSE A SIZE YOU LOVE. Start with a great fit in the shoulders, and then adjust the bust, waist, and hip widths if you need to. Use the formula and examples on pages 25–27 if you get stuck. Create a sweater that tells your body it's perfect.

AND, ABOVE ALL, REMEMBER TO HAVE FUN! Sweater knitting can be a complete blast.

I can't wait to see the beautiful garments you create.

Happy sweater-ing,

xo

Amy

YARN DESCRIPTIONS

Below are the fiber contents of all of the yarns used for the sweaters shown in this book.

PULLOVER

ROMANTIC: Quince and Co Tern (75% wool, 25% silk): 221 yd/202 m per 50g hank

MODERN: Blue Sky Alpacas Melange and Sport Weight (100% alpaca): 110 yd/101 m per 50g hank

CLASSIC: Swans Island Organic Washable Wool Aran Weight (100% merino): 100 yd/91 m per 50g hank

CARDIGAN

VINTAGE: Bijou Spun Sport Weight by Bijou Basin Ranch (100% yak): 328 yd/300 m per 100g hank

CASUAL: Rowan Yarns Lima (84% alpaca, 8% merino, 8% nylon): 120 yd/110 m per 50g ball

CLASSIC: Blue Sky Alpacas Techno (68% alpaca, 22% silk, 10% merino): 120 yd/110 m per 50g hank

VEST

VINTAGE: Imperial Yarns Tracie Too (100% wool): 395 yd/361 m per 113g hank

CLASSIC: Stonehedge Fiber Mill Shepherd's Wool Worsted (100% merino): 250 yd/229 m per 4 oz hank

AVANT GARDE: Quince and Co Osprey (100% wool): 170 yd/155 m per 100g hank

COWL

BOHEMIAN: Harrisville Designs Silk & Wool (50% silk, 50% wool): 175 yd/160 m per 50g hank

CASUAL: Shibui Staccato (70% superwash merino, 30% silk): 191 yd/175 m per 50g hank and Baby Alpaca (100% alpaca): 255 yd/233 m per 100g hank

ROMANTIC: Blue Sky Alpacas Brushed Suri (67% alpaca, 22% merino, 11% bamboo): 142 yd/130 m per 50g hank

TUNIC

BOHEMIAN: Shibui Staccato (70% superwash merino, 30% silk): 191 yd/175 m per 50g hank

CASUAL: Green Mountain Spinnery Alpaca Elegance (50% wool, 50% alpaca): 180 yd/165 m per 2 oz hank

SPORTY: Lorna's Laces Masham Worsted (70% English wool, 30% masham wool): 170 yd/155 m per 100g hank

WRAP

SPORTY: Lorna's Laces Sportmate (70% wool, 30% Outlast™ viscose): 270 yd/247 m per 100g hank

BOHEMIAN: Classic Elite Yarns Classic Silk (50% cotton, 30% silk, 20% nylon): 135 yd/123 m per 50g ball

MODERN: Brooklyn Tweed SHELTER (100% wool): 140 yd/128 m per 50g hank

TANK

AVANT GARDE: Shibui Linen (100% linen): 246 yd/225 m per 50g hank

SPORTY: Foxfire Fiber & Designs Cormo Silk Alpaca (70% cormo wool, 20% prime alpaca, 10% bombyx silk): 190 yd/174 m per 70g hank

MODERN: Swans Island Worsted (100% merino): 250 yd/229 m per 100g hank

BOLERO

ROMANTIC: Rowan Yarns Fine Lace (80% alpaca, 20% merino): 437 yd/400 m per 50g ball

AVANT GARDE: SweetGeorgia Yarn Trinity Worsted (70% merino wool, 20% cashmere, 10% silk): 200 yd/183 m per 115g hank

VINTAGE: Quince and Co Puffin (100% wool): 112 yd/102 m per 100g hank

---

RECOMMENDED READING

These are my favorite books on sweater knitting, design, and finishing:

SWEATER DESIGN IN PLAIN ENGLISH by Maggie Righetti

KNITWEAR DESIGN WORKSHOP by Shirley Paden

VOGUE KNITTING—THE ULTIMATE KNITTING BOOK by Vogue Knitting Magazine Editors

THE PRINCIPLES OF KNITTING by June Hemmons Hiatt

KNITTING FROM THE TOP by Barbara G. Walker

THE KNITTER'S HANDY BOOK OF SWEATER PATTERNS by Ann Budd (also see her *The Knitter's Handy Book of Top-Down Sweaters*)

FINISHING SCHOOL by Deborah Newton

THE KNITTER'S BOOK OF FINISHING TECHNIQUES by Nancie Wiseman

CAST ON, BIND OFF by Cap Sease

ABBREVIATIONS

BO: bind off

CC: Contrast Color

CO: cast on

DPN(S): double-pointed needle(s)

K: knit

K2TOG: knit 2 stitches together

K TBL: knit through back loop

LT (LEFT TWIST): Knit second st on needle through back loop, then knit first st and drop both sts from needle together.

M1-L (MAKE 1 LEFT): Insert left needle, from front to back, under strand of yarn which runs between next stitch on left needle and last stitch on right needle; knit this stitch through back loop. 1 stitch increased.

M1-R (MAKE 1 RIGHT): Insert left needle, from back to front, under strand of yarn which runs between next stitch on left needle and last stitch on right needle; knit this stitch through front loop. 1 stitch increased.

M1-P (MAKE 1 PURL): Insert left needle, from front to back, under strand of yarn which runs between next stitch on left needle and last stitch on right needle; purl this stitch through back loop. 1 stitch increased.

MC: main color

P: purl

P2TOG: purl 2 stitches together

P3TOG: purl 3 stitches together

PSSO: pass slipped stitch over

PT (PURL TWIST): P2tog, leaving stitches on left-hand needle, insert right-hand needle from back between stitches just worked and purl the second stitch again, slip both stitches from needle together.

RS: right side

RT (RIGHT TWIST): Skip the first st, knit the second st, then knit the skipped st. Slip both sts from needle together.

SL: slip 1 st as if to knit unless specified otherwise.

SM: slip marker

SSK (SLIP, SLIP, KNIT): slip 2 stitches individually as if to knit, then knit those 2 stitches together through the back loops.

SSP (SLIP, SLIP, PURL): slip 2 stitches individually as if to knit, then purl those 2 stitches together through the back loops.

ST(S): stitch(es)

TBL: through back loop(s)

WS: wrong side

WYIF: with yarn in front

YO: yarn over

BASIC STITCH PATTERNS

1X1 RIB (worked in rows or in the round over an even number of sts):
Every row: *K1, p1; repeat from * to end.

2X1 RIB (worked in rows over a multiple of 3 sts + 2):
Row 1 (RS): K2, *p1, k2; repeat from * to end.
Row 2: P2, *k1, p2; repeat from * to end.

2X1 RIB (worked in the round over a multiple of 3 sts):
Every round: *K2, p1; repeat from * to end.

2X2 RIB (worked in rows over a multiple of 4 sts + 2):
Row 1 (RS): K2, *p2, k2; repeat from * to end.
Row 2: P2, *k2, p2; repeat from * to end.

2X2 RIB (worked in the round over a multiple of 4 sts):
Every round: *K2, p2; repeat from * to end.

GARTER STITCH (worked in rows):
Every row: Knit.

GARTER STITCH (worked in the round):
Round 1: Knit.
Round 2: Purl.

SEED STITCH (worked in rows over an odd number of sts):
Every row: K1, *p1, k1; repeat from * to end.

SEED STITCH (worked in the round over an even number of sts):
Round 1: *K1, p1; repeat from * to end.
Round 2: *P1, k1; repeat from * to end.

STOCKINETTE STITCH (worked in rows):
Row 1 (RS): Knit.
Row 2: Purl.

STOCKINETTE STITCH (worked in the round):
Every round: Knit.

REVERSE STOCKINETTE STITCH (worked in rows):
Row 1 (RS): Purl.
Row 2: Knit.

REVERSE STOCKINETTE STITCH (worked in the round):
Every round: Purl.

ACKNOWLEDGMENTS

THIS BOOK IS DEDICATED TO MY FATHER, who always encouraged me to chase my dreams.

Books are massive, complicated, tricky things, and I'm extraordinarily lucky to have had such wonderful help with mine. My warmest and most mushy-gooey thanks go to Jonathan, Jacob, and Daniel. Their partnership and support on this project, and a thousand others, astounds and delights me. You give me courage and humor, and you make even the rough days joyful. Thank you.

Thanks also to the incredible STC Craft team: For a second time, you helped me transform rough, inarticulate ideas into something wonderful. Melanie Falick and Cristina Garces, my patient and insightful editors; our technical editor Sandi Rosner, who tackled these challenging patterns with complete aplomb; Karen Schaupeter, the best photostylist ever; Mary Jane Callister, who captured the spirit of the book perfectly in her wonderful layouts; Karen Pearson, whose easy nature and extreme skill resulted in these exquisite photographs; our models Jackie, Morgan; Courtney, Kiki, DeeDee, and Francesca, who made the sweaters (and the whole room) shine; Lauren, Kelly, Deb, Karen, Anjeanette, Jennifer, Jenn, Julie, Amanda, Wanietta, and Kate—sample knitters extraordinaire. Thanks to Linda Roghaar, whose concise and caring hands helped bring the idea for this book to life.

I was thrilled to once again have the very best materials for the samples you see on these pages. Thanks to Blue Sky Alpacas, Quince and Co., Swans Island, Rowan, Bijou Basin Ranch, Harrisville Designs, Shibui, Classic Elite, Brooklyn Tweed, Lorna's Laces, Foxfire Fiber & Designs, Imperial Yarns, Stone Hedge Fiber Mill, and SweetGeorgia Yarns for your beautiful yarns. Thanks also to Jennie the Potter, who provided the exquisite custom buttons for the Avant-Garde Bolero.

My heartfelt and sincere thanks to the many amazing women who take my classes, support one another in the Ravelry groups, follow along with the blog, welcomed my first book, and continue to allow me to join in on their sweater journeys. I am humbled by your passion and excitement.

Thanks must also go to the wonderful people with whom I'm privileged to work. Lauren, Andromeda, Jonathan—I can't think of a better team, or one I've enjoyed being a part of more. Finally, my fiercest thanks to Jackie, for encouraging me to believe, and showing me the way.

Published in 2015 by Stewart, Tabori & Chang
An imprint of ABRAMS

Text and illustrations © 2015 Amy Herzog
Photographs © 2015 Karen Pearson

Library of Congress Control Number: 2014942999

ISBN: 978-1-61769-139-3

Editor: Melanie Falick
Designer: Mary Jane Callister
Production Manager: Anet Sirna-Bruder

The text of this book was composed in Neutraface Slab, Benton Sans, and Courier.

Printed and bound in China.
10 9 8 7 6 5 4 3 2 1

Stewart, Tabori & Chang books are available at special discounts when purchased in quantity for premiums and promotions as well as fundraising or educational use. Special editions can also be created to specification. For details, contact specialsales@abramsbooks.com or the address below.

ABRAMS
THE ART OF BOOKS SINCE 1949

115 West 18th Street
New York, NY 10011
www.abramsbooks.com